13A £2.99

C000152434

The Indian Diaspora

Themes in Indian Sociology

Series Editor: B. S. Baviskar

Other Books in the Series

Themes in Indian Sociology, Volume 4

The Indian Diaspora

Dynamics of Migration

Editor
N. Jayaram

Foreword by
S. L. Sharma

Sage Publications

New Delhi • Thousand Oaks • London

Copyright © Indian Sociological Society, 2004

All rights reserved. No part of this book may be reproduced or utilised in any form or by any means, electronic or mechanical, including photo-copying, recording or by any information storage or retrieval system, without permission in writing from the publisher.

First published in 2004 by

Sage Publications India Pvt Ltd
B–42, Panchsheel Enclave
New Delhi 110 017

Sage Publications Inc
2455 Teller Road
Thousand Oaks, California 91320

Sage Publications Ltd
1 Oliver's Yard, 55 City Road
London EC1Y 1SP

Published by Tejeshwar Singh for Sage Publications India Pvt. Ltd, typeset at InoSoft Systems in 10 pt Souvenir Lt BT and printed at Chaman Enterprises, New Delhi.

Library of Congress Cataloging-in-Publication Data

The Indian diaspora: dynamics of migration / editor N. Jayaram;
    foreword by S.L. Sharma.
        p.   cm. — (Themes in Indian sociology)
Includes bibliographical references and index.
        1. East Indians—Foreign countries. 2. India—Emigration and
    immigration. I. Jayaram, N., 1950– II. Sharma, S. L. III. Series.

DS432.5.I49   304.8'0954—dc22   2004   2003028144

ISBN: 0–7619–3218–6 (US–HB)   81–7829–347–1 (India–HB)
          0–7619–3219–4 (US–PB)   81–7829–318–X (India–PB)

Production Team: Jai S. Prasad, Radha Dev Raj and Santosh Rawat

Dedicated to the
Late Professor G. S. Ghurye, Founder–President of
the Indian Sociological Society

Contents

Series Note

The Indian Sociological Society (ISS) was established in December 1951 by Professor G. S. Ghurye and his colleagues in the Department of Sociology at the University of Bombay. The ISS soon launched its biannual journal, *Sociological Bulletin*, in March 1952. Since then the journal has appeared regularly for the last 50 years.

Started on a modest scale, each issue of the journal usually did not contain more than a 100 pages. During the initial years, the print did not exceed a few hundred copies. The *Bulletin* has now matured into a respected professional journal both nationally and internationally. Since 1989 it is a fully refereed journal admired for its academic content and the high quality of its production. Very few professional associations in India and other developing countries have been able to achieve and sustain the kind of scholarly reputation acquired by the *Sociological Bulletin*.

The ISS celebrated its Golden Jubilee in 2001, and to mark the occasion, it decided to publish a series of seven volumes, called *Themes in Indian Sociology*, based on articles published in the journal during the last five decades. When the proposal was placed before the Managing Committee of the ISS, it received wholehearted support and several colleagues came forward to help implement it. The 100 issues published during the period contained about 500 articles on a variety of subjects concerning society and culture in India and abroad. The authors' list included almost all the leading names in Indian sociology and social anthropology. For the students of sociology and allied disciplines, it was a virtual goldmine of sociological knowledge. Some of the papers were considered landmarks in the development of the discipline and had acquired the status of 'classics' in sociological literature.

Unfortunately, some of the issues were out of print and scholars faced difficulty in consulting them for study, teaching and research.

The Managing Committee decided to republish some of the seminal papers in suitable volumes under appropriate themes to make them easily available. The committee identified a number of scholars who were specialists in their respective fields, and asked them to edit these volumes. Senior colleagues, well-known for their expertise in different fields, were asked to act as academic advisors and to write appropriate forewords for the volumes with which they were associated.

Each editor selected 10 to 15 articles related to his/her theme, arranged them in a meaningful sequence, and wrote a comprehensive introduction to place the articles in the context of overall development of the field. The editor has also given a list of articles related to the field but not included in the volume, discussing briefly what they contain and why they could not be included. This has made each volume a self-contained guide to the concerned field.

We have great pleasure in offering the following seven volumes under the series:

1. *The Sociology of Gender*. Editor, Sharmila Rege. Foreword by Karuna Chanana.
2. *Urbanization in India: Sociological Contributions*. Editor, R. S. Sandhu. Foreword by V. S. D'Souza.
3. *Sociology of Religion in India*. Editor, Rowena Robinson. Foreword by C. N. Venugopal.
4. *The Indian Diaspora*. Editor, N. Jayaram. Foreword by S. L. Sharma.
5. *Tribal Communities and Social Change*. Editor, P. M. Chacko. Foreword by K. S. Singh.
6. *The Family through Abstract and Lived Categories*. Editor, Tulsi Patel. Foreword by A. M. Shah.
7. *On Civil Society: Sociological Contributions*. Editor, N. Jayaram. Foreword by Satish Saberwal.

I hope these volumes will be useful to students, teachers and researchers in sociology, social anthropology and other social sciences. I would like to record my thanks to Omita Goyal and her colleagues at Sage Publications for their wholehearted support to the project. I am grateful to my colleagues in the ISS who came forward to work on these volumes as editors and academic advisors. This is a result of their willing cooperation.

B. S. Baviskar
Series Editor
Themes in Indian Sociology

Foreword

The study of *Indian Diaspora* has emerged as an important branch of knowledge in recent years. In fact, there have appeared two parallel traditions of research and analysis: literary and social scientific. In the social scientific study of overseas Indians, three disciplines, i.e., history, anthropology and sociology have been particularly active. In terms of its concerns, sociological research has evolved through three phases so far which, for want of better terms, may be designated as cultural, structural and political. In the initial phase, appearing in the 1980s, it was dominated by the cultural perspective which focused on the study of cultural dynamics of the diasporic community, particularly on the questions of cultural continuity and change, identity and integration, and resilience and adaptation. In the 1990s, there appeared the structural perspective with its focus on the study of structural dimensions such as gender in Indian diaspora, caste in Indian diaspora, regional identities in Indian diaspora, including Punjabi diaspora or Gujarati diaspora, etc., and the issues of racial discrimination. While the research on the structural aspects of Indian diaspora is still continuing with vigour, lately the question of the role of the Indian state and its diasporic policy has also captured the imagination of the scholars. Three questions in particular have begun to engage the attention of both the social scientists and the policy makers alike: (*a*) what has the Indian state done for the Indian communities in various parts of the world?; (*b*) what has the Indian diaspora done for or against the Indian state?; (*c*) what should the Indian state do to cultivate and harness the Indian diaspora as a resource for Indian development?

The contributions comprising the present volume focus on the cultural dynamics in Indian diaspora. They bring alive the questions of social adjustment of Indian emigrants in Britain, cultural persistence and adaptation among Indian and Pakistani families as well as people of Indian origin in Canada; uneven 'inclusion' of Indian emigrants in Mauritius; the phenomenon of 'sandwich' culture; comparative analysis of race relations, ethnicity, class and culture among the Indians in Trinidad and Malaysia; the influence of Indian Islam on fundamentalist trends in Trinidad and Tobago; dynamics of language in Indian diaspora; and the emerging theoretical perspectives on Indian diaspora.

It is evident from the contents that the thrust of this volume is on the question of the cultural dialectics and change in Indian diaspora. The volume represents thematic unity along with rich diversity of research on the subject. N. Jayaram deserves to be complimented on his imaginative choice of integrative theme and the thoughtful selection of articles. His introductory essay 'The Study of Indian Diaspora', provides an insightful overview of the theme as well as a systematic framework for its study. His crisp summary of each article included in the volume is very perceptive and succinct.

Given the multidisciplinary character of the study of Indian diaspora and the quality of contributions included in the volume, I am sure that the scholars and researchers interested in the subject will find the volume highly valuable and rewarding.

S. L. Sharma
Panchkula

Preface

The study of *Indian Diaspora* has emerged as a rich and variegated area of multidisciplinary research interest. Among the disciplines contributing to this field of immense theoretical potential as well as imminent policy import, sociology has been in the forefront. Not surprisingly, from as early as 1965, *Sociological Bulletin*, the official journal of the Indian Sociological Society, has been publishing articles on the Indian diaspora. Put together in this volume are nine selections of seminal significance from its pages. The choice of each one of them was determined by a specific rationale—historicity, thematic coverage, methodological orientation, and theoretical perspective.

The texts of the selections have been reproduced as they were originally published by the *Bulletin*, though obvious grammatical errors and printing mistakes have been corrected. The *Bulletin*'s referencing style has changed over time and the bibliographic details provided by the selections have not been the same. I have sought to present the references in a uniform format, but in a few cases the details are incomplete.

The selections here deal with the empirical reality of Indian diaspora, and the theoretical and methodological issues raised by it. Thematically, they cover social adjustment, family change, religion, language, ethnicity and culture, and cultural integration and syncretism. In terms of locale they traverse Britain, Canada, Malaysia, Mauritius and Trinidad. Thus, encompassing the classical and modern diaspora, the anthology not only seeks to arrive at the generalities of the global Indian diaspora, but also to highlight its specificities across space and time. Together with its analytical introduction and a select bibliography, this volume of essays, it is hoped, would be a useful reference work for all those interested in Indian Diaspora as an area of academic study.

It was very kind of Professor B. S. Baviskar, former President of the Indian Sociological Society, to have invited me to undertake this interesting academic endeavour, and I am grateful to him for his encouragement. I owe a special word of thanks to Professor S. L. Sharma, the academic advisor for this volume. His comments on the draft of my 'Introduction' have enriched it, and his 'Foreword' to the volume is a bonus. I take this opportunity to thank my erstwhile colleagues in the Department of Sociology at Goa University for supporting my engagement with this project. For nearly three decades now I have received the affection, guidance and support of Professor Satish Saberwal. As a small token of my gratitude I am happy to offer this volume to him.

N. Jayaram
Mumbai

1

Introduction: The Study of Indian Diaspora

N. Jayaram

To study a banyan tree, you not only must know its main stem in its own soil, but also must trace the growth of its greatness in the further soil, for then you can know the true nature of its vitality. The civilization of India, like the banyan tree, has shed its beneficent shade away from its own birthplace.... India can live and grow by spreading abroad—not the political India, but the ideal India.

—Rabindranath Tagore (cited in Tinker 1977: iii)

The banyan tree has thrust down roots in soil which is stony, sandy, marshy—and has somehow drawn sustenance from diverse unpromising conditions. Yet the banyan tree itself has changed; its similarity to the original growth is still there, but it has changed in response to its different environment.

—Tinker (1977: 19)

Migration and dispersion are natural phenomena, widely familiar both in the world of plants and in the animal kingdom. Human beings have been no exception. In the case of human beings, anthropology has recorded nomadism as a stage preceding their settlement as communities. Even after their evolution as communities, human beings have been experiencing temporary, seasonal or permanent migration from their original habitat. The implications of such migrations vary in terms of factors such as the nature of the community's boundary, the reasons for the migration of its members, the nature of the recipient society, the magnitude of migration, the distance that the migrants traverse and so on.

In human migration two unique factors need to be recognised: migration does not mean the mere physical movement of people. Migrants carry with them a sociocultural baggage which among other things consists of (a) a predefined social identity, (b) a set of religious beliefs and practices, (c) a framework of norms and values governing family and kinship organisation, and food habits and (d) language. More important, the migrants are not inevitably irrevocably cut off completely from the land of their breed. They themselves may retain physical and/or mental contact with their homeland, often characterised by what is called 'the myth of return'. Their significant others, their folk back in the homeland as well as sections of the population in their land of adoption, may identify them as originating from and/or belonging to their homeland. This facet of migration has important implications for the formation of ethnicity among a migrant community and its relationship with other ethnic groups.

The phenomena surrounding such human migration are best conceptualised under the rubric *diaspora*. Etymologically, the term diaspora is derived from the Greek composite verb *dia-* and *speirein* (infinitive), literally meaning 'to scatter', 'to spread' or 'to disperse'. It was originally used to refer to the dispersion of Jews after the Babylonian exile in 586 BC and to the aggregate of Jews or Jewish communities scattered in exile outside Palestine. In current parlance, however, the term is applied to describe any group of people who are so dispersed (see Baumann 2000).

People of the Indian subcontinent have been known to have migrated to different countries for various reasons at various periods of its history. Among the immigrants of diverse nationalities, overseas Indians constitute a sizeable segment. It is estimated that besides six million Indian citizens, there are over 20 million people of Indian origin all over the world (Government of India 2001: 680). Taking 5,000 as the minimum figure, overseas Indians are found in as many as 53 countries (see R. K. Jain 1993: 2–3). The people of Indian origin form the single largest ethnic community in Fiji (49 per cent), Guyana (53 per cent), Mauritius (74 per cent), Trinidad and Tobago (40 per cent), and Surinam (37 per cent). They form substantial minority communities in Asian countries like Hong Kong, Malaysia, Singapore, Sri Lanka, and in South Africa and East Africa. They have a significant presence in Australia, Canada, the United Kingdom and the United States of America.

Having almost unique sociocultural histories and being subjected to different economic and political situations, the Indian communities abroad have evolved as distinct diasporic entities. They are nevertheless *Indian* as they manifest in varying degrees the survival, persistence or retention of several social patterns and cultural elements whose roots and substance can be traced to India. In some of these communities, for various reasons, conscious efforts are being made to revive some of these patterns and elements—a kind of 'renaissance' of Indian culture, as declared by some diasporic Indians (see Jayaram 2003).

Living in multicultural societies and being characterised by an ethnic identity, the Indian communities abroad have been invariably required to negotiate the problem of ethnicity. They have been engaged in active economic and cultural competitions. They have experienced ethnic discrimination, either explicit or covert. Sometimes they have been even involved in violent ethnic conflict and fierce political struggles.

Not surprisingly, diasporic Indians have been under academic focus for sometime. In its Third Survey of Research in Sociology and Anthropology (covering the period 1979–89), the Indian Council for Social Science Research thought it appropriate to include 'Indian Communities Abroad' as a focal theme (see R. K. Jain 1993). Several symposia, seminars and conferences have been organised on Indian diaspora under the auspices of such agencies or institutions as the Global Organisation of People of Indian Origin (New York), India International Centre, Indian Sociological Society, Indo-Canadian Shastri Institute, etc., besides universities in India and abroad. Recognising the relevance and significance of the study of *Indian Diaspora*[1] as an area of academic study, the University Grants Commission established in 1995 the Centre for the Study of Indian Diaspora at the University of Hyderabad.

This chapter is divided into two parts: Part one[2] presents a brief outline of the history of Indian diaspora, discusses the nature and scope of *Indian Diaspora* as an area of academic study, and examines the key disciplinary perspectives and strategic approaches that can be adopted. It does not seek to present a state-of-the-art review on *Indian Diaspora*. Studies have been cited only to illustrate or substantiate the points made. Ravindra K. Jain (1993) provides an extant survey of the literature on Indian communities abroad and Vertovec (1991a) reviews the writings on Indo-Caribbean culture and society. Perceptive essays can be found in anthologies compiled by Clarke, Peach and Vertovec (1990), Gosine (1992 and 1994), Kurian and Srivastava (1983), Motwani, Gosine and Barot-Motwani (1993), Schwartz (1967), Singh (1979), *Sociological Bulletin* (1989) and Vertovec (1991b). Region or country-specific essays have also been compiled: On Canada by Israel (1987) and Kanungo (1984), on East Africa by Ghai (1970), on Fiji and the Pacific Islands by Crocombe (1981) and Subramani (1979), on South Africa by Arkin, Magyar and Pillay (1989), on South East Asia and South Asia by Singh (1982 and 1984), on New Zealand by Tiwari (1980), on the United Kingdom by Burghart (1987), on Trinidad and the Caribbean by Birbalsingh (1989a), Dabydeen and Samaroo (1987 and 1996), Gosine (with Malik and Mahabir) (1995), La Guerre (1985), Singh (1987), and on the United States of America by Chandrasekhar (1983) and Gosine (1990b). Barrier and Dusenbery (1989) have compiled an anthology on the Sikh diaspora.

Part two surveys the coverage of Indian diaspora in the pages of the *Sociological Bulletin* over the last 50 years, and introduces the selections appearing in this volume.

I

The History of Indian Diaspora

In the study of *Indian Diaspora*, it is customary to distinguish between two main phases of emigration: 'Overseas emigration in the 19th century' and '20th century migration to industrially developed countries' (see R. K. Jain 1993: Contents). For analytical convenience, these could be termed the colonial and the post-colonial phases of Indian diaspora. It is, no doubt, possible to identify overlaps between these two phases: The emigration of Indians that began in the second quarter of the 19th century continued into the early decades of the 20th century. The trickle of emigration of Indians to the industrially developed countries, which assumed phenomenal proportions in the post-colonial phase, could be noticed in the 19th century itself. Nevertheless, it is important to recognise the distinctive nature of these two phases of migration, for their causes, courses and consequences.

Studies on Indian diaspora have largely focused on one or the other of the aforementioned phases. This is easy to understand considering the magnitude of the populations involved, and the variegated nature of their economic status and political predicament in different diasporic situations. Furthermore, some of these diasporic communities have been topical or their members themselves have begun manifesting an acute sense of 'community self-awareness'. Not less important, in many of these cases, archival records and other secondary data can be found with greater ease, and the conventional techniques of historical, anthropological and sociological research can be easily adopted.

Indian Diaspora in Ancient Times

It should be emphasised, however, that the emigration of Indians has a much longer history than what the reference point of colonialism seems to suggest. In the history of ancient India, we come across accounts of the Buddhist *bhikkus* who travelled into remote corners of Cental and Eastern Asia. Maritime history of pre-colonial India records evidence of continuous contact between the kingdoms of the Coromandel coast and the islands of South-East Asia. The contact of the Palas of Bengal with the Sailendra kings of Indonesia and the expeditions of the South Indian Cholas which vanquished the great Indonesian empire of Sri Vijaya are repeatedly referred to by scholars (see Tinker 1977: 1). Several elements of the Hindu and Buddhist religion, mythology and culture have survived in Southeast Asia, and most notably in Thailand and Bali (see Vincent Smith 1958). 'Yet none of these contacts led to a distinctive Indian population overseas' (Tinker 1977: 1).

The trade with East Africa, however, led to a permanent Indian settlement there. In a footnote, McNeill (1963: 210) observes that 'there is some reason to think that a colony of Indian merchants lived permanently in Memphis, Egypt from about 500 BC' (see also Sastri 1959). In the 19th century, when 'European explorers like Burton first ventured into the interior [in Africa] they were guided on their way by Indian merchants' (Tinker 1977: 2–3). These early migrants to

East Africa belonged mainly to small trading communities like the Ismailis, Bhoras and Banyas of the Gujarat region. Their counterparts covering Ceylon, Burma, Malaya, Thailand and Indonesia were mainly Nattukkottai Chettyars of Chettinad in the Tamil region of South India.

Research on the pre-colonial Indian diaspora is scant and sketchy. Even the available data are scattered in historical works. Documenting the sources of such data is necessary. With the help of historians, compiling the basic research material on the subject may even be possible.

Indian Diaspora during European Colonialism

In terms of the magnitude of emigration and its spread, the European colonisation, marked by the penetration of mercantile capitalism in Asia, was the most crucial phase in Indian diaspora. Large-scale emigration of Indians into far-off lands was facilitated by the integration of peripheral economies into the emerging world capitalist system, the onset of a revolution in transportation and communication and the opening of the Suez Canal.

The phenomenal trade surpluses earned by the European mercantile class in the wake of geographical discoveries were invested in mines and plantations in Asia, Africa and elsewhere. This created an enormous demand for a cheap and regulated labour force. By the first quarter of the 19th century, the demand for labour was accentuated by the ever expanding colonial economy, the growing opposition to slavery and its eventual abolition (by England in 1833, by France in 1848 and by Holland in 1863), and the inability of the European countries to meet the shortfall in labour by deploying their own labour force. A combination of factors made India (and China) an extant reservoir of cheap, docile and dependable labour, especially to work on the plantations.

Tinker (1993) provides one of the most comprehensive surveys of the emigration of Indian labour overseas during the colonial era. Broadly three distinct patterns of Indian emigration are identifiable in this period: (a) 'indentured' labour emigration, (b) 'kangani' and 'maistry' labour emigration and (c) 'passage' or 'free' emigration.

The indentured labour emigration, so called after the contract[3] signed by the individual labourer to work on plantations, was officially sponsored by the colonial government. It began in 1834 and ended in 1920. The overwhelming majority of the labour emigrants under this system were recruited from North India. These labour emigrants were taken to the British colonies of British Guiana, Fiji, Trinidad and Jamaica, the French colonies of Guadalupe and Martinique, and the Dutch colony of Surinam.

The *kangani* (derived from Tamil *kankani*, meaning foreman or overseer) system prevailed in the recruitment of labour for emigration to Ceylon and Malaya (see Jayaraman 1975: 6). A variant of this system, called the *maistry* (derived from Tamil *maistry*, meaning supervisor) system was practised in the recruitment of labour for emigration to Burma. The *kangani* or *maistry* (himself an Indian immigrant) recruited families of Tamil labourers from villages in the erstwhile Madras Presidency. The labourers so recruited were legally free, as they were not bound by any contract or fixed period of service. These systems, which began in the first and third quarter of the 19th century, were abolished in 1938.

Emigration from India did not cease with the abolition of indenture and other systems of organised export of labour. There was a steady trickle of emigration of members of trading communities from Gujarat and Punjab to South Africa and East Africa (Kenya, Tanzania and Uganda), and those from South India to Southeast Asia.[4] Most labourers emigrated to East Africa to work on the construction of railroads. These emigrants were not officially sponsored: they themselves paid their 'passage', and they were 'free' in the sense that they were not bound by any contract.

Indian Diaspora in the Post-Colonial Period

A new and significant phase of emigration began after India became independent in 1947. Broadly, three patterns can be identified in the post-independence emigration: (*a*) the emigration of Anglo-Indians to Australia and England, (*b*) the emigration of professionals and semi-professionals to the industrially advanced countries like the United States of America, England and Canada, and (*c*) the emigration of skilled and unskilled labourers to West Asia.

The emigration of the Anglo-Indians is one of the least studied facets of Indian diaspora. Feeling marginalised in the aftermath of India's independence, many of these descendants of intermarriage between Indians and the English left India for England in the first instance. Finding that they were not racially and ethnically acceptable to the English, several of them emigrated to Australia, which has become a second 'homeland' to a significant section of the Anglo-Indians.

The large-scale and steady emigration of doctors, engineers, scientists, teachers and other semi-professionals to the industrially advanced countries of the West is essentially a post-independence phenomenon, and particularly so of the late 1960s and the 1970s. It somewhat declined with the adoption of stringent immigration regulation by the recipient countries. This pattern of emigration, often described as 'brain drain', is essentially voluntary and mostly individual in nature. With the second and subsequent generations having emerged, and the emigrant population enjoying economic prosperity and sociocultural rights, this stream of emigration has resulted in vibrant Indian communities abroad.

To be contrasted with the above is the emigration of skilled and unskilled labourers to West Asia in the wake of the 'oil boom' there (see Gracias 2000, and Nair 1991 and 1994). This emigration is voluntary in nature, but its trends and conditions are determined by labour market vagaries. It is a predominantly male migration, characterised by uninterrupted ties with the families and communities back in India. This cannot be otherwise, as in many of the West Asian countries the immigrant labourers cannot settle down, and have neither property rights nor the freedom to practice their own religion (other than Islam).

The Scope of *Indian Diaspora*

Brief as it may be, the foregoing historical sketch is sufficient to highlight the complex and variegated nature of the phenomenon brought under the rubric *Indian Diaspora*. As such, the scope of *Indian Diaspora* as an area of academic study encompasses a variety of topics. This section outlines a catalogue of important themes and issues that can be (and often are) pursued under this scope. The research questions raised by these themes and issues, it must be noted, can hardly be answered exclusively by any conventional discipline from its own theoretical and conceptual apparatuses. In other words, the agenda of *Indian Diaspora* as an area of academic study is necessarily multi-disciplinary in nature.

(1) Demography of Population Movements

At the outset, it is important to know the key demographic aspects of the emigration of people from the Indian subcontinent during various *periods*. During different periods, the *magnitude* of people emigrating and their *destination* have varied.[5] These in turn are influenced by the *policies* (if any) governing emigration prevalent during those periods. That is, time, magnitude, direction and policy enter as key variables in the analysis of Indian diaspora. They may be relevant, nay indispensable, in understanding specific aspects of Indian diaspora. They also form a focal theme for a more specialised study, which may be called the *Demography of Indian Diaspora*.

A significant demographic aspect of Indian diaspora that needs detailed analysis is the sex-ratio imbalance. The emigration of Indians in the first instance has generally been a male phenomenon. This problem was grave in the case of indentured emigration during the colonial era. The acute shortage of women had both short-term and long-term consequences. With reference to the post-colonial emigration too, and especially as for the labour emigration to West Asia, the predominance of males is noticeable. The implications of this and the balancing mechanisms at work are important facets for sociodemographic investigation.

Both in the colonial and the post-colonial phases of Indian diaspora, some emigrants returned home for various reasons. This is termed *reverse migration*. While in the normal course the returnees are individuals and families (see Nair 1991), under extraordinary circumstances reverse migration may assume massive proportions: the return of Indians from Burma (now Myanmar) on the eve of the Japanese invasion of that country during World War II and from Kuwait during the Gulf War (see P. C. Jain 1991) are cases in point. Reverse migration is one of the least studied aspects of Indian diaspora.

(2) Causes of and Conditions for Migration

The decision of an individual or a group of people to leave the homeland in the first instance, and then to settle down in an alien land is influenced by various reasons, which may be broadly categorised as *the push factors* and *the pull factors*. Given these factors, which may operate in combination, the prevalent conditions determine the actual migration. Among these include the presence of an agency facilitating emigration, the policy framework governing movement of population both in the homeland and in the recipient country, convenient and economical mode of transportation, etc.

An analysis of the factors responsible for emigration is important as these factors determine whether a given stream of emigration was *voluntary* (i.e., by choice) or *involuntary* (i.e., due to necessity). Such an analysis will also clarify if a given mass emigration had functioned as a safety-valve for some regions of the country or some sections of its population during particular periods in history, due to the prevalent economic, political or social conditions.

A study of the factors responsible for emigration could also provide a bench mark for comparing diasporic communities with their 'remembered past'. In fact, for a better understanding of some communities of Indian origin in Africa, Asia and the Caribbean, it would be necessary to reconstruct the late 18th century and early 19th century rural socioeconomic set-up in parts of India. Such an exercise has often been undertaken to delineate the factors influencing the emigration of Indians during the colonial period, especially under the indentured system (see Kondapi 1951, Mangru 1987: 53–78, Saha 1970, Tinker 1993: 39–60 and Vertovec 1992: 6–12).

(3) The Background of Emigrants

Historically, the emigrants from India have been a heterogenous lot. They are varied in terms of their regional, religious, caste, occupational, linguistic and cultural backgrounds. As crucial independent variables, data on these factors are indispensable for explaining the differential evolution of Indian communities abroad in general, and the differences noticeable among sections of a given diasporic community in particular. A knowledge of the background of emigrants in conjunction with the demography of population movements is also crucial for interpreting the dynamics of social institutions and sociocultural patterns (see items 7 and 8) of Indian communities abroad.

(4) The Process of Emigration

The process of emigration, especially if it is on a large-scale (as in the colonial era) or of a particular category of labour force (as for example, computer specialists or trained nurses), involves agencies and mechanisms of emigration. The emigration may be officially sponsored, as the indentured labour immigration was, or it may be channelled by private entrepreneurs or informally sponsored by relatives and friends. The entire gamut of recruitment, agency and the modalities employed by the emigrants is a significant aspect in the study of *Indian Diaspora*.

(5) The Changing Composition of the 'Host' Country

The plight of Indians as a diasporic community abroad is to a considerable extent determined by the ethnic, religious and socioeconomic composition of the 'host' country. Such countries are often described as plural societies. The concept of *plural society* is more than a descriptive label, and it rests on certain assumptions about which scholars are not in agreement. In fact, notwithstanding its uses, as a theoretical perspective in the analysis of diasporic situations it is fraught with controversies (see Baber 1987; Robotham 1980 and 1985; and M.G. Smith 1965: Ch. 4, 1983 and 1987). As a descriptive label, 'multicultural society' appears to be more appropriate.

In discussions on the relationship of the Indian community with others in multicultural polities, one often comes across the phrase 'host society'. Since Indians are an emigrant (and thereby a 'guest') community in such alien (and thereby 'host') polities, the expression 'host society' seems apparently acceptable. However, a closer review of these societies/polities would reveal that in certain cases, the expression could be misleading. With the native population having been almost annihilated, as in Trinidad, the so called 'host society' may consist of only immigrant communities with varying lengths of diasporic history.[6] Thus, a knowledge of the changing composition of the country in which the Indians have emerged as a diasporic community is a *sine qua non* for a proper understanding of the latter.

(6) The Dynamics of the 'Host' Society

It is obvious from the foregoing that Indians as a diasporic community cannot be understood *sui generis*. The evolution of an Indian community abroad is closely linked to the general history of the host country. The economic, political and social changes taking place there have an impact on the Indians as a diasporic community. Accordingly, the dynamics of the 'host' society becomes an integral part of a study of *Indian Diaspora*, providing as it were the backdrop against which the evolution and predicament of a diasporic community can be understood.

(7) The Social Organisation of the Diasporic Community

Crucial to the evolution of Indians as a diasporic community has been their ability to adapt in an alien setting the institutions characteristic of the social organisation of their ancestral land. The most important of these have been family, the rites (marriage) for establishing it and the network of relationships (kinship) resulting from or reinforced by it. Caste system, which had been the primordial principle of social organisation in the homeland, was another such institution. At a much broader level was the *panchayat*, the council of village elders, which arbitrated in community disputes and regulated community life.

In some diasporic situations, during the colonial phase (e.g., in the Caribbean, Mauritius and Fiji), the conditions were not conducive to the continuation of the traditional institutions. These institutions and the associated social practices even got deinstitutionalised. With the settlement of Indians as a community, however, the traditional institutions were reconstituted with varying degrees of effectiveness. Caste system almost disappeared, and even in communities where the semblances of its elements are noticeable, it is neither a 'structural principle' nor is it 'functionally relevant' (see Schwartz 1967). Though we come across references to the *panchayat* during the early stages of community formation, as in Trinidad (*see* Klass 1961: 211–20), it is no more to be found. Family is one institution which was effectively reconstituted, though even this was adapted to the local socioeconomic conditions. Thus, the organisation of Indians as a diasporic community bears the stamp of the dynamics of 'host' society (*see* item 6).

Not surprisingly, the social institutions of the Indian communities abroad have attracted and continue to attract the attention of anthropologists and sociologists studying Indian diaspora. Generally, studies on social institutions have been descriptive in nature, often comparing those institutions with their counterparts prevalent in India. Such a comparison carries the risk of confusing 'difference' for 'change'. Any analysis of change is necessarily diachronic and requires a point of departure in time. It is such a point of departure that is contemplated in item (2). Viewed in a diachronic perspective, analyses of social institutions in Indian diaspora have immense potential for theoretical advancement, as they can explain the 'essentiality' of an institution, and its rootedness or otherwise in the Indian (Hindu, Muslim, or Sikh) culture.

(8) The Cultural Dynamics of the Diasporic Community

Akin to the social organisation of the Indian communities abroad is the question about the sociocultural baggage carried by the first generation emigrants from India. This baggage consisted of religion, language, music, art, dress, cuisine, etc. often in the folk form but in their regional variants. The experience of these cultural elements in different diasporic situations has been varied: some of these elements have disappeared; some have survived or persisted; others have experienced assimilation, syncretism or change and a few elements have been sought to be revived. The relative dynamics of the cultural elements in diaspora is an instructive field of investigation. The conditions of persistence, assimilation, change and revival, the relative ability of a particular element to adapt itself to new and changing conditions, and the sequences of changes in cultural elements are some key aspects that could be covered in such an investigation.

(9) The Question of Identity

In many diasporic situations, especially in multiethnic polities and where the people of Indian origin are numerically significant, the question of their image and identity has been critical. In the colonial phase, the British stereotyped Indian emigrants as 'coolies'. Even when the upwardly mobile Indians became professionals, the prefix 'coolie' was always attached to their professional designation: In South Africa Mohandas Karamchand Gandhi was often called 'the coolie lawyer'. Similarly, the traders of the East African coastline were called 'passenger Indians': 'The meaning was that they came to Africa on their own initiative as passengers paying their own fares; and yet, the nickname seemed to have an implication that they were travellers, sojourners, not settlers or immigrants' (Tinker 1977: 3). In the literature on the subject we also come across references to such expressions as 'East Indians', 'Girmitiyas', 'the Asians', and the prefix 'Indo-' being attached to Indians forming nationality groups in a country (like the 'Indo-Americans', 'Indo-Canadians', 'Indo-Guyanese', 'Indo-Trinidadians', etc.).

Many expressions describing diasporic Indians are local coinages, either by the Indian community itself or by its significant others, while some are labels coined by scholars studying them. Underlying these images and expressions is the process of mutual perception by the diasporic Indian community, on the one hand, and its significant others, on the other. The question of identity ('self-image' and 'other-image') is thus an integral part of the study of *Indian Diaspora*.

Intrinsically related to the question of identity are the behaviour patterns designated by the term ethnicity. The evolution of ethnicity among diasporic Indians in relation to their significant others in multiethnic polities and the dynamics of ethnic relations are other areas falling under the study of *Indian Diaspora*. With reference to countries where the ethnic relations involving Indians have become complicated, Tinker (1977: 138–39) raises the following key questions:

... do the Asians [Indians] create their own difficulties by their own way of life, and by remaining separate from the host society; or do their troubles arise mainly from excess of chauvinism or racism in the country of their adoption? Do they offend because they are, visibly, both pariahs and exploiters in alien societies? Or are they scapegoats, singled out for victimisation because their adopted country (or its government) needs an alibi for poor performance in the national sphere?

Expressions of ethnic identity and articulations of ethnic interests could be seen in the associations and fora formed by Indians in the diaspora. The nature and orientation of such associations in the Indian communities which have been in existence abroad for over a century are different from those in communities which have come into existence in the last few decades. The formation of associations on regional, linguistic and caste lines is generally peculiar to the latter. The structure and functioning of ethnic Indian associations abroad deserve more scholarly attention (see Bhat 1993 and Bacon 1996: 22–58). Moreover, Mitra (1997: 76–77) has argued that electronic communication systems offer an opportunity to the diasporic communities to produce new identities and that they are using different means to achieve this.

(10) The Struggle for Power

In polities where Indians have been numerically significant, their ethnic orientation has been tied to struggle for political power. That is, the issue of ethnicity has a tendency to get politicised. Governmental policies and actions are perceived and reacted to in ethnic terms. In some countries, the struggle for political power has crossed the bounds of democracy and has even led to violent conflicts and the suppression of the Indian community. This has also resulted in the exodus of the Indian community, as with the Indo-Guayanese emigrating to North America, the Hindustani Surinamese emigrating to The Netherlands, the East African Sikhs emigrating to the United Kingdom and the Indo-Fijians emigrating to New Zealand and Canada. The political predicament of the Indian communities abroad and their involvement in the struggle for political power form a distinct focus of the study of *Indian Diaspora*.

(11) The Secondary Emigration

Besides political upheavals and oppressions in their country of adoption, the diasporic Indians have moved out of their country of first settlement in search of greener pastures (see Gosine 1990a). Some of them, though rarely, and mostly as individuals, have even experienced subsequent emigration. While the 'twice-removed' Indians (Bhachu 1985 and 1991) were initially treated as refugees, they have now established themselves as diasporic communities in their second land of adoption. In some cases, as in the United Kingdom and Canada, these 'second' diasporic communities have to negotiate with the Indian diasporic communities already existing there (see Bhachu 1991, and Buchignani and Indra 1981). Thus, the phenomenon of the second and subsequent diaspora throws up new facets for research.

(12) Orientation of the Diasporic Indians to the Ancestral Land

As Safran (1991: 84) has observed, it is a general characteristic of diasporics that 'they continue to relate, personally or vicariously, to the homeland in one way or another, and their ethno-communal consciousness and solidarity are importantly defined by the existence of such a relationship'. Thus, the diasporic Indians do not sever their relationship with their ancestral land. The nature of this relationship is highly variant in different diasporic situations: with a mental relationship with 'imagined India' at one extreme, to periodical visits to India at the other extreme. The image that the diasporic Indians have of India, what does that image mean to them and what is the relationship between the diasporic Indians and Indians are some topics for investigation in the study of *Indian Diaspora* (see Jayaram 1998a).

In this context, it must be observed that the rapid advancements in the electronic media, and particularly the computer mediated communication technologies, have created, what Appadurai (1997: 4) calls, 'diasporic public spheres'. The diasporic people, Indians included, are 'increasingly using these technologies to re-create a sense of virtual community through a rediscovery of their commonality' (Mitra 1997: 58). This phenomenon opens up fascinating possibilities for the study of Indian diaspora (see Lal 1999).

An important manifestation of the continued contact that the diasporic people maintain with their ancestral land is the remittances that they make home periodically. While these remittances are welcome considering the precious foreign exchange that they bring into the country, they have also significant impact on the families and areas from which the immigrants hail (see Amjad 1989, Helweg 1983, Lall 2001, Nair 1994, Nayyar 1994 and Oberai and Singh 1980).

(13) Orientation of the Ancestral Land to the Diasporic Indians

Conversely, the orientation of the ancestral land to the diasporic Indians is also a significant but neglected subject of study in *Indian Diaspora*. This orientation can be approached from two different points of view: (*a*) the formal stand of the Government of India about the Indian communities abroad (see Lall 2001), as revealed by its policies and programmes and (*b*) the informal relationships which exist between Indians and their relatives and friends in the diaspora.

(14) Other Themes

Some diasporic communities have received scant attention and they need to be studied as they are characterised by special features: the Anglo-Indians who emigrated to Australia are one such case. The Indian Jewish emigrants (the Bene Israelis of Maharashtra, the Cochini Jews and the Baghdadi Jews) who answered the call of the founders of Israel for an 'ingathering of Jews' from all over the world are another case (see Das 1996 and Kushner 1973). Similar cases include the Indians in Burma (Myanmar) (see Chakravarti 1971), Thailand (see Hossain 1982), Singapore (see Arasaratnam 1970, and Siddique and Purushottam 1982) and other South and East Asian countries (see Singh 1982 and 1984).

There have been some diasporic communities in India, e.g., the Chinese and Armenians in Calcutta, the Tibetans in Dharmshala and Karnataka, and the Jews and the Africans. The evolution of these communities in the country and their integration with the mainstream society need to be studied. Studies on these communities will provide insights into the nature of India as a 'host' society.

Approaches to the Study of Indian Diaspora

The specific topics falling within the purview of the foregoing broad themes can be and have been approached from the perspective of different disciplines. Given the complex nature of *Indian Diaspora* as an area of academic study, the scholars with a specialist background in one discipline have been required to cross the boundaries of their discipline. Tapping data on a particular topic, using concepts for interpreting data on hand, and the use of theoretical and methodological perspectives to enlarge the scope of generalisation and to join debates at a broader level are some transdisciplinary strategies adopted by scholars. A few scholars have even been explicitly interdisciplinary in their orientation.

Emphasising chronology, the historical approach yields accounts of the phases of emigration and the early life situations of the Indian emigrants in the 'host' countries (see Tinker 1993). Anthropological and sociological approaches have largely shared a common platform: Using the conventional research techniques and theoretical frameworks of their disciplines, these approaches yield rich ethnographic accounts of the Indian communities abroad and analyse the dynamics of social institutions and sociocultural elements in those communities (e.g., R. K. Jain 1970, Jayaraman 1975, Klass 1961 and Williams 1991). There have been instances of geographers combining the techniques of and the insights from these disciplines (see Clarke 1986 and Shah 1980). Political scientists have followed suit, especially in their analysis of the interface between ethnicity and politics in multiethnic societies where the Indian community is a key constituent (e.g., see Premdas 1995a, 1995b and 1996).

Besides historians, anthropologists, sociologists, geographers and political scientists, scholars working in the fields of languages (see Damsteegt 1988), linguistics (see Durbin 1973, and Mohan and Zador 1986) and literature (see Birbalsingh 1986 and 1989b and *Caribbean Quarterly* 1986) have been interested in Indian diaspora. Their interest, however, is more restricted, though they too use the work of scholars from other fields. Based on their experience, a few diplomats have reported on the position and problems of Indian communities in some countries (see Bhatia 1973, Hiremath 1992–93 and Ramchandani 1976). There have also been analyses of policies and laws governing immigration in some countries (see Wood 1983).

Largely, studies on Indian diaspora have been country-specific. Some scholars have enlarged their coverage by focussing on a specific issue or topic of Indian diaspora in a given region. This is understandable considering the constraints of opportunity, time and resources encountered by scholars. Thus, comparative studies of Indian diaspora have been few (see Arasaratnam 1970, R. K. Jain 1988, Jayawardeva 1980, Look Lai 1993, Mahajani 1960 and Vertovec 1994). Restudies of a diasporic community (see Klass 1961 and 1991) and comparisons between 'the old immigration' and 'the new immigration' (see Helweg 1991) are rare.

Whatever the disciplinary orientations from which the study of Indian diaspora is approached, broadly two theoretical frameworks have been adopted in its analysis: *the sociocultural perspective* and *the political economy perspective* (see S. L. Sharma *infra* chapter 2). Focussing on cultural identity and integration of the diasporic communities, the sociocultural perspective has largely operated from within the parameters of conventional structural-functionalism. It addresses the questions of sociocultural continuity and change among the diasporic communities on the one hand, and the dynamics of these communities in the context of multiculturalism on the other.

Drawing insights from a variety of Marxist and non-Marxist socioeconomic thinking, the political economy perspective focuses on the economic and political aspects of the phenomenon of Indian diaspora. This perspective emphasises the historical context of the diaspora, the mode of economy of the 'host' country and the place of the diasporic Indians in it, and the nature of the state in the 'host' country. While these two theoretical perspectives are different, both in their substantive interests and conceptual apparatus, they can only be complementary to each other in providing a more comprehensive understanding of Indian diaspora.

To conclude, it may be reiterated that the study of *Indian Diaspora* is *not* a discipline by itself, but only an area of specialised study utilising the data, concepts, methods and theories of many disciplines. Its import for policy formulation, both in India and the countries where Indians are a diasporic community, is often emphasised. However, scholars working in the area are queried by their comrades in the discipline as to its theoretical significance.

Societies with large or significant sections of immigrant population are social laboratories where the salient theoretical perspectives of social science disciplines can be tested. Diasporic situations enable us to trace and analyse certain key social processes like the formation of ethnic identity, the shaping of ethnic relations, the reconstitution of institutions, the reconstruction of life-worlds, etc. Since diasporic situations require interaction of cultures, they provide unique avenues for understanding the dynamics of culture.

II

Indian Diaspora in *Sociological Bulletin*

For over 35 years, the study of *Indian Diaspora* has been a subject of interest to the *Sociological Bulletin*. Beginning with G. S. Aurora's analysis of the process of social adjustment of Indian immigrants in Britain which appeared in its Volume 14(2) in September 1965 (see *infra* chapter 3), articles focussing on various aspects of the Indian diasporic communities have periodically, though infrequently, appeared in the pages of the *Bulletin*. According it a pride of place, under the guest-editorship of S. L. Sharma, the *Bulletin* brought out a special number (Vol. 38, No. 1, March 1989) on 'Indians Abroad'. From these various articles, nine selections of lasting value on the subject are reproduced in the volume. I must confess, however, that the process of selection has not been easy: Specific rationale—historicity, thematic coverage, methodological orientation and theoretical perspective—determined each selection. Not that other articles are of less relevance or significance, but that constraints of space regrettably precluded many others. A list of all articles on Indian diaspora carried by the *Bulletin* is included in a separate section in the *Select Bibliography on The Indian Diaspora*.

The first systematic attempt to analyse the various perspectives for studying the Indian diaspora was provided by S. L. Sharma (see *infra* chapter 2). After identifying the different types of writing on Indian diaspora (the historical, diplomatic and anthropological) and examining the colonial and the nationalist discourses on the problems of Indians abroad, he contrasts at length two sociological perspectives for understanding and interpreting the phenomenon of Indian diaspora: The functional perspective, which he appropriately prefers to call 'the sociocultural perspective', which is rather predominant, focuses on cultural continuity and change which inevitably follows the change of national domicile of an individual or a group. More specifically, this perspective 'tends to concentrate on the question of cultural identity and integration'. The political economy perspective, with its various versions (the Marxist, non-Marxist, and Neo-Marxist), brings to sharp relief the political and economic aspects of the diaspora. History, economy, class and power are its central explanatory categories. In conclusion, Sharmà reflects on the theoretical significance of the study of Indian diaspora.

G. S. Aurora's article on the Indian immigrants in Britain (Vol. 14, No. 2, September 1965, see infra chapter 3), was the first one to be published in the Bulletin on the subject. Based on the data that he gathered from Punjabi-speaking industrial labourers during 1957–59, he sought to analyse the 'process of adjustment' that they underwent in 'the foreign social environment'. Considering that they were the first generation immigrants, they were keen to avoid conflicts with the host society, and if possible to get assimilated into it. Since the immigrants were not a homogenous social and cultural group, the process of adjustment they experienced also varied. Aurora noticed that 'The idioms whereby class identifications are expressed are also the idioms whereby an immigrant may establish his cultural bona fides...'. His analysis revealed that in terms of their adjustment the immigrants were broadly either 'accommodationists' or 'integrationists'. Following Max Gluckman, Aurora argues that 'the structural forms which a community takes in its process of adjustment in a new social environment are evolved as a result of a constant interaction between its endo-trait complexes and the exo-trait complexes'.

Chaudry M. Siddique's article on the immigrants in Canada (Vol. 26, No. 2, September 1977, see infra chapter 4) is analytically special: It deals with the changes experienced by the first generation Indian and Pakistani families. It compares these families with those in their country of origin and the white Canadian families in Saskatoon. Starting with the axiom that migration inevitably involves disruption and readjustment in family life and behaviour, Chaudry delineates changes that have taken place in the household division of labour and decision-making. While the change towards the 'Canadian pattern' is discerned, the structural separation of the immigrant families from their larger kin networks and the experience of living abroad are found to account for the variations in the trends of change within the community.

A state-of-the-art account of research on people of Indian origin in Canada is attempted by Norman Buchignani (Vol. 38, No. 1, March 1989, see infra chapter 5). His review of the Indo-Canadian Studies as an area of special study reveals it to be an anomalous development: studies being primarily oriented towards the discipline of the author and to the theoretical literature within it, divergent methodologies separating researchers, descriptive work eschewing comparison and the total isolation from South Asian studies. He calls for 'an eventual unification of discourse' for a better understanding of Indians in Canada. His observation that certain topics would be best addressed by researchers whose primary expertise is in India is noteworthy for the development of *Indian Diaspora* as an area of academic study.

Calling for 'a separate and careful study' of Muslims in Indian diaspora, Nasser Mustapha (Vol. 46, No. 2, September 1997, see *infra* chapter 6) examines the influence of Indian Islam on the fundamentalist trends in Trinidad and Tobago. Muslims constitute 6 per cent of the total population of this twin-island Caribbean republic, and 95 per cent of these Muslims are of Indian origin. Mustapha tries to dispel the notion of a monolithic Muslim community by showing how a variety of Islamic fundamentalisms can coexist: 'Muslims experience more conflict and tension among themselves than with other religious denominations in the society'. He observes that while the influence of the Middle East has been growing over the past decade, the Indian influence remains strong.

Dealing with the Trinidadians of Indian origin, N. Jayaram (Vol. 49, No. 1, March 2000, see *infra* chapter 7) analyses the dynamics of language in Indian diaspora. He traces the linguistic element in the sociocultural baggage brought by their ancestors during the indenture era, examines the metamorphosis and attrition that this element experienced in the course of over 150 years of their presence in Trinidad and documents the efforts at reviving and rejuvenating the linguistic element of their cultural heritage and reflects on the prospects thereof. He concludes that while Hindi may develop as a 'language' among the Indo-Trinidadians, Indo-Trinidadians are not likely to become a distinctive 'speech community'.

Ravindra K. Jain (Vol. 38, No. 1, March 1989, see *infra* chapter 8) provides a comparative analysis of the Indian diaspora in two widely different national settings, namely, Trinidad and Malaysia. The focus of his comparison is on the interplay and relative significance of race relations, ethnicity, class and culture in defining the varying identity of the Indians in these two countries. He argues that different frameworks of analysis—that of race relations in Trinidad and that of ethnicity in Malaysia—are useful in studying diasporic situations. He treats caste as a 'cultural variable', passing into race in Trinidad and ethnicity in Malaysia, and observes that social stratification—in terms of such dimensions as class, status and power—are not 'the determinant framework of Indian identity in the overseas context'.

Following Jeffrey Alexander's multi-dimensional model of 'inclusion', S. R. Mehta (Vol. 38, No. 1, March 1989, see infra chapter 9) examines the marginal status of the diasporic Indians in Mauritius: On the external axis, the Indo-Mauritians show partial 'inclusion' into the economic, social and religious spheres of civil solidarity, though they have made their mark in the political sphere. On the internal axis, their race, kinship and religion preclude them from being included in the civil solidarity; while they do share language (i.e., Creole) as a cultural trait of the Mauritians. In brief, 'the Indo-Mauritians present a case of uneven "inclusion" into the core solidarity and civil social set-up of Mauritius'.

In his theoretically stimulating article, Yogesh Atal (Vol. 38, No. 1, March 1989, see infra chapter 10) explains the nature of 'sandwich culture' occasioned by the diaspora. He observes that in diaspora the inevitable orientation towards two cultures leads 'to accretions and attritions' and the development of 'a new pattern of interrelationship between different elements'. He introduces the concept of 'sandwich culture' as complementary to that of 'resilience', and highlights the enormous theoretical potential of these concepts in understanding diaspora. While the concept of 'sandwich culture' is applicable at various levels (from that of an entire country to that of refugee communities), Atal clarifies, the subcultures of outside groups in an alien land are of immediate interest to understanding diaspora.

Thus, these nine selections deal with the empirical reality of the Indian diaspora, and the theoretical and methodological issues raised by it. Thematically they cover social adjustment, family change, religion, language, ethnicity and culture, and cultural integration and syncretism. In terms of locale they traverse Britain, Canada, Malaysia, Mauritius and Trinidad. Thus, encompassing the classical and modern diasporas, the anthology not only seeks to arrive at the generalities of the global Indian diaspora, but also to highlight its specificities across space and time.

Notes

1. For analytical clarity, I have italicised the designation *Indian Diaspora* to distinguish it as an area of academic study from its substantive focus, namely, the sociocultural phenomenon of Indian diaspora.

2. In preparing this part, I have drawn heavily on my article 'The study of Indian diaspora: A multidisciplinary agenda' (Jayaram 1998b). For permitting this, I thank the Centre for the Study of Indian Diaspora, University of Hyderabad, which had published it as its Occasional Paper No. 1.

3. In Fiji, this contractual system was called *girmit* (the Hindi-ised version of 'agreement'), and the labourer entering such a contract was called a *girmitia*.

4. Thomaz (1985) has drawn attention to the presence of Indian merchant communities in Malacca under the Portuguese rule.

5. For instance, in the colonial era, emigrants to South Asia and Southeast Asia were predominantly drawn from South India, whereas those to East Africa were Gujaratis and Punjabis and those to the Caribbean hailed from the Gangetic plain. Similarly, in the post-colonial phase, Anglo-Indians have predominantly emigrated to Australia.

6. Tinker (1977: ix) uses 'dominant population' as an alternative to 'host society' in the analysis of the Indian predicament in diaspora. However, when the Indians are themselves a numerically dominant community, in Mauritius, Guyana or Fiji, this expression can hardly be useful; and, it may even be misleading. For instance, in Mauritius, the Indians being the majority ethnic group may *appear* to be the 'host' community in relation to other minority ethnic groups. Or, their numerical dominance notwithstanding, under certain circumstances, the Indians may be at the receiving end, as is clear from their history in Fiji and Guyana. Thus, it would be relevant and necessary to specify aspects of dominance in analysis of the location and predicament of the Indian community in a diasporic situation. Incidentally, 'settlement society' and 'receiving society' have been often used as alternative expressions.

References

Amjad, Rashid. 1989. *To the Gulf and Back: Studies on the Economic Impact of Asian Labour Migration.* Geneva: United Nations Development Programme.

Appadurai, Arjun. 1997. *Modernity at Large: Cultural Dimensions of Globalization.* New Delhi: Oxford University Press.

Arasaratnam, Sinnappah. 1970. *Indians in Malaysia and Singapore.* London: Oxford University Press.

Arkin, A. J.; K. P. Magyar and G. J. Pillay (eds.). 1989. *The Indian South Africans.* Pinetown: Owen Burgess.

Baber, Willie L. 1987. 'The Pluralism Controversy: Wider Theoretical Considerations', *Caribbean Quarterly*, 33(1–2): 81–94.

Bacon, Jean. 1996. *Life Lines: Community, Family, and Assimilation among Asian Indian Immigrants*. New York/Oxford: Oxford University Press.

Barrier, N. Gerald and Verne A. Dusenbery (eds.). 1989. *The Sikh Diaspora: Migration and the Experience Beyond Punjab*. Delhi: Chanakya Publications.

Baumann, Martin. 2000. 'Diaspora: Genealogies of Semantics and Transcultural Comparison', *Numen* (International Review for the History of Religions), 47(3): 313–37.

Bhachu, Parminder. 1985. *Twice Migrants: East African Sikh Settlers in Britain*. London: Tavistock Publications.

———. 1991. 'The East African Sikh Diaspora: The British Case', in Steven Vertovec (ed.): *Aspects of the South Asian Diaspora*. New Delhi: Oxford University Press, pp. 57–85.

Bhat, Chandrashekhar. 1993. 'Indian Ethnic Associations in London: Search for Unity in Diversity', in Chandrashekhar Bhat, Laxmi Narayan Kadekar and K. Ranga Rao (eds.): *Sociology of Development and Change*. Delhi: Orient Longman, pp. 210–28.

Bhatia, Prem. 1973. *Indians' Ordeal in Africa*. Delhi: Vikas Publishing House.

Birbalsingh, Frank. 1986. 'Indians in the Novels of Edgar Mittelholzer', *Caribbean Quarterly*, 32(1–2): 16–24.

———. (ed.). 1989a. *Indenture and Exile: The Indo-Caribbean Experience*. Toronto: TSAR in association with the Ontario Association for Studies in Indo-Caribbean Culture.

———. 1989b. 'Jamaican Indians: A Novelist's View', in Frank Birbalsingh (ed.): *Indenture and Exile: The Indo-Caribbean Experience*. Toronto: TSAR in association with the Ontario Association for Studies in Indo-Caribbean Culture, pp. 91–99.

Buchignani, Norman and Doreen Marie Indra. 1981. 'Inter-group Conflict and Community Solidarity: Sikhs and South Asian Fijians in Vancouver', *Canadian Journal of Anthropology*, 1(2): 149–57.

Burghart, Richard (ed.). 1987. *Hinduism in Great Britain: The Perpetuation of Religion in an Alien Cultural Milieu*. London: Tavistock.

Caribbean Quarterly. 1986. Special Issue on 'East Indians in West Indian Literature', 32(1–2).

Chakravarti, N. R. 1971. *The Indian Minority in Burma: The Rise and Decline of an Immigrant Community*. London: Oxford University Press.

Chandrasekhar, S. (ed.). 1983. *From India to America: A Brief History of Immigration; Problems of Discrimination; Admission and Assimilation*. La Jolla: A Population Review Book.

Clarke, Colin G. 1986. *East Indians in a West Indian Town: San Fernando, Trinidad, 1930–70*. London: George Allen and Unwin.

Clarke, Colin; Ceri Peach and Steven Vertovec (eds.). 1990. *South Asians Overseas: Migration and Ethnicity*. Cambridge: Cambridge University Press.

Crocombe, Ron (ed.). 1981. *Pacific Indians: Profiles from 20 Countries*. Suva: Institute of Pacific Studies, University of South Pacific.

Dabydeen, David and Brinsley Samaroo (eds.). 1987. *India in the Caribbean*. London: Hansib Publishing Limited.

———. (eds.). 1996. *Across the Dark Waters: Ethnicity and Indian Identity in the Caribbean*. London and Basingstoke: Macmillan Education.

Damsteegt, Theo. 1988. 'Sarnami: A Living Language', in R. K. Barz and J. Siegel (eds.): *Language Transplanted: The Development of Overseas Hindi*. Wiesbaden: Harrassowitz.

Das, Chitta Ranjan. 1996. 'Israel's Jews from India', *The Eastern Anthropologist*, 49(3–4): 317–48.

Durbin, Mridula Adenwala. 1973. 'Formal Changes in Trinidad Hindi as a Result of Language Adaptation', *American Anthropologist*, 75(5): 1290–1304.

Ghai, Dharam P. (ed.). 1970. *Portrait of a Minority: Asians in East Africa*. Nairobi: Oxford University Press.

Gosine, Mahin. 1990a. *Caribbean East Indians in America: Assimilation, Adaptation and Group Experience*. New York: Windsor Press.

———. (ed.). 1990b. *Dot-head Americans: The Silent Minority in the United States*. New York: Windsor Press.

———. (ed.). 1992. *The Coolie Connection: From the Orient to the Occident*. New York: Windsor Press.

———. (ed.). 1994. *The East Indian Odyssey: Dilemmas of a Migrant People*. New York: Windsor Press.

Gosine, Mahin (with Dipak Malik and Kumar Mahabir). 1995. *The Legacy of Indian Indenture: 150 Years of East Indians in Trinidad*. New York: Windsor Press.

Government of India. 2001. *India 2001: A Reference Annual*. New Delhi: Publications Division, Ministry of Information and Broadcasting.

Gracias, Fatima da Silva. 2000. 'Goans away from Goa: Migration to the Middle East', *Lusotopie 2000* (Lusophonies asiatiques, Asiatiques en lusophonies). Paris: Editions Karthala, pp. 423–32.

Helweg, Arthur W. 1983. 'Emigrant Remittances: Their Nature and Impact on a Punjabi Village', *New Community*, 10(3): 435–43.

———. 1991. 'Indians in Australia: Theory and Methodology of the New Immigration', in Steven Vertovec (ed.): *Aspects of the South Asian Diaspora*. New Delhi: Oxford University Press, pp. 7–35.

Hiremath, J. R. 1992–93. 'Indian South Africans: A Contemporary Portrait', *Africa Quarterly*, 32(1–4).

Hossain, Zakir. 1982. *The Silent Minority: Indians in Thailand*. Bangkok: Chulalongkorn University Social Research Institute.

Israel, Milton. (ed.). 1987. *The South Asian Diaspora in Canada: Six Essays*. Toronto: The Multicultural History Society of Ontario.

Jain, Prakash C. 1991. 'Rehabilitating the Returning Migrants from the Gulf', *International Studies*, 28(3): 307–15.

Jain, Ravindra K. 1970. *South Indians on the Plantation Frontier in Malaya*. New Haven: Yale University Press.

———. 1988. 'Overseas Indians in Malaysia and the Caribbean: Comparative Notes', *Immigrants and Minorities*, 7(1): 123–43.

———. 1989. 'Race Relations, Ethnicity, Class and Culture: A Comparison of Indians in Trinidad and Malaysia', *Sociological Bulletin*, 38(1): 57–69.

———. 1993. *Indian Communities Abroad*, New Delhi: Manohar.

Jayaram, N. 1998a. 'Social Construction of the Other Indian: Encounters between Indian Nationals and Diasporic Indians', *Journal of Social and Economic Development*, 1(1): 46–63.

Jayaram, N. 1998b. 'The Study of Indian Diaspora: A Multidisciplinary Agenda' (Occasional Paper No. 1). Hyderabad: Centre for the Study of Indian Diaspora, University of Hyderabad.

————. 2003. 'The Politics of "Cultural Renaissance" among Indo-Trinidadians', in Bikhu Parekh, Gurharpal Singh and Steven Vertovec (eds.): *Culture and Economy in the Indian Diaspora*. London: Routledge, pp. 123–41.

Jayaraman, R. 1975. *Caste Continuities in Ceylon: A Study of the Social Structure of Three Tea Plantations*. Bombay: Popular Prakashan.

Jayawardena, Chandra. 1980. 'Culture and Ethnicity in Guyana and Fiji', *Man*, 15: 430–50.

Kanungo, Rabindra (ed.). 1984. *South Asians in the Canadian Mosaic*. Montreal: Kala Bharati.

Klass, Morton. 1961. *East Indians in Trinidad: A Study of Cultural Persistence*. Prospect Heights, Illinois: Waveland Press.

————. 1991. *Singing with Sai Baba: The Politics of Revitalization in Trinidad*. Boulder, Colorado: Westview Press.

Kondapi, C. 1951. *Indians Overseas, 1838–1949*. New Delhi: Indian Council for World Affairs.

Kurian, George and Ram P. Srivastava (eds.). 1983. *Overseas Indians: A Study in Adaptation*. New Delhi: Vikas Publishing House.

Kushner, Gilbert. 1973. *Immigrants from India in Israel*. Tucson: The University of Arizona Press.

La Guerre, John G. (ed.). 1985. *Calcutta to Caroni*. St. Augustine, Trinidad: Extra Mural Studies Unit, The University of the West Indies (2nd edition).

Lal, Vinay. 1999. 'The Politics of History on the Internet: Cyber-Diasporic Hinduism and the North American Hindu Diaspora', *Diaspora*, 8(2): 137–72.

Lall, Marie-Carine. 2001. *India's Missed Opportunity: India's Relationship with the Non Resident Indians*. Aldershot, Hampshire: Ashgate Publishing Limited.

Look Lai, Walton. 1993. *Indentured Labor, Caribbean Sugar: Chinese and Indian Migrants to the British West Indies, 1838–1918*. Baltimore and London: The Johns Hopkins University Press.

Mahajani, Usha. 1960. *The Role of Indian Minorities in Burma and Malaya*. Bombay: Vora and Co.

Mangru, Basdeo. 1987. *Benevolent Neutrality: Indian Government Policy and Labour Migration to British Guiana*. London: Hansib Publishing Limited.

McNeill, William H. 1963. *The Rise of the West: A History of the Human Community*. Chicago: The University of Chicago Press.

Mitra, Ananda. 1997. 'Virtual Commonality: Looking for India on the Internet', in Steven G. Jones (ed.): *Virtual Culture: Identity and Communication in a Cybersociety*. London: Sage Publications, pp. 55–79.

Mohan, Peggy and Paul Zador. 1986. 'Discontinuity in a Life Cycle: The Death of Trinidad Bhojpuri', *Language*, 62: 291–319.

Motwani, Jagat K.; Mahin Gosine and Jyoti Barot-Motwani (eds.). 1993. *Global Indian Diaspora: Yesterday, Today and Tomorrow*. New York: Global Organization of People of Indian Origin.

Nair, P. R. Gopinathan. 1991. 'Asian Migration to the Arab World: Kerala (India)', in Godfrey Gunatilleke (ed.): *Migration to the Arab World: Experiences of Returning Migrants*. Tokyo: United Nations University, pp. 19–55.

Nair, P. R. Gopinathan. 1994. 'Migration of Keralites to the Arab World', in B. A. Prakash (ed.): *Kerala's Economy: Performance, Problems, Prospects*. New Delhi: Sage Publications.

Nayyar, Deepak. 1994. *Migration, Remittances and Capital Flows: The Indian Experience*. Delhi: Oxford University Press.

Oberai, A. S. and H. K. Manmohan Singh. 1980. 'Migration Remittances and Rural Development: Findings of a Case Study in the Indian Punjab', *International Labour Review*, CIX(2): 229–41.

Premdas, Ralph R. 1995a. *Ethnic Conflict and Development: The Case of Fiji*. Aldershot, Hants, England: Avebury/Ashgate Publishing Ltd.

———. 1995b. *Ethnic Conflict and Development: The Case of Guyana*. Aldershot, Hants, England: Avebury/Ashgate Publishing Ltd.

———. 1996. 'Ethnic Identity in the Caribbean: Decentering a Myth' (Monograph Series No. 1). New Haven, Connecticut: Center for Latin American and Caribbean Studies, Yale University.

Ramchandani, R. R. 1976. *Uganda Asians: The End of an Enterprise*. Bombay: United Asia Publications.

Robotham, Don. 1980. 'Pluralism as an Ideology', *Social and Economic Studies*, 29(1): 69–89.

———. 1985. 'The Why of the Cockatoo', *Social and Economic Studies*, 34(2): 111–51.

Safran, William. 1991. 'Diasporas in Modern Societies: Myths of Homeland and Return', *Diaspora*, 1(1): 83–99.

Saha, Panchanan. 1970. *Emigration of Indian Labour, 1834–1900*. New Delhi: Peoples Publishing House.

Sastri, Nilakanta. 1959. 'Ancient Indian Contacts with Western Lands', *Diogenes*, 28: 44–53.

Schwartz, Barton Morley. 1967. (ed.): *Caste in Overseas Indian Communities*. San Francisco, California: Chandler Publishing Co.

Shah, S. 1980. *Aspects of the Geographic Analysis of Asian Immigrants in London*. DPhil thesis, Oxford University, Oxford.

Siddique, Sharon and Nirmala Purushottam. 1982. *Singapore's Llittle India: Past, Present, and Future*. Singapore: Institute of South East Asian Studies.

Singh, I. J. Bahadur (ed.). 1979. *The Other India: The Overseas Indians and their Relationship with India (proceedings of a seminar)*. New Delhi: Arnold-Heinemann.

———. (ed.). 1982. *Indians in South-East Asia*. New Delhi: Sterling Publishers.

———. (ed.). 1984. *Indians in South Asia*. New Delhi: Sterling Publishers.

———. (ed.). 1987. *Indians in the Caribbean*. New Delhi: Sterling Publishers.

Smith, M. G. 1965. *The Plural Society in the British West Indies*. Berkeley, California: University of California Press.

———. 1983. 'Robotham's Ideology and Pluralism: A Reply', *Social and Economic Studies*, 32(2): 103–39.

———. 1987. 'Pluralism: Comments on an Ideological Analysis', *Social and Economic Studies*, 36(4): 157–91.

Smith, Vincent A. 1958. *Oxford History of India*. London: Oxford University Press.

Sociological Bulletin. 1989. Special Number on 'Indians Abroad' (Guest ed.: S. L. Sharma), 38(1).

Subramani (ed.). 1979. *The Indo-Fijian Experience.* St. Lucia, Queensland: University of Queensland Press.

Thomaz, Luis Filipe. 1985. 'The Indian Merchant Communities in Malacca under the Portuguese Rule', in Teotonio R. de Souza (ed.): *Indo-Portuguese History: Old Issues, New Questions.* New Delhi: Concept Publishing Co., pp. 56–72.

Tinker, Hugh. 1977. *The Banyan Tree: Overseas Emigrants from India, Pakistan and Bangladesh.* Oxford: Oxford University Press.

———. 1993. *A New System of Slavery: The Export of Indian Labour Overseas, 1830–1920.* London: Hansib Publishing Limited (2nd edition).

Tiwari, Kapil (ed.). 1980. *Indians in New Zealand.* Wellington, New Zealand: Prince Milburn.

Vertovec, Steven. 1991a. 'East Indians and Anthropologists: A Critical Review', *Social and Economic Studies*, 40(1): 133–69.

———. (ed.). 1991b. *Aspects of the South Asian Diaspora* (Oxford University Papers on India, Vol. 2, Part 2). New Delhi: Oxford University Press.

———. 1992. *Hindu Trinidad: Religion, Ethnicity and Socio-Economic Change*, London: Macmillan Education.

———. 1994. '"Official" and "Popular" Hinduism in Diaspora: Historical and Contemporary Trends in Surinam, Trinidad and Guyana', *Contributions to Indian Sociology*, 28(1): 123–47. Reprinted in David Dabydeen and Brinsley Samaroo (eds.): *Across the Dark Waters: Ethnicity and Indian Identity in the Caribbean.* London and Basingstoke: Macmillan Education, 1996, pp. 108–30.

Williams, Brackette F. 1991. *Stains on My Name, War in My Veins: Guyana and the Politics of Cultural Struggle.* Durham, N. C.: Duke University Press.

Wood, John R. 1983. 'East Indians and Canada's New Immigration Policy', in George Kurian and Ram P. Srivastava (eds.): *Overseas Indians: A Study in Adaptation.* New Delhi: Vikas Publishing House, pp. 3–29.

2

Perspectives on Indians Abroad*

S. L. Sharma

Recent decades have witnessed an upsurge of literature on Indians settled abroad. Mainly three types of writings can be distinguished: historical, diplomatic and anthropological. The historical works provide an account of the phases of emigration of Indians and their early life situations in foreign lands.[1] The diplomatic works read like country reports on the status and problems of Indians beyond seas.[2] The anthropological works are in the nature of ethnographic accounts with their accent on cultural continuity and change.[3]

Varieties of writings apart, the existing literature shares three notable features in common. One, much of it is in the form of country-specific profiles. Cross-country comparisons are few and far between.[4] Two, most of it is descriptive, with analytical ideas and imaginative hypotheses in short supply. Three, for most part, it tends to project the problem in colonial perspective.

There are broadly two ways in which the problem of Indians abroad has been looked at: the colonial and the nationalist. The

*Originally published in *Sociological Bulletin*, Vol. 38, No. 1, March 1989, pp. 1–22.

*I am grateful to Professor Partha N. Mukherji, Dr M. N. Panini and Dr Sherry Sabbarwal for their valuable comments and suggestions which helped me refine this article.

colonial way[5] maintains that Indians went abroad driven by their domestic economic compulsions, or greed or avarice; that they were 'heathens', lazy, cunning and quarrelsome; that they tended to cling tenaciously to their culture in order to make up for the loss on economic front or to cope with their status loss on the social front; that they were so carried away by their desire to grab wealth and power that they had no compunction at throwing the natives out of employment and power in the latter's own lands; and, that their difficulties in foreign countries were largely of their own making. All this is clearly indicative of the way colonialists and their ideologues look at the problem and would have us look at it.

As against this, the nationalist way[6] contends that in most cases Indians did not go abroad on their own, but were indeed taken, taken under various arrangements as instruments of colonial domination; that they were not led by their own predatory instincts, instead they were lured and duped by colonial designs; that they did not plunder the country they went to, instead they served its development needs and worked hard to better the lot of its residents; that they were not lazy but industrious, not cunning but thrifty, not indolent but enterprising; that they had been tolerated only as long as they were prepared to play second fiddle to the natives, but once they began to assert their rights they were pushed out; and, that their difficulties in foreign lands were not of their own making, but of the making of neo-colonial powers which keep playing political games in the Third World countries.

In the study of Indians abroad it is the functionalist orientation that predominates. This is evident from the fact that the existing literature is preoccupied with the question of the cultural identity and integration, to the relative neglect of the question of class and power. It is a pity that no systematic attempt has been made to look at the problem in terms of other perspectives, including that of Marxism. This precisely is what I propose to do here; that is, to view the problem of overseas Indians in terms of prevailing sociological perspectives.

Accordingly, this article is organised in three parts, besides the preliminaries. In the first part, I will illustrate and extend the functional perspective on Indians abroad which, in the interest of more appropriate characterisation, I prefer to call the sociocultural perspective. In the second part, I will look at overseas Indians in terms of the political-economy perspective which has received scant attention in the existing literature. In the third part, I propose to reflect on the theoretic significance of the study of Indian immigrants in particular and immigrant communities in general.

Before proceeding further it will be in order to know some basic facts about Indians settled abroad, their estimated numbers, their pockets of concentration, their distribution across nations, and their regional derivations and settlements. This will help us put the subsequent discussion in perspective.

Estimates vary about the number of Indians settled abroad. In fact, these vary widely from as low as 3.5 million to as high as 13 million.[7] Exact figures are hard to find partly because a number of countries include Indians in the category of Asians or South Asians in their enumeration and partly because of the unreported presence of Indians in several countries. From the available accounts, however, it appears that the number of Indians abroad is more than 10 million which is equivalent to roughly two per cent of the present total population of India.

Indians are not the only people who have ventured out of their homeland in such vast numbers. Their number looks small when compared to overseas Chinese (about 20 million) and overseas British (over 50 million).[8] Their relatively lesser numbers notwithstanding, Indians form large enough numbers outside India and significant enough groups in several countries to merit serious research attention as well as civil concern.

Spread over most parts of the world, Indians are found more in some regions than in others. They are concentrated in South, Southeast and Southwest Asia, in South Africa and East Africa, in Western Europe, North America and the Caribbean. Taking 1,500 as the minimum figure, overseas Indians are found in as many as 53 countries. They form a majority in at least three foreign countries: Mauritius (74 per cent), Fiji (49 per cent) and Guyana (53 per cent). They are close to majority in Trinidad and Tobago where they are 40 per cent as against 43 per cent of the blacks. They form a substantial group in Malaysia, Singapore and Sri Lanka where they are more than 10 per cent of the total population of each country. In the remainder countries they figure as a small but distinctive group forming less than three per cent of the total population of each.

In respect of their regional derivations and settlements there are noticeable some broad interesting patterns. There is a preponderance of South Indians, particularly Tamils, in South and Southeast Asia and South Africa, of East Indians in West Indies, of Punjabis and

Gujaratis in Africa, Europe and North America. This is not to underestimate the presence of Indians of other regional origins in these parts of the world, but just to indicate that there are some perceptible regional linkages between the regions of origin and of settlement. In terms of their mobility and spread, however, Sikhs have the distinction of venturing far and wide, with Patidars (Gujaratis) following them.

Sociocultural Perspective

Taking the study of the sociocultural aspects of immigration as its main concern, this perspective addresses itself to the question of cultural continuity and change following change of the national domicile of an individual or a group. More pointedly, it tends to concentrate on the question of cultural identity and integration.

A look at the recurrent themes in the existing literature on overseas Indians indicates clearly how sociocultural perspective predominates it. There are three such recurrent themes. The first is that overseas Indians tend to recreate Indian social structure wherever they go. The second is that they tend to hold fast to their native culture in their lands of adoption. The third is that their mode of adaptation is marked by a clear preference for economic integration more than cultural assimilation.

I intend to review here some of the formulations pertaining to these themes. Among other things, I would like to argue that much is made in the existing literature of the so-called magnificent cultural obsession of Indian immigrants. I also propose to advance a hypothesis of differential modes of adaptation and the factors thereof. I will do so in the light of my understanding acquired from methodical observations and inquisitive discussions with Indians in several parts of the world, particularly the Caribbean, North America, Western Europe and Asia, of which I have some first-hand knowledge.

As in India, so abroad: the social structure of overseas Indians is marked by a multiplicity of communities based on regional, linguistic, religious, or in some places, caste lines. Region and religion seem to be more important determinants of their social organisation than language and caste. The evidence of it can be seen in the greater popularity of regional associations and religious organisations than pan-Indian organisations.

Based on cross-cultural evidence, Fisher hypothesises that the tendency of ethnic divisiveness is found more among those Indian immigrants who hope to repatriate to India (1980: 90). Such immigrants keep channels of communication and exchange open between themselves and their families back home. Scouting for mate selection in the homeland, maintenance of property, frequent visiting and sending remittances are some of the ways in which immigrants maintain ties on a continuing basis.

I find this hypothesis rather problematic. This is so because it ignores the schismatic orientation of Indian immigrants towards repatriation. At one level, most of the Indian immigrants harbour a desire to ultimately return to India. At another level, a very small number of them is really serious about it. If the former is taken as true, the hypothesis loses its punch. If the latter is the case, how come that parochial ethnic organisations are so preponderant, as reported by Fisher himself. At any rate, it needs a deeper probe.

Coming to the second theme, Indians are known for jealously preserving their cultural identity. They continue to cling to their norms of endogamy, marital stability and family solidarity, kin orientation, religion and mother tongue. They are always nostalgic about Indian food and their women tend to stick to their lovely *saris*.

As for the mechanisms of their cultural preservation, mention must be made of temples and gurdwaras, practice of *keertan* and *akhand path*, audio cassettes of devotional songs, video cassettes of *Ramayan* and *Mahabharat*, festivals and functions, and ethnic associations and organisations. What is more, even picnics provide occasions to reinforce old cultural practices. For instance, I was truly astonished to see *antakshari* (a verbal game in which the last letter of the verse recited by one participant has to be used as the starting letter of the verse by another participant) played in Sanskrit hymns in a picnic of Indians in Salt Lake City in USA.

Overseas Indians adhere to their traditional culture so ostensibly that at times it appears that they are more Indian in their cultural orientations and practices than resident Indians in India. Take, for instance, the Sikhs who are quick to take to modern ways in India but they tend to be rather orthodox abroad. Even those Indians who couldn't care less for their culture in India become quite observant of it in foreign lands.

Why do Indians get so faithful to their culture in foreign lands while at home they seem to favour Western culture? Several explanations come to mind. One, that they find in their culture a defence mechanism against a sense of insecurity in alien settings. Two, that they might be banking on their culture as a compensatory mechanism for the loss of status in foreign lands. Three, maybe there is something in the Indian culture—perhaps its adhesive quality—that accounts for it. Four, may be it is a sense of pride of belonging to one of the oldest cultures of the world that makes them so reverent to it. Fifth, it may well be so because the immigrants get stuck to their conception of Indian culture of the time when they had left India and remain blissfully unaware of the changes it has undergone since then.

As important as it is, the question of cultural identity of overseas Indians needs careful scrutiny. It involves several issues. The first is the issue of how Indians abroad perceive their self-identity. Do they view themselves as Indians or as Punjabis, Gujaratis, etc.? In other words, do they identify themselves in terms of pan-Indian identity or in terms of a parochial ethnic category. According to Fisher (1980) Indians have difficulty in organising as Indians. More often than not they tend to identify themselves in terms of narrow ethnic categories. By and large Fisher is right. The only thing I may add is that perhaps it is the context that determines their self-identity. It seems that while dealing with the non-Indians they tend to take on pan-Indian identity. But when it comes to interacting among themselves their regional, linguistic or religious identities take precedence. A second issue is how others look upon Indians. Are they viewed as Indians or as Asians? That depends on several things including their relative numerical strength in the host country. Wherever Indians form a substantial group, they are viewed as Indians having a distinctive identity. In the countries where their number is small and the ethnic groups of other nationalities are also present they tend to be bracketed with the other Asians.

Even at the risk of sounding outrageous, it may be remarked that perhaps too much is made in the existing literature of the instinct of cultural preservation and identity of Indians in foreign settings. For one thing, perhaps every ethnic group tends to stick to its culture in strange surroundings about as fastidiously as do the Indians. Are Chinese immigrants any different from Indians? It requires a comparative study of various immigrant communities, including Indians, to maintain that the Indians stand out among others. For another, there is no dearth of contradictory evidence to show that any number of Indians have abandoned their culture in favour of the cultures of their adopted lands. Third, there is a generational context to it. While the first generation immigrants tend to stick to Indian culture with vigour, the second and subsequent generations give evidence of distancing from it. This, however, depends on a host of other factors also which we will look into a little later. There is, of course, no denying the fact that it causes a great deal of agonising inter-generational cultural conflict.

This brings us to the third theme, that is, the question of the course or modes of adaptation. A scholar like Greeley (1976: 53), for instance, has sketched a six–stage process which the immigrant communities are believed to go through in their course of adaptation. These six stages are: cultural shock, organisation and emergent self-consciousness, assimilation of the elite, militancy, self-hatred and anti-militancy, and emerging adjustment. In my view, it seems remote that there is such a thing as one uniform course of adaptation. The course of adaptation is likely to vary from community to community depending on many factors. In any case the hypothesis of a uniform course does not strike a unanimous chord among the scholars.[9]

Concerning the mode of adaptation, once again the same story. It is apparently wrong to speak of a uniform mode of adaptation followed by Indian immigrants. There are at least three identifiable modes: (a) assimilation, (b) cultural preservation with economic integration and (c) ethnic politicisation for power cultivation. These refer to three processes, namely, merger, adjustment and striving for dominance. In some countries Indian immigrants give evidence of the first mode, namely assimilation. From my personal knowledge I can speak of it for Jamaica. Grenada may be cited as another example.

The second mode of adaptation seems to be more widespread. Indian immigrants in Southeast Asia, in East Africa, in Britain, and in the USA and Canada give ample evidence of it. Some of the recent studies of Indian immigrants in the USA have the following to observe: that in the cultural domain Indians tend to preserve their identity while in the economic domain they are quick to integrate (Gordon 1964); that they remain Indian in their primary groups but act Americanised in their secondary groups (Saran 1985). Similar observations have been made by Mahajani (1960: vii) for Indians in Burma (now, Myanmar) and Malaysia.

Evidence of the third mode of adaptation comes from countries like Mauritius, Guyana, Trinidad, Fiji and Sri Lanka where Indians have carved out a place for themselves in the power politics of the place. While in Mauritius they have been lucky to have smooth sailing, in other countries they have run into rough weather on account of their being locked in power game with the natives or other dominant ethnic communities.

How to account for the varying modes of adaptation? One of the ways to do so is to identify the factors responsible for it. No systematic attempt has been made so far to catalogue such factors. At best we come across only passing references to some of them, such as demographic, generational, religious, cultural, etc. Note that all of these belong in the category of the sociocultural factors. There is another set of factors, namely, politicoeconomic, such as colonialism, state, class and level of development which has received little, if any, attention. This only substantiates my earlier observation that the study of Indians abroad is dominated by the sociocultural perspective.

It will be useful to prepare an inventory of the factors which are likely to impinge on the mode of adaptation of an immigrant community. In the interest of systematic exposition these may be grouped into the following six sets:

1. Background conditions and characteristics of immigrants.
2. Their demographic, generational and organisational status in the country of immigration.
3. Their economic performance and power position in the host country.
4. Response of host community, culture and religion.
5. Level of development and manpower needs of the host country.
6. State policy in respect of immigrants.

In the first set are included the following factors: time and conditions of emigration; motives behind emigration; sponsoring agencies and arrangements; racial, religious, caste, class and community backgrounds of the emigrants, their regional and rural–urban backgrounds, their level of education, occupational skills and professional status; and their command of the language of the country of immigration.

Notable among the factors of the second set are: number and proportion of the natives, Indian immigrants and other immigrant communities in the total population of the host country; majority/ minority status of the Indian immigrants, their concentration and dispersion, their rural–urban distribution, their generational composition, their homogeneity and heterogeneity, their ethnic associations and religious organisations, and their cultural exclusivism and inclusivism.

The third set comprises the following factors: proportions of immigrants in the various sectors of the host economy; proportions of Indian immigrants therein, their employment status vis-à-vis natives, their economic performance, their income levels, their status as achiever or non-achiever, their class alliances, their contribution to the development of the host economy as perceived by them and by the natives, their hold over the host economy; their involvement in the power sector, the degree and form of their participation in domestic politics, their hold over the host polity; their proportions in legislatures, administration and judiciary; the threats that they pose to the natives in the fields of employment, professional attainment, income levels and power.

The fourth set entails the following: the generalised attitude of the natives towards immigrants in general and Indian immigrants in particular, their sense of racial and cultural superiority or inferiority, their perception of the status of the immigrant culture, their openness to or tolerance of the immigrant culture, their perceived images of the immigrants along with stereotypes and stigmas attached to them, their ethnic prejudices and cultural hostility against the immigrants and their attempts at religious conversion of the immigrants.

The level of economic development of the host country and her manpower needs are the crucial factors which make the fifth set.

Covered in the sixth and final set are the factors pertaining to state policy—a variable of supreme importance. These include: immigration laws, civic status of immigrants, their rights and obligations; contracts and agreements, decrees and disabilities, restrictions on their property rights and on access to positions of power; the cultural policy of the host state in respect of immigrants; the state of relations of the host state with the home state of immigrants; and the policy of the home state in respect of its people abroad.

Having listed the factors, it will be only apt to show how they affect the mode of adaptation of Indian immigrants. On account of constraint of space I can do no better than illustrate the importance of one factor each of the three of the above six categories. Take, for instance, the caste factor from the first set. It is well known that a vast majority of Indians in the Caribbean hail from low caste backgrounds and for the same reason were marginal to the Great Tradition of Hinduism even in India. As such, it is hardly surprising that their mode of adaptation carries an imprint of Little Tradition in the Caribbean. This is markedly different from the mode of adaptation of the Indian immigrants in North America who are largely drawn from relatively higher caste backgrounds and whose mode of adaptation for the same reason is marked by the prominence of Sanskritik Hinduism.

Take the demographic factor from the second set. Andreski (1964) contends that 10 per cent is the 'critical minimum' population for an immigrant group to be able to positively maintain its cultural identity. His observation seems to hold good for Indian immigrants in the countries where they are in the strength of 10 per cent. This, however, should not be taken to mean that they have necessarily lost their distinctiveness wherever they are less than 10 per cent of the total population. All that it means is that 10 per cent is the safe bet. To this we may add another idea, the idea of 40 per cent as the 'critical optimum' for an immigrant group to become a force to reckon with in the domestic politics of the host country. This is evident from the political prominence of Indians in countries like Mauritius, Guyana, Trinidad and Fiji where Indians are 40 per cent or more of the total population.

Take the religious factor from the sixth category. Christian missionaries made concerted efforts to convert Indians both in Jamaica and Trinidad. They succeeded in Jamaica where Arya Samaj movement, a Hindu organisation, did not operate, presumably because of the small number of Indians there. They failed in Trinidad and Tobago because of the counteracting role of Arya Samaj. This in part accounts for the distorted Indian identity in Jamaica and a persistent Indian identity in Trinidad and Tobago.

Three of the above six categories of factors numbering one, two and six encompass factors of sociocultural nature, while the remaining three embody factors of politicoeconomic order. I propose to discuss the latter under the political economy perspective, to avoid repetition.

Political Economy Perspective

True to its name, political economy perspective brings in sharp focus political and economic aspects of the phenomenon in question. There are several versions of it: Marxist, non-Marxist and neo-Marxist. Without going into the finer distinctions of its versions, it should suffice to indicate that we are concerned here with its classical Marxian version. The basic elements of the Marxian political economy are: historical context, mode of production, class relations and nature of state. At a philosophical level, it tends to postulate a determinate relationship between objective conditions and subjective conscious-ness. Accordingly, it takes history, economy, class and power as its central explanatory categories.

To begin with the historical context, nothing is so central as the context of colonialism for situating the problem of overseas Indians in a proper perspective. Considering the centrality of the colonial context, it will be only appropriate to distinguish three phases of the history of emigration of Indians to foreign lands: pre-colonial, colonial and post-colonial. In the pre-colonial phase Indians went overseas in relatively small numbers as conquerors, scholars and tra-ders mainly from South India to Southeast Asia, which was like a trickle compared to the torrent of Indian emigration during the colonial phase. With the rise of British imperialism there was massive emigration of people from one part of the Empire to the other. This was necessitated by the imperial need for cheap labour for its plantations, following the abolition of slavery. It is during this phase that a vast majority of Indian immigrants went as indentured and *kangany* labourers to the Caribbean and Fiji islands, Malaysia and Mauritius, and other parts of the British dominion. Apparently, they went there as instruments of colonialism. Similarly, with the massive growth of the industrial sector in Britain, the Empire needed more and more of factory labour, particularly after World War II which wiped out much of its manpower base. As a result, the local working classes chose to move out of their traditional occupations which were no longer lucrative. Into this gap the Indians were drawn, once again as instruments of colonialism. As the colonies attained freedom, there began the post-colonial phase which is only a few decades old. A remarkable feature of this phase is the emigration of white-collar professionals from India to the developed parts of the capitalist West, particularly to the USA, Canada and Britain. This has given rise to the question of brain drain.

From the above facts it is clear that the political economy of colonialism as well as of imperialism provides the key to an understanding of the problem of overseas Indians in proper perspective. It reveals that Indians, in most cases, did not thrust themselves on other countries. They were indeed inducted as captive labour by the imperial powers. Finally, it also shows the primacy of the economic factor in accounting for the emigration of Indians as well as their incorporation into the select sectors of the economies of the host countries.

Coming to the mode of production, the 'plantation mode of production' is of paramount importance for understanding the lot of Indians abroad. As an economic system, the plantation mode of production in the colonial context was an example par excellence of ruthless exploitation of plantation workers, permitting not so much as a sign of protest, let alone unionisation. In fact, in no other system was the dependency of the working class on the managerial/proprietary class so sharp and salient as in the plantation system.

As a social system, it consisted of displaced ethnic groups and degraded and deprived individuals with a weak sense of community. For all practical purposes it was totally regimented and highly oppressive. As a cultural system, it symbolised acceptance of a perverse value system which made a man feel important if his woman was summoned to management bungalows.

The impact of plantation mode of production on the sociocultural life of the overseas Indians was too profound to be described. It affected them in the severest of the ways. It violated their human dignity, destroyed their family life and ruined their *dharma*.[10] It robbed them of their morals and manners, punctured their value system and undermined their sense of legitimacy in marital and kinship relationship. In short, it inflicted untold sufferings on them and badly damaged their psyche. It is indeed amazing to note that they have managed to keep their cultural tradition alive in some form, in spite of all the onslaughts on it.

The above description applies more to the plantations in the Caribbean than to those in Malaysia and elsewhere. But the difference is only a matter of degree and not of kind. By and large the plantation mode of production had a messy effect on the sociocultural life of those who got trapped into it.

The story of the impact of the mode of production will remain incomplete without a reference to the industrial mode of production which drew a large number of Indians to some advanced nations. The same pattern of initial immiserisation of early Indian workers occurred in British factories as in the Caribbean plantations. The Indian workers in British factories were subjected to racial discrimination, economic deprivation and sociocultural denigration (Chandan 1986 and Desai 1963). They were not allowed to form unions and were subjected to all sorts of humiliation. It is only in some of the post-industrial societies that the recent Indian immigrants are relatively better off than their earlier counterparts in the underdeveloped countries.

Thus, there seems to be a connection between the level of development of a country and the socioeconomic lot of the Indian immigrants there. This perhaps is understandable in terms of the availability of opportunities. At their present stage of development some of the advanced countries need more and more of qualified professional and technical manpower to run their advancing economy. Since they have shortage of it, they find it profitable to import such manpower. That is the reason why Indian professionals are welcome there, though in a selective manner. For the same reason, the recent Indian immigrants find the going good in such countries. In the underdeveloped countries, on the other hand, there is scarcity of opportunities which leads to severe competition between the natives and immigrants, making things harder for the latter.

Turning to the class situation it will be revealing to first look into the class backgrounds of Indian immigrants in their home country, then locate them in the class structure of their host countries, and finally trace the change, if any, in their class position over time. The class backgrounds of Indian emigrants have varied with the phases of emigration. In the pre-colonial phase the emigrants generally hailed from better socioeconomic backgrounds. During the colonial phase they were mostly drawn from low caste and class backgrounds. In the post-colonial phase middle and upper-middle class backgrounds seem to predominate.

As regards their class position in the host country, ordinarily it tends to correspond with their class background in the home country. That holds true for all the three phases. Accordingly, the Indian immigrants of the pre-colonial phase were generally able to command respectable positions in their countries of settlement. The immigrants of the colonial phase found themselves at the bottom of the class hierarchy in their countries of destination. Similarly, the immigrants of the post-colonial phase form part of the new middle-class in their countries of adoption.

There is, however, one important irritant for the immigrant professionals in the USA, and that is the FRG (Foreign Registered Graduate) stigma.[11] For sheer chance of having had their initial professional training in India they are dubbed as second-rate professionals vis-à-vis their local counterparts. They feel exceedingly bad about this organised status discrimination, partly because in many cases they feel that they are in fact more competent than their local counterparts and partly because they find it hypocritical on the part of the host society to profess the principle of merit and equality but practice the contrary. More explicit in the medical profession, the 'foreign' stigma operates in subtle ways in other professions also.

Concerning the change in the class position of the Indian immigrants three points are worth noting. First, there has emerged an Indian peasantry out of the estate labour in the Caribbean, but the Indian estate labour in Malaya could not make that grade. This is attributed by Jain (1988) to the differences in the two systems of recruitment, namely, indenture and *kangany*, under which Indians were brought to the Caribbean and Malaysia, respectively. Because of its strictly contractual nature, the indenture system allowed occupational freedom to its recruits at the termination of the contract, which offered them the option of a passage back home or in lieu of that a piece of agricultural land, thus facilitating the rise of Indian peasantry in the Caribbean. On the other hand, the *kangany* system did not provide access to land to the estate worker. He went on being accommodated from one plantation to the other by the contractors with whom he had village or regional affinity. All this prevented him from turning into a peasant. Second, there is some evidence of a fond hope in popular circles in both the Caribbean and Malaya of the evolution of 'a middle-class' out of Indian plantation workers. Based on his observation of the trend of Indian immigrants increasingly taking to cane farming in the Caribbean, Johnson (1972) hopes for the emergence of a Victorian middle-class among them. Similar optimism was expressed by Narayanan, a union leader, for the Indian rubber tappers in Malaya who he hoped would 'cease to be labourers and become the new middle-class of the country, the new scooter-owning class' (*Strait Times*, 28 May 1962). Third, in actual fact, the chances of the emergence of a middle-class from the ranks of plantation workers do not appear to be bright. Striking a realistic note, Jain (1988) expresses his apprehensions about the potential of the Indian cane farmer in the Caribbean and rubber tappers in Malaya to make it into the middle class.

How about class mobility among the Indian immigrants of the post-colonial phase? It is essential to emphasise first that unlike their earlier counterparts they have escaped the process of immiseration. More important, they seem to be upwardly mobile. In respect of their economic success and prosperity, they are in fact making news.[12] Having made economic fortunes in their new abodes they prefer to acquire residential property rather than own means of production. They seem to be keen to invest in India but somehow the Indian government has not yet been able to take full advantage of this gesture. The number of Non-Resident Indian (NRI) investment schemes notwithstanding, the NRI investment has not really picked up yet.

The younger generation of Indians in the USA and Canada are doing wonderfully well, as is evident from their enviable accomplishment in the educational field. The adult professionals are second to none in their fields of professional activity. If anything, they are making new records. Their overall performance is so remarkable that it has led to reaction formation among some sections of the US society which manifests itself in the racist attacks on Indians by the so-called dotbusters.[13]

There is one more aspect of class relations which merits serious consideration. This is the interface of ethnicity with class. It is often found that Indians are discriminated in the field of employment as against the locals for no other reason but their being immigrants. This discrimination does not remain confined only to the economic field but extends to other fields also. As a consequence of this there develops an ethnic solidarity cutting across class boundaries. Some scholars (Chauhan 1988 and Sharma 1988) have gone to the extent of projecting this phenomenon in terms of 'class-for-itself'. But this issue is too complex to be resolved without focused and serious research.

Finally, the power factor. It has three facets relevant to the present context: colonial, state and community power structure. Not all colonial powers have had the same character; there were internal differences between them because of which they exerted differential effects on the lot of overseas Indians. For all that we know the experience of Indian immigrants in British colonies is different from that of their counterparts in French colonies. Generally, Indian immigrants have had smooth sailing in French colonies and rough in British colonies. A look at Indians in French Guyana and British Guyana proves the point.

The potential of the host state to influence the lives of immigrants can hardly be underestimated. It may affect not only their status and culture but also their life chances. In ways both legal and extralegal, it may play havoc on the immigrants. Indian immigrants had suffered such mighty havocs of the state in several countries including Zanzibar, Uganda and Burma where draconian decrees were passed to harass them to the point of expulsion. Even today they are bearing the brunt of state directed discrimination and oppression in some countries such as Guyana, Fiji and Sri Lanka. Given the upsurge of the son-of-the-soil ideology in many states, the position of Indian immigrants is likely to become vulnerable there, except in such pluralistic societies as the USA and Canada.

No less important is the role of the home state in safeguarding or sacrificing the interests of the people of its origin settled abroad. The Indian state has generally followed a policy of advising overseas Indians to identify themselves with their country of adoption. Sound advice this so long as the state of the host country owns them also, identifies itself with them and treats them at par with other citizens. This, however, is not always the case. For the same reason, overseas Indians are generally critical of the policy of the Indian state to leave them to their fate. Right or wrong, it is widely held that the non-interventionist policy of the Indian state even when intervention is warranted is to blame in part for the indignities that have been heaped on Indians in many foreign countries, including Burma, Uganda and Guyana.

The involvement of Indian immigrants in the domestic power game of their adopted country is yet another factor that is likely to affect their lives. There are countries where Indians have taken to power politics in a big way. Mauritius, Guyana, Trinidad and Tobago and Fiji are the countries where Indians have plunged headlong in national politics. Except for Mauritius, everywhere else they have burnt their fingers and invited the wrath of the sons-of-the-soil or of other power groups. Indications are that Indians in the USA are itching for making forays into the power sector after having proved their mettle in the economic and professional fields. Given the pluralistic and democratic character of the US polity, they may have luck there. But the experience of it elsewhere counsels restraint.

A comment on the recurrent phenomenon of confrontation between Indian immigrants and locally dominant community in the host country: on the face of it, it looks like ethnic or communal conflict. But there is generally a politicoeconomic dimension to it. Indian immigrants have run into conflict situations often in the countries where they happened to take control either of the economy or polity of the host country. It is this divide of economy and polity between two ethnic communities that seems to be at the root of seemingly ethnic or communal conflict. Ordinarily Indian immigrants first tend to hold the reign of economy and then seek to capture power. This naturally hurts the dominant community of the host country which seeks to retaliate with a sense of vengeance.

Such, then, is the view of Indians abroad from the political economy perspective. How very different this view is than the one from the sociocultural perspective outlined earlier. This, however, should not be taken to mean that the two are alternative perspectives. No, they are only different, as they seek to illuminate different facets of the same reality. For the same reason they are indeed complementary. Taken together they provide a more comprehensive view of the life world of overseas Indians than taken singly.

Theoretic Significance

Some subjects have greater potential for theoretical abstractions than others. The study of immigrant communities is one such subject. This is so because it provides a special testing ground for some of the seminal ideas of the prevailing sociological perspectives.

Legally speaking, immigration connotes entry of a non-resident into a country to take up permanent residence there. Sociologically speaking, it implies more than that. It signifies a situation of interaction between two cultural systems, in some cases between a traditional and a modern cultural system. It also means a change in the existential conditions of immigrants with all its implications for the change in their consciousness. It represents a turning point in the lives of immigrants to confront a strange new world and to make sense of it. It also involves a possibility that immigrants may modify and reconstruct their life-world. To a discerning mind it should be clear from the above that immigrant communities provide fascinating laboratories for testing some of the basic ideas of functionalism, Marxism, ethnomethodology and phenomenology.

It will be only apt to show the promise that the study of overseas Indians holds for theoretical purposes. First, for the functional perspective. Culture is the prized explanatory category of functional analysis. Little wonder, therefore, that culture emerges as a key factor in the functional analysis of Indian society. This is evident from the prevailing hypotheses in the functional literature on Indian society: the hypothesis of sanskritisation, of modernisation through adaptive transformation of tradition and of Hinduism as an impediment to economic development. Long debated in Indian sociological circles, all the three accord primacy to culture as an explanatory variable. For a more stringent test of these hypotheses, I think, overseas Indians provide an ideal group. A study of the patterns of adaptation among overseas Indians will enable us to assess the strength of the hold of traditional culture on their mode of living in the alien settings. Similarly, a study of modernisation of Indian immigrants in some of the well-known modern countries like the USA, Canada or Britain will help us better appraise the pattern of interaction between Indian tradition and modernisation. It is one thing to see how Indian tradition responds to modernity in India, that is, in its homeland and quite another to see how it conducts itself in relation to modernity in the West, that is, the homeland of modernity. In the same way, a study of the economic performance of the Hindu immigrants in diverse foreign settings will be revealing to clarify and qualify the relationship between Hinduism and economic development.

Next the Marxian perspective. One of the important Marxian propositions is that the material conditions of our existence determine our consciousness, and that with the change in our existential conditions a corresponding change occurs in our consciousness. Indian immigrants, or for that matter immigrants of any nationality, provide an appropriate group to examine the validity of the above proposition. It is common knowledge that people go abroad driven by diverse considerations, but chiefly by economic. So it is with Indians, who in more cases than not have gone overseas out of economic motivation, be it search for jobs or betterment of one's economic lot. It also goes without saying that immigration implies a change in the existential conditions of immigrants. A careful study of the continuity and change in the culture of the Indian immigrants, in their world view and value orientations may yield significant evidence on the nature of relationship between economy and culture, with particular reference to the question of determinacy or indeterminacy of this relationship.

The main concern of the ethnomethodological perspective is with discovering people's methods of making sense of their social world. Accordingly, it begins by calling into question the 'taken-for-granted world', treating it as 'problematic' so that the methods people invoke to make sense of it can be discovered. There can be no more appropriate occasion for it than that of the first encounter of immigrants with the strange ways of the country of their adoption. To the natives most aspects of their everyday life are so familiar that they are just 'taken-for-granted' which in turn appear to be 'problematic' to the immigrants who are strangers. In his essay on 'The stranger', Schutz (1971) rightly views the immigrant as a perfect example of stranger. Thus, a study of Indian immigrants, particularly of the recent arrivals, may be a valuable source of insights into the methods people use to make sense of their sociocultural world.

Finally, we have the phenomenological perspective with its stress on the interface of subjective and objective in the construction of social reality. Fully appreciative of the objective, phenomenological sociology attaches remarkable importance to the subjective. From the phenomenological point of view it will be profitable to see how overseas Indians use their stock of knowledge, their typifications and their intersubjective experiences to come to terms with the new life-world. Equally valuable will be to probe deep into the subjective to know their pains, their torments, their dilemmas and the bearing of this all on the modification and reconstruction of their life-worlds.[14]

So much about the sociological significance of the study of overseas Indian communities. Studies of other immigrant communities may pave the way towards a sociology of immigrant communities. For bringing out the full theoretic significance of the study of immigrant communities, it will be necessary to undertake their comparative studies. Such comparative studies may yield some generalisations of wider significance, some propositions which may hopefully form the basis of a sociological theory of immigrant communities. A fascinating hope this, it deserves to be turned into a project.

Notes

1. For a flavour of historical writings, see Haraprasad Chattopadhaya (1970 and 1979).

2. For works produced by diplomats, see Prem Bhatia (1973) and I. J. Bahadur Singh (1979, 1982 and 1987).

3. For anthropological monographs, see Aurora (1976), Chauhan (1988), R. K. Jain (1970) and Morris (1968).

4. For comparative analysis, see Mahajani (1960), Tinker (1976 and 1977), Fisher (1980) and R. K. Jain (mimeographed).

5. That is the way Idi Amin of Uganda and Col. Sitiveni Rabuka of Fiji have looked at Indian immigrants.

6. This view is articulated by Pandit Govind Ballabh Pant in his speech in the Assembly in 1935, parts of which are reproduced by Bhagwan Singh in his article titled 'What Pandit Pant had said' (National Herald, 19 September 1988).

7. See Tinker (1977: 11). For current population estimates of Indians abroad see Singh (1979) and P. C. Jain (1982).

8. See Tinker (1977: 11).

9. There emerged a sharp difference of opinion on this question among the participants in a panel discussion on 'Indians abroad: Identity and integration' organised on the occasion of the 10th Uttar Pradesh Sociological Conference held at Varanasi on 7–9 January 1989. Holding a brief for the uniformity thesis Satyendra Tripathi advanced a hypothesis of a three-step course of adaptation: subservience, resurgence and dominance; the first implying sociocultural demoralisation, the second resurgence of sociocultural identity and the third economic success-based political mobilisation. Rejecting the thesis of uniformity, I. S. Chauhan argued that Indian immigrants had followed a historic-specific course of adaptation in each country and that it would be futile to look for a uniform pattern.

10. This is observed, among others, by C. F. Andrews who visited Indian immigrants in Fiji in 1915 and often heard them complain that their 'dharma has been ruined'. He found that the 'fact was glaring' and 'it was true'. For details see Ram Swamp's article 'Fiji Hindus face persecution' (Indian Express, 13 May 1989).

11. According to a recent report, the International Association of American Physicians (IAAP) has brought to the notice of the US Congressional body complaints of discrimination against fully-trained and qualified foreign medical graduates including Indians, virtually reducing them to the status of 'second-rate doctors'. For details, see Indian Express, 11 May 1989.

12. Based on an analysis of the 1980 US Census data, Peter Xenos, Herbert Barringer and Michael Levin in their article (mimeographed) have shown how Indian immigrants in the USA are doing better than other immigrant groups, their economic performance being superior to that of all other communities, including Whites and Japanese. The average Indian earns 17 per cent more than the average white and nine per cent more than the average Japanese. The authors attribute this remarkable performance to the exceptionally high level of education

of the US Indians which, in turn, is reflected in the occupational structure. Forty-two per cent of the Indian males are engaged in white-collar professions as against 10 per cent of the Whites. The same with the females: 27 per cent of Indian women are in the professions as against 13 per cent of the whites.

13. Over the past few months several Indian residents in the US have been assaulted on the streets by a gang calling itself 'Dotbusters'—dot being the *bindi* Indian women wear on their forehead.

14. Based on a case study of an Indian family, Kathy Cox reports on how Indians miss in the US their social life of India: 'And while they easily accept the bounty that has come with emigration: economic success, a comfortable life style and a high standard of living, they ponder the cultural consequences, especially its impact on their children. They miss their family, their friends, the powerful attachments that come with a strong sense of community' (*Express Magazine*, 21 August 1988).

References

Andreski, Stanislav. 1964. *The Use of Comparative Sociology.* Berkeley: The University of California Press.

Aurora, G. S. 1976. *The New Frontiersmen: Indians in Great Britain.* Bombay: Popular Prakashan.

Bhatia, Prem. 1973. *Indians' Ordeal in Africa.* Delhi: Vikas Publishing House.

Chandan, Amarjit. 1986. *Indians in Britain.* New Delhi: Sterling Publishers.

Chattopadhaya, Haraprasad. 1970. *Indians in Africa: A Socio-Economic Study.* Calcutta: Booklands.

———. 1979. *Indians in Sri Lanka: A Historical Study.* Calcutta: OPS Publishers.

Chauhan, I. S. 1988. *Leadership and Social Cleavages: Political Processes among the Indians in Fiji.* Jaipur: Rawat Publications.

Desai, Rashmi. 1963. *Indian Immigrants in Britain.* London: Oxford University Press.

Fisher, Maxine. 1980. *Indians of New York City.* New Delhi: Heritage Publishers.

Gordon, Milton. 1964. *Assimilation in American Life.* New York: Oxford University Press.

Greeley, Andrew M. 1976. *Why Can't They Be Like Us?* New Delhi: Prentice-Hall of India.

Jain, Prakash C. 1982. 'Indians Abroad: A Current Population Estimate'. *Economic and Political Weekly,* 16(8): 299–304.

———. 1985. *Colonialism, Class and Race Relations: The Case of Overseas Indians.* PhD thesis, Carleton University, Ottawa.

Jain, Ravindra K. 1970. *South Indians on the Plantation Frontier in Malaya.* New Haven: Yale University Press.

———. 1988. 'Overseas Indians in Malaysia and the Caribbean: Comparative Notes', Mimeographed.

Johnson, Howard. 1972. 'The Origins and Early Development of Cane-Farming in Trinidad: 1882–1906'. *The Journal of Caribbean History,* 5 November: 46–74.

Mahajani, Usha. 1960. *The Role of Indian Minorities in Burma and Malaya*. Bombay: Vora and Co. Publishers.

Morris, H. S. 1968. *Indians in Uganda*. London: Weidenfeld and Nicolson.

Saran, Parmatma. 1985. *The Asian Indian Experience in the United States*. New Delhi: Vikas Publishing House.

Schutz, Alfred. 1971. 'The Stranger: An Essay in Social Psychology', in *School and Society: A Sociological Reader*. London: Routledge and Kegan Paul in association with Open University Press.

Sharma, K. L. 1988. *Society and Polity in Modern Sri Lanka*. New Delhi: South Asian Publishers.

Singh, I. J. Bahadur (ed.). 1979. *The Other India*. New Delhi: Arnold Hienemann.

————. (ed.). 1982. *Indians in South-East Asia*. New Delhi: Sterling Publishers.

————. (ed.). 1987. *Indians in the Caribbean*. New Delhi: Sterling Publishers.

Tinker, Hugh. 1976. *Separate and Unequal: India and the Indians in the British Commonwealth, 1920–1950*. Vancouver: University of British Columbia Press.

————. 1977. *The Banyan Tree: The Overseas Emigrants from India, Pakistan and Bangladesh*. Oxford: Oxford University Press.

3

Process of Social Adjustment of Indian Immigrants in Britain*

G. S. Aurora

Greenend (pseudonym) is a small borough near a great commercial city of Great Britain. From the brochure issued by the borough town council we learn that it is '... a progressive community of over 55,000 inhabitants with all the amenities associated with a large borough'.[1] The borough is famous for its industries; for, quite a few of the goods with famous trademarks originate in this borough. It has over 'two hundred industries from saddle-making to civil engineering contractors, who have been responsible for great projects...'.[2] But the borough is probably more famous, both in Britain and the Punjab, as the 'host', since 1951, to a large community of Punjabi-speaking people. They were employed (till 1960—the period for which the author has personal knowledge) mostly as industrial labourers in a few of the industrial firms in and around the borough.

I was with this community during the two years of its early, formative life, that is, during 1957–59, as a sociological investigator.

*Originally published in *Sociological Bulletin*, Vol. 14, No. 2, September 1965, pp. 39–49.

*I am grateful to Dr A. Béteille and Dr M. S. A. Rao who went through the manuscript of this chapter and enriched it with their valuable suggestions.

In this article I will try to analyse some of the initial sociological processes of adjustment of the immigrants to the foreign social environment.

According to an estimate, which the borough council made during December 1958, there were 110 houses owned by Indians. From an impressionistic survey of the Indian houses in April 1959, I calculated the Indian population of the borough to be approximately 1,250, nearly 2.6 per cent of the total population of the borough. Despite the small percentage, this population was very conspicuous. Their conspicuousness, as compared to other immigrants such as the Poles, the Welsh and the Irish, could be attributed not only to their skin colour, an obvious reason, but also to two other facts, namely, their being by and large a male community[3] and the very pronounced difference between their culture and that of the British 'host' community.

The British community in the borough was not culturally uniform and in fact neither was the Indian community. It is important to keep in mind this cultural heterogeneity of the two communities while we notice points of cultural uniformity within the immigrant and the host communities. Experience shows that sociological generalities too often become popular stereotypes.

Greenend and the boroughs adjoining it were affected by two population movements in the last half-a-century. First, owing to the establishment of various industries local working-class communities came into being. At the same time, some of the districts of the borough took in the overflow of the 'country-minded' professional and middle classes from the city. This resulted in the creation of two kinds of localities, namely, those of the working-class and the middle-class. The middle-class localities had large double and single storied houses situated farther away from the centre of the town and near to the park and the green belt. The working-class localities were situated near the commercial centres, the industries and the railway station. There were streets where more well-to-do and better paid working class people occupied accommodation similar to that of the middle class people. These streets had newer and larger double-storied houses.

Different grades of property owners in the area set before the immigrants models of class behaviour to be emulated, imitated or rejected. The class structure of the host society also suggested to the immigrants various adaptations by which they could avoid conflicts with the host society and if possible, even get assimilated into the desirable groups. The idioms whereby class identifications are expressed are also the idioms whereby an immigrant may establish his cultural bona fide; baggy trousers and drinking draught beer in the public-bar identify a man with the working classes, leather bag and dark suit with the middle classes.

The immigrant Indians too could not be labelled a homogeneous group. Nevertheless, there were many features of the Indian community which singled it out as a subculture. For example, practically all the Indian workers living in Greenend came from the Punjab. They were mainly of peasant stock. An overwhelmingly large number among them were Jats (tillers–farmers) from Jullundhar and Hoshiarpur districts of the Punjab. But all the immigrants were not Jats, nor were they uniformly of agricultural background; there were other castes represented among them as well—such as the Chamars, Rais, Khatris, Brahmins, Rajputs, etc. Among them were lower middle-class ex-government servants such as *patwaris* (revenue officials, grade III), police constables, army personnel, craftsmen, former school teachers and young unemployed graduates, etc. The English-educated section among them, though smaller, acted as the 'pacemaker' group. It set the pace of communal action for effecting adjustment—largely through organised efforts, but also by their accommodating behaviour. The behaviour pattern of the Indians therefore could not be uniform. There were, in fact, significant divergences in the adjustment policy of different segments within the Indian community.

Most of the Indians were employed as industrial workers in different factories in and around the borough. Some of the factories employed large numbers of Indians as unskilled labourers. But there were also a few concerns where a small number of skilled Indian workers were employed. Since most of the Indians were agriculturists, they were used to manual labour of an unskilled kind and could, therefore, adjust easily to the hard work in British factories.

Factories which employed Indian workers in large numbers did so after considerable deliberations. By introducing labour of a foreign ethnic stock they were taking many risks, not only because the capacity of the Indian labourer to handle expensive machinery was unknown but also because their employment was resented by the British workers. Racial tension often resulted in conflict between the white and the coloured and in its wake disturbed the industrial organisation. Again, the employment of the Indians presaged organisational adjustments. For example, since a majority of them could not speak English, they had to be organised in such a manner that some of the English-educated Indians could always be found at hand to act as interpreters. The problem of maintaining smooth personal relations between workers of different ethnic stocks made the work of personnel management much more complex. Despite these difficulties some of the factories employed the Indians en masse; the reason being that they were eager workers and generally submitted to the commands of the managements without hesitation.

The skilled workers and the English-educated workers were more easily absorbed in the diverse industries.

II

The adjustment of the Indian community in the British 'environment' can be conceived in terms of social processes of accretion and re-formation of group structures. Accretion or gathering together of Indians occurred as a natural consequence of the social fact that the individual migrants continued to be members of their 'parent' village communities even after they moved away from their traditional habitat. Re-formation of group structures is a necessary consequence of the ingathering of people with similar cultural backgrounds. The term 're-formation' is used in preference to 'formation' to suggest continuity of the groupings in terms of sentiments. For example, although the composition of the commensal units changes from a joint or a primary family to a 'family' (of exigency) consisting of closely related, distantly related, unrelated or a combination of these, some of the expectations and sentimental bonds remain similar to those of the 'parent' families.

In a sense the migration of the Indians was not 'individual' but social, since each migrant went in response to communal pressures upon him. This fact could be ascertained by an analysis of the migration at each stage. The decision regarding an individual's migration was arrived at with the consensus of the effective social unit such as the joint family or the primary family. The family's attitude to the question of migration was intimately tied up with the experience of the villagers and relatives whose kin had migrated. If they received handsome remittances from the emigrants, they broadcast their new prosperity and thus inspired others to send their eager young men to *vilayat*. This often required sacrifices on the part of the joint families. For example, not only had Munjeel's[4] brother provided him with the necessary capital to migrate abroad but had also supported his family after his departure for a considerably long duration. In other cases, portions of family land and jewellery were sold to muster enough money for the emigration. The organisation of travel also showed irrefutable signs of a mass movement. It was organised by 'travel agents' who forged passports on a mass scale, chartered planes and moved illiterate peasants from home in India to 'home' abroad. In Britain the aggregation of the Indians occurred almost naturally around the localities where their relatives, villagers and countrymen had established residences.

The Greenend Indian community could not be thought of as simply an extension of the Punjabi regional community in a foreign environment, since the Indians did not go to Britain as a 'tribe' but as individuals and families. If it was a 'segment' of the Punjabi community, it was a most unusual segment. It was composed of individuals and partially re-formed 'families' from various parts of the Punjab. The sentiments which, in the first instance, united it were not only the sentiments originating from traditional, face-to-face relations between close-knit families and village neighbourhoods but were also the sentiments of a more abstract kind which broadly unite secondary groups. Thus many a newcomer, though sponsored by some relative or a fellow villager made his initial acquaintances with other Indians as a brother-Punjabi (*Punjabi bhra*), brother-Hoshiarpuri, brother from Shanker tehsil (*Bhra Shankar val da*) or brother Jat (*Jat bhra*).

The above noted terms may be thought of as the idioms of their culture, reflecting the specific regional character. Each of these idioms serves as a principle for structural organisation. It is obvious that the function of the idioms of a culture is to organise as well as reflect the organisation of the social relations within the community.

Now each of the above terms (idioms) denotes a sentimental unity which is not based on actual reciprocal relations but rather on the similarity of cultural values; they could not, therefore, serve as adequate guides for establishing face-to-face relations. For establishing these types of relations the idioms normally used among their 'parent' primary groups were employed. Some of the most important idioms employed in these contexts were *jat* (caste), *pind* (village), *jajman–kamin* (patron–client), *yar–beli* (friends), *apni palti* or *apne bande* (faction), *ghar* (house, household), *tubber* (family), *khandan* (minimal lineage) *bradri* (maximal lineage), *vadachhota* (high status–low status), *paise vala–gharib* (rich–poor), *padya–anpad* (educated–uneducated). In the new conditions some of the idioms lost some of their importance, while others became very important. For example, *jat* or caste idiom, though remaining a significant organisational principle, had weakened to some extent as the following quotation makes clear:

> In a meeting of the IWA (Indian Workers Association) of the borough, one of the participants complained that a particular leader had treated as though he were a *Chamar*. At once another member got up and said, 'In Britain we are all Indians and not Chamars or Jats. Chamars are as good as any other caste and the word should not be used at all'. Every one in the meeting agreed.[5]

On the whole the social class idioms tended to become more important, for example 'money' and 'education' were two idioms which dominated as ideas. A frequently employed channel of upward mobility in social status was the peddling business. House-owning was another way of social ascent. It was a more secure form of investment though the returns were fixed. People usually tried to exaggerate the fatness of their purses or pay packets. That English education should be highly valued is also not difficult to appreciate as the social situation was such that the English-educated were indispensable as the 'bridge' element with the host society.

The changing meaning of family, lineage and village idioms made a most interesting study. These idioms were exceptionally important in the formation of initial primary groupings. But very often some idioms such as the family (*tubber*) and 'household' (*ghar de*) had to undergo a radical extension in their meaning since the configuration of roles and sentiments within the partially re-formed primary groupings was often radically different. Consider for example the following case:

> Munjeet's commensal group consisted of the following: Ujjagar, a friend of Munjeet, a Punjabi but not from the same district; Kuldeep, a fellow villager and caste-man of Ujjagar and Munjeet himself. What brought them together as a joint commensal unit was not only the fact that they were Punjabis, but also interest and effort in making the house, a certain similarity of background and the need to share each other's burdens, both material and emotional.[6]

A method of comprehending the changing configuration of roles and sentiments would be by analysing the actual meaning given by the Indians to various idioms denoting structural relation and effective distance. The following array of terms is arranged in their order of decreasing emotional content:

Mera bhra (my brother)
Apne he bhra, which on second enquiry may be referred to *apne he bhravan verga* (one like a brother)
Apne ghar da (one of the household or family)
Apni bradri da (one of the clan)
Apne pind da (belonging to the same village as the speaker).

Now these terms did not refer only to the actual structural situation but also to affective relations between individuals who in reality were not always similarly related. A neighbour (in India) might often be referred to as *mera bhra* (my brother) and only further enquiry revealed the real relation. A *pind da* (fellow-villager) was often referred to as *ghar da* (of the same household). In the context of the unusual out-group situation there was a tendency towards the dislocation of the traditional in-group position as a result of which in-group identifications shifted outwards. The terms referring to a particular affective relationship tended to be used for the next group of intimate relations.

III

Re-formation of the primary groups is a corollary to the process of accretion. This process is influenced by the cultural tendencies of the in-group as well as the impact of the culture of the out-group (in this case the British society). In the aforementioned paragraphs, I have dealt with cultural affinity as a factor of cohesion. However, the affinity of the in-group does not rule out differentiation and regulated antagonism, but rather presupposes it. Different segments within the Indian community had certain differences of interests, as well as differences of approach to problems of relations with the British society. This was reflected in the general 'policies' of adjustment of these segments. I was able to differentiate two broad categories of Indians with further subdivisions within each category.

A great majority of the Indians belonged to what I characterised as the 'accommodationists' because their policy was one of ad hoc accommodation with the host society. Their aim was to adjust their cultural behaviour via-à-vis the host society only to the extent that allowed them to still preserve their cultural identity. Another reason for their accommodationistic attitude was that they were not motivated by feelings of identification with the culture of the host society. The accommodationists aimed primarily at fulfilling their economic goals of earning money. This is not to deny that even in their case acculturation did take place. Their mode of behaviour as regards dress, language and acceptance of some of the broad values of the British society also underwent a degree of change. But their acculturation advanced only to the extent where contact with the British at the informal level became less irksome. For example, they adopted the British working-class dress except for the necktie and the cap, and the institutions of queuing, use of zebra-crossings and municipal urinals, keeping their empty milk bottles in wire crates at their door steps, etc. However, on the whole, they tended to lead an intense in-group life centred around their residences, the *gurdwara* and some 'haunts' in the coloured quarter established by the earlier (old-timer) Indian migrants to Britain. The accommodationists were, by and large, composed of the rural elements. Only a small percentage of them were English-educated. Being unfamiliar with urban and Western values they were forced to live in compact groups, so that a small number of English-educated persons among them could serve as a 'bridge' with the larger society. The educated among the accommodationists were the petty officials such as former school masters, police sub-inspectors and non-commissioned army officers, etc. Occasionally there were also educated Jats who had strong enough links with their rural family members. The relation between the 'educated' and the 'uneducated' elements was not of one-way dependence but rather of mutual interdependence and conflict. The 'uneducated' often supported the business ventures of the 'educated' by providing them with capital. They also helped them by being their loyal followers in the politics of the community. The conflict between the two was expressed in competition for jobs. This was a sore point particularly with the 'uneducated' who did not often have as good a chance of getting employment as the 'educated', because of the employers' preference for the English-speaking Indians. The 'uneducated' usually tried to compensate for their language disability by working hard and offering unquestioning obedience.

The structure of relations within the in-group has also to be viewed as being consistently influenced by its culture contrast with the out-group. One of the important points of tension was the difference in the mode of living of the normal British working-class family and the numerically significant accommodation segment of the Indian community. The British family is usually a small, well-organised, closed group. The British like to feel that their 'house is their castle' where they can lead a reserved life amongst polished floors and furniture and television shows. This of course does not mean that they have no contact with their neighbours. In fact, 'in well-established areas the neighbourhood spirit is very much alive, societal interaction is more frequent and the community's pressure for conformity is fairly high. The curious housewife in between her floor polishing and hanging clothes drops a furtive glance into the neighbours' backyards or rear windows to keep herself informed of the latest developments. On her shopping tours she meets other housewives with whom she shares her secrets'.[7] Now in this atmosphere the Indian accommodation houses were a misfit. About 60 per cent of the Indian houses were entirely 'bachelor' households where between 10 and 14 males lived. Each tenant of the house hired a bed for between 15 shillings and one pound. When too many immigrants arrived sometimes two persons slept in the same bed. The overcrowding naturally meant low standards of hygiene and tidiness. On the average the Indian houses were noisier. This contrast of the Indian houses with the British led to a certain antagonism between the British community and the Indians which in turn considerably influenced the internal relations in the Indian community. A small segment consisting of English-educated persons from urban classes and urbanised Jats were adopting Western middle-class modes of life and aiming at what we may term integration within the British culture. Quite a few of them were able to purchase their own houses where an attempt was made to conform to the prevalent British standards of hygiene and privacy. These attempts of the educated to segregate themselves from the uneducated mass and identify themselves with their British hosts was often bitterly commented upon by the uneducated Indians.

A subgroup within the 'integrationists' married or lived in common-law unions with European females. This very often led to their gradual isolation from the integrationist segment of the Indian society. I quote from my thesis a description of this category and the circumstances in which it emerged:

Houses where the wife of the landlord is an English or an European woman are closest to the 'respectable' British standards. The family usually keeps the major portion of the house for its own use and lets only the single rooms to the 'student type'[8] immigrants. The behaviour of the landlady towards the tenants is the typical 'landladyish'. Thus the tenant is best when he is quiet and tidy, pays his rent regularly, has few friends who come to visit him and does not bring in women. Though they may not have any friendly contact with their neighbours they are sensitive to 'what the neighbours would say'. They keep their front garden nicely tended, the door and the facade of the house properly painted. Floors are kept clean and polished, the kitchen is as modern as possible within their means. The reception room has a television, carpets and three piece sofa sets. In short, in every respect it is a 'British' house. When the Indian husband is not at work, he spends most of the time at home, shunning the company of Indians as far as possible. His interests are his studies, his children or various household chores. Though psychologically identified with the British society he realises the difficulty of being accepted by them on an equal and friendly footing. His wife herself is an outsider to her close family circle, who (the wife's family) do not take kindly to her having accepted a dark partner. Often she is the product of an unhappy family for whom her 'Indian' is a refuge, but at the same time she cannot totally accept what the community of her 'husband' has to offer her. Under these circumstances they are very much turned within. Sometimes these couples are friendly to one another or a few 'student types'. Compared to the rest of the community they can be aptly described as 'isolates'. Below I note a case which illustrates why radically mixed houses may become isolates:

Avtar lives with a white widow. Both of them work and have been able to acquire a nice house in a more respectable part of the borough. The standard of furnishing of the house is the same as that of their English neighbours. Part of the house has been let to a Welsh couple.

Avtar has brothers and cousins in Greenend. He used to live with them before he developed a serious relationship with Jeanie. I once visited him with Chaman (a student type) who works in the same factory. Chaman told Avtar that his brother was in real trouble with his foreman because he had been 'trying to be funny' with a woman in the factory and as an elder brother he must restrain him. Avtar said he (the brother) thought himself too clever. He said that his brother did not know how to behave and that is why he had separated from him and was living on his own. Later Chaman told me that his brother and relatives complained that ever since he began living with 'that white woman', his attitude had completely changed. He had become very jealous and haughty (which meant that he did not want to mix with them.) It is understandable that Avtar's younger brother should not have much regard for him.

Husband–wife relationship has a certain sacredness about it; but how can a relationship between a 'morally loose' white woman be regarded with that attitude? At the same time Avtar knows that his 'wife' is not getting the respect which, he considers, she must have. He is also afraid that even his closest relatives may not he able to resist the temptation of having a try at her.[9]

Avtar's 'isolation' from the bulk of the community was obviously an indicator of the fact that as a result of his close contact with Jeanie he had begun to think in different terms from his compatriots. Whereas for a great majority of the Indians the white woman who started cohabiting with an Indian without going through the rites of marriage was obviously immoral, Avtar, on the other hand, had understood Jeanie's cohabitation with a married man like himself as primarily a result of love which, in accordance with British romanticism, purifies the stigma attached to an 'unconventional bond'.

IV

In this article I have attempted to analyse some processes of social adjustment of an Indian immigrant community with the British society. I have illustrated my generalisations by drawing upon a part of the data which I had collected to describe the life and problems of the Indian community in Great Britain. It has been my contention that the structural forms which a community takes in its process of adjustment in a new social environment are evolved as a result of a constant interaction between its endo-trait complexes (for example, the kinship system, caste system, factions, system of values, etc.) and the exo-trait complexes[10] of the host culture. Since there is uniformity neither in the host culture nor in the culture of the immigrants, there is no single 'policy' of adjustment on the part of the immigrant community; the same is true of the 'host' community.

Notes

1. 'Greenend' handbook, 1959, p. 9.
2. Ibid.
3. The voters list compiled in October 1958 included 327 Indian names; of these barely 11 were female names.
4. G. S. Aurora: *Indian Workers in England.* Unpublished thesis, University of London. London, 1960, Appendix III, p. 30.
5. Ibid., p. 187.
6. Ibid., pp. 33a–35a.
7. Ibid.
8. A 'student type' supports a middle-class style of life and at least pretends to be a part-time student.
9. Ibid., p. 126.
10. For the terms 'endo-traits' and 'exo-trait', see M. Gluckman: 'Analysis of a Social Situation in Modern Zululand', *Bantu Studies*, 14, 1940.

4

On Migrating to Canada: The First Generation Indian and Pakistani Families in the Process of Change*

Chaudry M. Siddique

Despite a growing number of Indian and Pakistani immigrants in the ethnic mosaic of Canadian Society,[1] surprisingly very few empirical studies of their family life have been reported to date.[2] The need for a systematic investigation of family life and behaviour in this immigrant community, therefore, seems well justified. The present article may be considered only a limited attempt in this direction. Using data from a larger project designed to study various aspects

*Originally published in *Sociological Bulletin*, Vol. 26, No. 2, September 1977, pp. 203–26.

*Thanks are due to Professors S. P. Wakil and Norman W. Bell for making available their data to write this paper. I am also thankful to Professors S. P. Wakil, Bhopinder Singh Bolaria, Linvill Watson, Gurcharn Singh Basran, Richard Laskin and Mr S. A. Nasim of the Department of Sociology, University of Saskatchewan, Saskatoon and two friends from the immigrant community for reading an earlier draft of the article. Professor James L. Turk of the University of Toronto made various methodological suggestions which are gratefully acknowledged. In giving the article its present form, the critical comments made by Professor Jim Frideres of Department of Sociology, The University of Calgary, were of great help; I am thankful to Professor Frideres.

of the immigrant Indian and Pakistani community of Saskatoon, this article looks at the patterns of family interaction as they emerge from member's comparative participation in the household division of labour and decision-making areas.

Specifically, the article has two-fold objectives. First, it explores the nature and direction of change in these interrelated aspects of family structure. To achieve this objective, in addition to our data on the immigrants, two other sets of data, one on the patterns of decision-making and division of labour in the immigrants' country of origin and the other on these very aspects of interaction among the white Canadian families, will be used. The former set of data will be drawn from relevant studies conducted in India and Pakistan, and the latter from a cross-sectional survey of white families living in East York, Toronto. Wherever possible, the available evidence on the immigrants' 'back home' interaction patterns will be compared with their current patterns, and the latter, in turn, will be compared with the Canadian patterns. It is hoped that this method, despite some limitations,[3] would help point out the direction of family change.

The second objective of the article is to offer a tentative explanation for the type of change which we shall observe in the decision-making and division of labour aspects of the immigrant family. As we proceed towards data analysis, we would explore some possible explanations. Here it may be noted that the very fact of migration to Canada has been seen as a major source of change. It is suggested that the migration by separating the immigrant families from their families of orientation and interconnected networks of kin, relatives and friends, who are generally considered as readily available voluntary source of concrete help and emotional satisfaction in the country of their origin have produced initial circumstances conducive to family change. Furthermore, migration has provided some additional conditions which seem to have facilitated the exposure of these immigrants to the value system of this highly differentiated society with a relatively more 'modern' ideology of family life. In this respect, the immigrant's length of stay in Canada and other Western countries—henceforth referred to as 'an experience of living abroad'—would be emphasised as an important variable in the causal chain of events leading to a varying amount of change in the community as a whole. This variable seems pertinent to the immigrant's socialisation in this new cultural setting and may influence their awareness of the structural pressures to change.

In sum, this article would emphasise two types of constraints, which appear to be of particular importance to understand family change in the immigrant Indian and Pakistani community: (a) the constraints which have resulted from the immigrant family's structural separation from its larger kin networks, and (b) the constraints posed by the host society—which may be actual or of perceived variety. Though we would stress the former type of constraint, the latter are no less significant. Since all the families of this study have experienced a relatively full impact of economic gains by migrating to Canada, they are likely to feel under some pressure to change their style of life and behaviour to the demands of the new peers in the Canadian society, even if the latter as a whole promotes 'ethnic pluralism'. The relevance of only some of these variables to changing patterns of division of labour and decision-making would be shown in the section where we compare different sets of data; however, a more extensive discussion of their theoretical importance would be presented in the last part of the article.

The Immigrant Data.[4] In the Saskatoon study, the data were collected on 50 families (including 12 Pakistani and 38 Indian families) who were residing in the city of Saskatoon in the summer of 1972 and the winter of 1972–73. A combination of the following two methods has been utilised for this research: the participant observation—the researcher himself being participant, and the interviewer. For the latter method, an Interview Guide[5]—consisting of over 200 items—was used, which was administered by two Canadian–Caucasian trained interviewers. For 20 cases, where the respondent allowed, the answers were tape recorded; for others, immediately after the interview was over, the 'mental notes' were recorded on separate note books. The average time spent per interview was two hours. The collected data covered all the family members, e.g., husband, wife, children and relatives in Canada, if any. The information gained through interviewing was then checked against participant observation data for reliability. Thus, the data used for this article came from two main sources: tape recorded and other interview data, plus the lengthy notes of the observer based on long informal talks with families on various occasions.

Characteristics of the Immigrant Community. The sociodemographic characteristics of the community may be briefly noted as follows. In all 50 families the husbands were working full-time whereas only 17 wives were in the work force. Forty-eight per cent husbands were holding professional jobs and other 44 per cent were in semi-professional jobs. The mean income for husbands was $15,360 and the modal annual income was $18,000. The mean years of formal schooling for husbands was over 19 and for the wives the figure was about 15; the modal number of years spent in formal schooling for husbands and wives were 21 and 14 respectively. It is obvious that in terms of socioeconomic status, these families represent a higher upper-class section of the Indian and Pakistani immigrants in Canada, and a high middle-class section of the Canadian ethnic elite in general (cf. Porter 1965).

Most of the families were young and small in size. For instance, the mean age for husbands and wives was 36 and 31 years respectively. The mean duration of marriage was slightly over eight years. Only four couples who were newlywed did not have children; the remaining 46 had at least one child. With one exception of a family of foreign-born woman,[6] in other families neither spouse has his or her relatives living permanently with them in Canada.

Analysis of Data and Findings

Before we present our findings, a note on the mode of analysis is in order. For the purpose of presentation and comparisons with other studies, part of the data is quantified; the qualitative data would be generally used to throw some light on the observed variation in the direction of change. In order to explore the possibility of a link between the emerging patterns of decision-making and division of labour and the immigrant's 'experience of living abroad,' 24 families, where the husband's duration of stay in Canada was six years or more, are considered as having 'greater experience' and the remaining 26, having relatively 'less experience' of living abroad, especially in Canada.[7] These two groups would be our point of reference for occasional comparisons *within* the immigrant community. And finally, it may be noted that instead of doing a separate analysis of data on the immigrant Indian *and* Pakistani families, we will treat them as *one* group.[8]

Family Decision-Making. From the Saskatoon study, the data on 13 decision-areas which concerned almost all of the families, are presented in Table 4.1. It is evident from the table that generally an overall joint pattern of decision-making characterises these immigrant families. For instance, the decisions regarding the location of residence, buying a home, buying major appliance, buying furniture, and going on or planning vacation were reported to be made jointly by 90 per cent, 76 per cent and 84 per cent families respectively.[9] However, on two items, the nature of father's job and buying clothes for children, the pattern of participation in decision-making swings to the extremes: in the former case husband's participation is extremely high as in 86 per cent families, he decides what job to take, while in the latter, it is the wife whose participation in 60 per cent cases exceeded that of husband's.

We may sum up here the general pattern as it emerges from the data shown in Table 4.1, so that it may be easily contrasted with decision-making patterns reported by other relevant studies. In addition to children's clothes, other similar areas of activity, where the wife's participation is greater than her husband's include children disciplining (32 per cent), grocery shopping (44 per cent), planning family budget (34 per cent), and her decision of taking up a job (40 per cent), while decision regarding life insurance policies (54 per cent) and buying a car (40 per cent) mostly concern the males. This distribution of decisions between husbands and wives leaves the following impression of the immigrant community: that generally males in this community participate in those decision-areas which are more or less of economic nature (earning and spending) and which are highly important as rated by the judges;[10] the wives, on the other hand, tend to participate in those decisions which are linked to their 'motherly role'.

Comparable findings from a representative sample of 211 middle-class white families of East York in metropolitan Toronto show some similarity between the decision-making patterns observed in the immigrant community and the 'Canadian patterns' in general. As in the case of the immigrant families, among the East York families— according to wife's report—the decisions regarding husband's job, buying a car and insurance were made by the husbands in 70 per cent, 55 per cent and 43 per cent families respectively; and the decisions regarding the amount of money to be spent on food and whether or not the wife should work were reported to be made by wife alone in about one-third of the sample. On the other hand, the decisions about vacation, renting or buying a house and the choice

Table 4.1: Decision-making among the Immigrant Indian and Pakistani Families of Saskatoon

Patterns of Partici- pation	Buying a Home	Children's Discipline	Working of Mother	Nature of Father's Job	Location of Residence	Grocery Shopping	Buying Major Appli- ances	Planning Family Budget	Amount and Type of Life Insurance	Buying Furniture	Going on or Planning Vacation	Buying Clothes for Children	Buying Car
Husband Always	12	10	20	86	4	8	10	14	54	8	6	2	40
Both Husband and Wife	82	58	40	12	90	48	76	52	46	84	86	38	50
Wife Always	6	32	40	2	6	44	14	34	0	8	8	60	10
Total	100	100	100	100	100	100	100	100	100	100	100	100	100

Note: Figures are given in percentages (N=50).

of medical practitioner[11] were highly equalitarian in this East York sample as both husband and wife reported to have 'exactly the same' participation in 64 per cent, 60 per cent and 36 per cent cases respectively (Bell 1976). While this brief comparison seems to indicate the direction to which the immigrant families are changing, a lack of comparative evidence on each decision item for India and Pakistan makes it difficult to talk about the extent of change. However, the studies reported by Gore (1968), Ross (1967), Goode (1970) and Kapadia (1962) for India and by Pepanek (1971) and Korson (1970) for Pakistan show that it is the 'eldest male'—generally the grandfather—who almost invariably makes all important family decisions in these countries. The range of his participation is not well specified; it may encompass decisions about buying a house, land and other property, marketing of crops, change of tenants, as well as the career choice of potential wage-earners and the type of college or university the growing up sons and daughters would go. He might influence the decisions regarding family budget, the exchange of small gifts among friends or relatives, disciplining of children and so on. Of course, the extent to which the eldest male influences these and other decisions may vary in rural and urban, upper, middle and lower-class families as well as in joint and nuclear families as noted by Ross (1967) and Gore (1968), but the fact remains that he is still the active participant in most of the decisions—though he is no longer the 'patriarch', he may have been some 50 years ago. Even in India and Pakistan, some change—albeit a small one—indicating some reduction in his role as a decision maker is well underway (cf. Goode 1970). Now the family of procreation consisting of husband–wife and children as well as some other members, e.g., husband's brother and sister can afford some liberty to discuss the matter, before it is decided upon. For instance 63 per cent respondents in Gore's (1968) sample reported to participate in family discussions leading to decision-making; another 19 per cent discussed the matter although the final decision was that of the eldest male, and about 11 per cent never discussed any family decision. But in such discussions, if at all they take place, only husband's brother or sister, and elder female, probably husband's mother, would more often express their views. The wife, whom we observed very actively participating in family decisions as she faces them here in Canada, had a relatively small, if not negligible, role in India and Pakistan. The fact that now she can make some independent decisions coupled with her greater overall sharing with her husband, show a clear direction of change towards greater egalitarianism. For instance, the mean for shared or joint decisions was 7.62; 56 per cent of the immigrant families fall above it, which indicates higher than average mutual sharing of decision.[12]

This direction of change in decision-making patterns evoked various explanations. Since with one exception,[13] in none of the families the eldest male or eldest female was living with them in Canada (at the time of this investigation), the question of their participation in family decisions does not arise. In the cases where either spouse had his or her brother or sister living in Canada, they maintained a separate residence. However, this does not preclude the possibility of eldest male's and other close relative's decision-making influence which they might wield through mail-correspondence, telephone calls and other sources. It is our observation that the sphere of this influence is generally limited to decisions regarding marriage and the purchase of highly expensive property in Canada. Thus, as one would expect the ultimate responsibility of such frequently occurring decisions, which we studied, is likely to fall on the couple. This would suggest that the physical separation of the immigrant family from the family of orientation, where the latter's influence tends to be minimal, itself constitute an important reason of changed patterns of decision-making. The findings of Gore (1968), Ross (1967) and Goode (1970) indicating a trend towards some degree of 'mild' equalitarianism in the nuclear family in India, which moved away from the elder members of the family, are consistent with our reasoning. However, in the case of this immigrant community this trend is more pronounced since in addition to its structural separation it obtains some other conditions, e.g., its member's attainment of higher education from western schools and their possession of prestigious occupations. As revealed by our extensive exploration of observational data, tape-recorded and written comments of the respondents, both these conditions, by facilitating the immigrant's exposure to western value system—including the ideal of 'equalitarian family life'—have contributed a great deal to change their 'traditional patriarchal attitudes' in the direction of greater egalitarianism. Also consistent with our expectations, this change in attitude and orientation and its impact on decision-making showed a somewhat more clear link with family member's experience of living abroad, especially in Canada. In order to describe this latter association, few excerpts from the observation data are presented below.

In one family, the husband (with 10 years experience of living abroad), who made most of the decisions, explained this pattern as follows, 'Well, my wife doesn't take much interest in making these decisions, this is why I have to take this responsibility. I always ask her to express her view, but she leaves everything to me. Perhaps she feels I am here for a longtime and I know better about certain things'. Even where despite an increase in the length of stay in Canada and other western countries the husband makes most of the decision, the fact of consulting the wife even if she really does not change the decision, indicates some change in this important domain of familial interaction. In various other instances, as the wife's own experience of Canadian culture increased, a rather marked degree of increase in her participation was observed. As one wife revealed:

> In the beginning I didn't know how to do shopping, whatever I need to buy for myself or for our child I had to ask my husband—now I know all big stores in the downtown and also I have an idea of buying various things—I even sometimes do a little shopping for my husband.... Last time I made my own choice of utensils and furniture....

The link between greater experience of living abroad and changing patterns of decision-making seems to appear through the following process: (a) with an increasing stay in Canada, the wife becomes able to familiarise with new decision areas where she might have to play some role, (b) once she learns these areas (some of them were simply unknown to her, while almost all of them were in the hands of the eldest male or female or her husband), she gains some confidence which enables her to make her independent decision or to influence her husband's judgement and (c) both these effects are likely to reduce her dependence on the husband. In combination, this process eventuates in her increasing participation in family decisions as well as in a pattern moving towards equality—since any addition in wife's participation compared to her role in her country of origin is considered basic to egalitarian direction of change, especially in the case of this immigrant community. On the other hand, in newly immigrant families, the pattern of decision-making remained more or less similar to the traditional one in which the male had to play a prominent role. The reasons for this seem contrary to those presented above. That is, the wife does not take an active part in decision-making perhaps because she feels this is not her area of jurisdiction, since it was not so in their country of origin. Second, she is not familiar with certain decisions and therefore, has to leave their making to her husband, who by now is well versed and integrated in the new setting. As one wife said, 'I don't know much about the complicacies involved in buying insurance, though I can see its advantages, naturally my husband has to take care of this'. Similarly, lack of confidence on the part of newly arrived wives make their participation less likely in certain decisions involving a large amount of money. Referring to the purchase of a car, one wife said, 'I am always afraid of making this type of decision myself. I would rather leave it to my husband...you know, one can't buy these and other expensive things like other routine stuff.... Of course, the choice of colour is going to be mine'.

As noted earlier, despite a varying degree of change in overall decision-making patterns, the decisions regarding father's job, and the discipline of children and buying their clothes etc., have shown a great deal of persistence in the traditional pattern. One might speculate that the husband has to make his choice with respect to his job because he is relatively free from the influence or guidance of the oldest members. Then, there are certain structural pressures, e.g., availability of jobs and the nature of training which may not only restrict his choice but make him to use his own judgement more often. Also since husband's job is most important of his achieved roles and perhaps has been instrumental in his decision of migrating to Canada, he may think it more appropriate to assume full responsibility to decide about it. In general, the immigrant wives quite willingly leave this decision to their husbands. One wife said, for instance, 'I don't think I have to make any suggestion regarding his job-choice. He has spent so much time (six years) completing his education, and now it is up to him to find out any profession which suits him most'. Another wife told, 'He is kind of a career oriented person, after living for a long time in this country (eight years) he knows better about the type of job which he could like'. No remarkable difference on this decision was found among immigrant families of long and short experience of living abroad. But a longer stay in Canada did differentiate families with respect to wive's exclusive concern with taking care of children; that is, in families having longer stay, the husbands showed a good deal of interest in various matters relating to their children. However, high participation of mother in these areas may be attributed to her role of a nurturer which is more sentimentally viewed among Indian and Pakistani families (cf. Goode 1970, Gore 1968, Ross 1967).

Family Division of Labour. Table 4.2 shows the frequency distribution of husband's and wife's participation in 10 household tasks—indicative of family division of labour. As in the case of decision-making, here too, one can see a trend towards equalitarianism, but it is relatively less pronounced. In terms of couples relative participation, we observe a high male-participation in washing cars (54 per cent), small appliance repairs (54 per cent), mowing lawn (46 per cent) and clearing snow from the front walk (44 per cent), and a high female-participation in keeping a record of family expenses (34 per cent), getting breakfast (60 per cent), making beds (76 per cent), taking care of babies/children (52 per cent) and doing dishes (54 per cent). An overall distribution of 10 tasks according to relatively greater or 'exclusive' involvement of one sex, indicated that the immigrant females do slightly more work (in quantitative terms) than the males around the home. And this seems generally true in India and Pakistan, where usually the females perform a major proportion of routine household chores. Comparative data on family division of labour for these countries lend some support to this observation. In one study Ross (1967: 52–67) through an intensive analysis of interviewing data on middle-class families of Mysore [now Karnataka] State, has shown a rather clear-cut division of labour into male and female areas of concern. She states, 'the kitchen work—such as planning the menu and cooking—was the exclusive duty of the women' while the males 'either supervised the family property—which included collecting rents or looking after the farm and doing the heavy farm work or earned an income in business, a profession or government service' (p. 54). This pattern slightly varied in joint and nuclear families, as well as among rural and urban and 'traditional' and 'modern' families. For instance, 'in most modern families women would sometimes buy important household items without consulting the men'. Ross (1967: 57) reports one respondent in her educated group saying that, 'Mother was an educated woman; so she helped father with his business as well as keeping house. When father was at home or had a holiday, he used to help a lot with the children and cooking'. Also, 'the preparation of evening meal' is a 'joint affair' in this family. Gore's (1968: 157–58) findings present a similar picture of division of labour. Of 330 families in his main sample, the 'only job' of women in three-fourth of the families was to do housework. The percentages

Table 4.2: Division of Labour among the Immigrant Indian and Pakistani Families of Saskatoon

Household Task Area

Patterns of Participation	Washing Car	Small Appliance Repairs	Keeping Record of Family Expenses	Getting Breakfast	Making Beds	Clearing Garage and Basement	Mowing Lawn	Clearing Snow from Front Walk	Taking Care of Babies/ Children	Doing Dishes
Wife Always	6	22	34	60	76	32	8	12	52	54
Both Husband and Wife	40	24	46	30	22	46	46	44	44	38
Husband Always	54	54	20	10	2	22	46	44	4	8
Total	100	100	100	100	100	100	100	100	100	100

Note: Figures are given in percentages (N=50).

showing exclusive involvement of women in household chores in rural, fringe and urban areas was 96, 90 and 57 respectively. In the joint family 80 per cent of the women compared to 69 per cent in the nuclear family took the complete responsibility of household work. This is perhaps because, in the nuclear family, husband shared a number of tasks, since external help to the wife was available to a lesser degree than in the joint family. Although Gore (1968) collected data on various division of labour areas especially relevant to Indian family, he does not show husband–wife comparative or joint participation in each area which makes any comparison with Saskatoon study almost impossible. Nevertheless, he inserts this general statement: that in Aggarwal community and probably in India, 'men earn and women take care of the home and the children'. Since none of the women in Gore's sample worked outside the home, while almost all the men held some sort of job, her exclusive concern with household chores may be attributed in part, to her greater availability at home and of course mainly to the traditions which not only demand from her a greater share of household work, but through socialisation, perpetuates this pattern by discouraging her from joining the labour force. In a research in progress, Wakil (1976) hopes to show a somewhat familiar degree of sex-segregation with respect to division of labour and decision-making in Pakistani society 'as a whole'. Earlier observations made by Korson (1970) and Pepanek (1971) seem to bear out Wakil's preliminary predictions.

If we contrast the findings of these studies, showing the division of labour as it exists in India and Pakistan, with our study of the immigrant families of Saskatoon, the direction of change seems clear, e.g., towards some degree of sharing. But still the tendency among the males and females to stick to their specialised roles generally in accordance with the traditional sex distinction is remarkable. For instance, the mean adherence to sex-roles was 4.96; about 64 per cent of the families fall above it, which indicates a high degree of adherence to traditional sex-roles.[14] Since in Western society, despite a strong emphasis on equalitarianism a somewhat similar (but more flexible) pattern does persist, in the case of this immigrant community, any indication of husband's participation in those areas which he himself might consider 'feminine', shows that some degree of change is underway. However, the extent of equalitarianism shown by East York families is much higher than what we observed in our investigation of these immigrant families. For example, in well over

50 per cent families of East York, both husband and wife reported a joint participation in most of the household chores, shopping and other tasks including taking care of children (Bell 1976).

As in the case of decision-making, we also explored various possible explanations for the type of change which we have indicated in the household division of labour. The families were asked if they feel some degree of pressure from their peers in the Canadian society to modify their traditional patterns. It is important to note that none of the respondents could attribute change in these aspects of family interaction to any sort of perceived or actual pressures. However, some of them did mention the relevance of outside influence to the emergence of husband–wife 'social companionship'—going to movies, ethnic programmes, variety shows and participating in voluntary associations as 'couples'. In order to account for this differential impact of constraints on family life in the new setting, one may argue that since decision-making and household task-performance fall in the more private domain on internal family activities, they are likely to remain relatively insulated against external influences. Perhaps this is why most of the families see the changing patterns of division of labour simply as a consequence of their migration and the lack of availability of general assistance offered by relatives and friends. As one husband explains:

> I and my wife have a lot of discussion together regarding decisions—We also jointly do all sorts of household chores—If she is busy with something else, I myself do so many things around here—like making tea, cooking, doing dishes—Back home my sister or mother could have done all these things for me. We miss that unpaid help and advice here....

The impact of two other variables, the employment status of wife, and an overall experience of the immigrant family in the western culture, on the changing patterns of division of labour appeared somewhat more pronounced. For instance, about 47 per cent husbands of the working wives did a great deal of household work, even greater than their wives, and approximately the same per cent showed a joint pattern. In the non-working wives' group, both relative participation of the husband and the volume of shared participation was low. In more than 42 per cent such families, wives' participation exceeded their husbands' and, this was much higher than the working wives' group. This is perhaps because the non-working wife has enough time which she can devote to these household chores. As one wife puts it, 'How do you spend your time if you don't work! So what I do, is keep myself busy with these things you mentioned. When my husband comes, from the office, he finds his dinner ready—after eating we can go out for a walk...'. Also in such families, the wives more frequently justified their greater concern with household chores by making reference to 'obligations' and 'duties' of wives. Where the wives worked outside the home, the husbands did help to relieve them from the possible strains of this dual task of office and housework. This was true despite the fact that all the immigrant husbands held full-time jobs and no remarkable variation occurred in professional, semi-professional, upper and middle-class families. Instead, some variation in the pattern of division of labour was noted according to the length of family's experience in the Canadian and other western societies. The responses of few individuals seem illustrative of this point. One husband, who has resided in various western countries said, 'Well the things are different here in this country. Back home I never did these things, but here you "must" do them. And perhaps this is how other Canadian families go about doing the household chores'. The families of relatively new immigrants showed a slightly different but mixed pattern. In two such families, where the husbands are in Canada for the past four years and the wives came about two years later, a pattern of division of labour pretty much similar to the traditional pattern existed. It is interesting to note that in some of the newly arrived families the wife's expectations of her husband are changing more rapidly than vice versa. In few instances, the wives felt that their husbands should help them 'a little more'.

Some other behavioural variations with respect to household help may be briefly noted. In the families where the couple belongs to the same nationality group, more than 50 per cent husbands rarely help their wives with household work in the presence of other members of similar ethnic background. However, this tendency of 'feeling ashamed of doing feminine work' was much higher among the husbands whose stay in Canada ranged between one to five years. One wife reveals that her husband 'sometimes washes dishes and prepares breakfast when he is not with his [ethnic] friends, but when other families visit, he will like to "order" for tea and other things'. In families where the wives were foreign born, the husbands, in general, did not show much reluctance in doing household chores in the presence of ethnic friends. While the equalitarian mode of participation remained a visible feature of these families, in certain cases the husbands even did more work around the house than their wives; on the other hand, more than half the wives had greater say in the making of family decisions. Such a pattern may be expected since the husbands who happen to marry women of a different religion and cultural background might have a greater predisposition towards 'equalitarian family life', which may have led them to change their traditional ideology of 'male supremacy' rather easily. There is some evidence to support the belief that the males who are not willing to accept the notion of equalitarian family and its consequences for marital life rarely marry western women (see Ames and Inglis 1973, Srivastava 1974 and Wakil 1974). However, as in the case of decision-making, here too, from our analysis of data on division of labour in the total population, we may speculate that with a more fuller exposure of these immigrant families to the Canadian culture and value systems, their traditional orientation is likely to soften to some extent and consequently they may adopt a more equalitarian pattern of doing household tasks. But the fact that some continuity of traditional patterns is discernable even among the families having longer stay in Canada, a complete equalitarian pattern of fifty-fifty variety is less likely to occur. And perhaps, in Canada too, this pattern is nonexistent!

Changing Patterns of Family Interaction: A Discussion of Relevant Variables

It is evident from this comparative analysis that some degree of change in the decision-making and division of labour aspects or family interaction in the immigrant community of Saskatoon is well underway. Although the emerging patterns are generally in the direction of Canadian patterns, at present, they seem to indicate an 'intermediate level of conformity'[15]—falling somewhere between the patterns of immigrants, countries of origin and Canada. However, in view of the traditional ideal modes of familial interaction, where usually the husbands make most of the decisions and the wives take care of household chores, this degree of change in the immigrant families is indeed remarkable and shows a somewhat significant departure from the traditional practices. In order to sketch a tentative explanation for the emerging patterns, we may briefly recapitulate some of the variables which we have emphasised in the foregoing analysis and link them with each in a more systematic way.

To restate, an obvious outcome of migration—as an instance of geographic mobility—is that it has led to a rather inevitable structural separation of the immigrant families from their respective families of orientation and larger kin networks. As a consequence of this, the immigrant families at their current place of residence have become 'nuclear' in their composition—consisting of husband–wife and children, if any, and no 'extended family' relative is permanently living with them. Thus, at least three interconnected variables, a neolocal residence, necessitated by migration, and latter's consequences of physical separation from the kinfolks and small size of the family may be held accountable for the restructuring of social networks and of familial interaction at the place of destination. These variables seem to operate concomitantly to induce a degree of change in the following way: (a) the eldest male, the eldest female and a number of 'other important family members' are simply absent from the scene, thus the question of their participation in family activities no more arises, and (b) the very absence of these relatives has put all familial responsibilities on the couple, which of necessity may have contributed to a high degree of sharing. In this respect, the following remarks of a wife may be noted, 'We feel living here alone, I mean away from parents and relatives, what we have to do we got to do ourselves. No one is here to help around, you know. So whether it is a matter of going out for shopping or taking care of household things (you just mentioned) we do together'. Thus, following Elizabeth Bott (1971), part of the change in familial interaction resulting from this mutual help and emotional involvement of husband–wife, may be attributed to the very fact of migration (or geographic mobility) which tends to isolate the couple from its close-knit network of relatives, friends and other sources of voluntary help and advice (see also McAllister 1973). The findings of various other empirical studies substantiate this view. Consistent with our study, Mogey (1955) for instance, observed that families who moved to a new housing estate in Oxford developed a less rigid division of labour, which in turn, was related to their lesser contacts with close relatives and former friends. Young and Willmott (1972) report that Bethnal Green families who moved to a housing estate at Debden practised a relatively more joint and flexible pattern of household task-performance and decision-making. Like Mogey, these authors also seek to establish a link between the change in family role-relationships and a low frequency of interaction with the kin networks and other sources of external help available to husbands and wives from their respective networks at the place of origin. Turner's (1967) data on 115 Leadgill couples lent some additional support to the view that geographic mobility tends to reduce segregation in familial interaction by decreasing the availability of a substitute source of concrete help or emotional gratification to the mobile couple.

In addition to geographic mobility, the variable of social mobility may also be held accountable for some degree of change in the immigrant families of this study. Before we show this link, it is important to note that all 50 families have experienced upward social mobility, as measured in terms of husband's attainment of higher education from western schools, working in prestigious occupations and the yearly income, compared to their own status before migration to Canada as well as to their parental status in their countries. Whereas geographic mobility leads to physical separation, social mobility generally results in what may be called social-psychological separation (Blau 1956). This view states that because of mobile and non-mobile individual's differential orientation to their respective reference group values and the consequent differing socialisation experiences, there remains very little in common to hold them together in the long run. As a result the mobile families are less likely to be influenced by the standards of doing things or making decisions adopted by their 'old folks' who remained at the status of origin. One might further stress the importance of social mobility by suggesting that after the temporal effects of geographic mobility start decreasing over a period of time, the social-psychological effects of social mobility make their appearance and gear the process of change rather more strongly. Since status is generally achieved by associating with those of equal or greater social success, the vertically mobile individual may have to sacrifice old ties and customs if he wants to gain acceptance by a more prestigious group (Blau 1956). And, as Parsons (1953) has suggested, the mobile person with high achievement orientation, when faced with this type of dilemma, is very likely to give preference to social acceptance of new peers over ties with the extended family relatives. Since the Indian and Pakistani immigrants—perhaps like other immigrants from developing countries—

in their decision of migrating to Canada were largely motivated by social and economic advantages, this view seems to cast some light on their expressed departure from the back home modes of behaviours. An initial weakening of loyalties to traditional way of life brought by migration, seem to have been intensified under the social-psychological impact of mobility. This is evident from their willingness to adopt relatively new patterns of family interaction practised by their peers in the Canadian society.

It may be pointed out here that besides their combined effects discussed in the context of social mobility, the variables of occupation, income and education, may singularly play an important role in the process of change. For instance, both high income and prestigious occupations, being important resources for the immigrants in the new setting, are likely to increase their exposure to the life style and behaviour patterns of the members of their terminal class. And since the characteristics of the stratum of destination are generally taken through a process of 'adult socialisation' (cf. Blau 1956), high level of education is more likely to facilitate this process, as well as to remove some of the difficulties which one may encounter in the course of adoption of new modes of behaviour. In addition, the educated people, because of their low level of traditional orientation, are more likely to have a rational look at the new culture which may motivate them to have an experience of its any aspect which they consider worthy of experimentation. In the case of this community, the immigrant husbands' greater acceptance of interchangeability of family roles may be attributed to their changed outlook marked by a favourable attitude toward western modes of behaviour. It is interesting to note that now they do not feel threatened by their wives' having greater say in the process of decision-making nor do they find their masculine status at stake by doing household chores of 'feminine' variety. Thus, given the urgency of structural constraints (as for example, the constraints created by physical isolation from kin networks), the variables of income, occupation and education seem to formulate an important set of 'intervening variables' which create some degree of predisposition to accept new modes of behaviour by facilitating the availability of necessary resources and conditions of change.

Since all the immigrant families have experienced geographic and social mobility—the variables which we have shown to account for the overall family change in the community as a *whole*—the extent to which patterns of family interaction vary *within* the community as well as the extent to which they are similar to Canadian patterns, may be attributed to their experience of living abroad. Considering change in interaction patterns as incremental over an extended period of time, the importance of longer duration of stay in the new cultural setting, which produces the type of attitude and behaviour conducive to necessary modifications, becomes extremely obvious. According to our observation, the immigrant families whose interaction patterns are changing in the direction of Canadian patterns, were generally those who had a greater experience of living in Canada (cf. Breton 1971). However, a rather 'complete' adoption of the behaviour patterns of the members of the host society, who have a long history of their own, is less likely in the case of new comers (Blau 1956). Second, since they are neither in a position to maintain strong ties with their former kin networks from which they have departed, they may equally find it difficult to practice old modes of family behaviour. While these may be considered very important reasons for the emergence of family interaction patterns which represent 'an inter-mediate level of conformity,' other relevant variables may also be noted as follows: the personal motivation to change, adherence to back home patterns, the presence of structural constraints, and the availability of visible cues and reinforcements etc. at the new setting.

Some of these variables may be briefly commented upon since they seem to throw some light on the observed patterns of family interaction. In this community, for instance, most of the wives seem to lack a real motivation to change. One important reason behind wive's greater reluctance to change may be seen in the fact that almost all of them came to Canada later than their husbands and therefore are not fully exposed to its value system as yet. Furthermore, unlike their husbands most of the wives did not pursue higher education in western schools nor did most of them join the work force, which may also account for their low integration in the western culture. Thus, the persistence of traditional modes of family inter-action may be attributed to wive's low experience of living abroad compared to that of their husband's. This is most true of non-working wives who generally lacked motivation to participate in the process of familial decision-making, but on the other hand, showed a greater interest in household chores. Interestingly, in a large number of families, the wive's low integration in the new cultural setting has given rise to the following two paradoxical consequences: value-conflict with the husband, and emotional dependency upon them. Obviously, the situation of value-conflict has arisen because of wive's lesser experience of living abroad and an 'incomplete' exposure to western values for the reasons explained above. On the other hand, their greater perception of the loss of kinship ties, which they have not overcome as yet due to the recency of their separation from kinfolks, had led to their increasing reliance upon the husband for emotional solace and satisfaction. Again the net outcome of this situation seems a high degree of husband–wife companionship which has made their normative expectations with respect to the allocation of familial roles rather more flexible. This is manifest from their mutual consultation and sharing of family activities without any visible degree of conflict and hostility. One may speculate that as more and more immigrant wives assume employment status, the process of family change is likely to be enhanced as a result of their exposure to the value system of the host society. However, it is difficult to say whether the patterns of family interaction would continue to represent 'an intermediate level' or would become completely similar to the Canadian patterns. In view of the emphasis placed on 'ethnic pluralism' by the Canadian society, which has enabled its ethnic groups to maintain back-home patterns of behaviour and style of family life if they wish, one might guess the continuity of this intermediate level for sometime, at least for the first generation. In fact, it is this low level of constraints posed by the Canadian society which, despite other necessary conditions of change, e.g., the constraints induced by the fact of migration, seems to account for the emergence of this intermediate level of conformity with respect to family decision-making and division of labour in the immigrant community.

In the end, it may be noted that because of the partial analysis of a larger set of data, the findings of this study may be considered preliminary and only of sensitising value. Another important reason which restricts the generalisability of these findings is the nature of our methodology which is rather 'crude'. Further, the explanations which we have discussed in this section are not definitive. Despite their apparent relevance to the problem explored in the article, and the empirical support they derive from observational data, these explanations may be considered of speculative nature at best. In order to formulate any systematic explanations for the changing interaction patterns, which may generate valuable hypotheses for empirical testing, additional data on this immigrant community are needed.

Notes

1. For instance, about 6,200 Indians and Pakistanis immigrated to Canada in 1972, and in this way constituted the sixth largest group of the total immigrants in that year (Information Canada 1974: 4).

2. At present, the findings of the following four studies made by Srivastava (1974), Ames and Inglis (1973–74), Kurian (1974) and Wakil (1974) are available. (The latter two studies are still under preparation.) All these studies are based on information gained from a relatively small number of respondents and none of them presents a comparative analysis of data.

3. Some obvious limitations which restrict the generalisability of our findings may be noted as follows: First, most of the studies which we will review in this article have asked different questions, therefore, neither the family aspects which are being analysed nor the items used to measure them are always identical with our own study. Second, given the family variations among the white Canadians, it may be quite misleading to speak of 'Canadians patterns' by using data from a cross-sectional study. Third, since within India and Pakistan, the family forms and modes of behaviour vary not only among different socioeconomic classes and the extent these classes are exposed to western ideas of liberalism but the rural–urban, regional, racial and religious differences cause a great deal of variation, it is difficult to clearly delineate the 'back home family patterns' and to use them as a point of reference to assess the degree of change in the immigrant families. Fourth, in view of these variations our implicit treatment of Canadian or western family as 'equalitarian' and Indian and Pakistani family as 'patriarchal' may not give a realistic picture of the family system as they operate in these cultural contexts; it is only in ideal-typical terms that such an assumption may be accepted for the sake of comparisons. Perhaps it is by giving some precedence to the substantive contribution of this research—albeit of sensitising nature—over these and other methodological lapses, that we feel to have some justification for undertaking the present comparative analysis. Another equally important reason is a lack of reported research on this rapidly growing community in the ethnic mosaic of Canadian society.

4. Main characteristics of East York families can be found in Turk and Bell (1972). This sample of 211 families largely consisting of second and third generation white Canadians, drawn by stratifying families according to stages in life-cycle, is considered to be 'representative of a total community—a stable, fairly homogenous lower middle-class to upper middle-class community' (p. 216). The characteristics of data, used from studies done in Pakistan and India, may be seen in the relevant sources cited in the text.

5. Copies of 'interviewing guide' are available from Professor S. Parvez Wakil of the Department of Sociology, University of Saskatchewan at Saskatoon, Canada.

6. There were 13 families with foreign-born women; in that four women were American, three Canadian, two German, two Filipino and one Kenyan. Out of these, in one family, the wife who was from Saskatoon had her mother living with her who 'just moved in' at the time her daughter's first child was born.

7. Since, except 13 families of foreign-born women, in all other families the average duration of husbands' stay in Canada (six years) and the average number of years they have been away from their countries of origin (9.8 years) was greater than their wive's, the cutting points dividing families into these two groups are based on *husband's stay only rather than wive's*. According to this division, 11 families of foreign-born wives fall in the category of 'greater experience of living abroad'—since their husbands were also those who left their countries of origin earlier than most of the other individuals. Also a large number of husbands classified as having 'greater experience of living abroad' reported to have lived in one or two countries other than Canada, especially England and the USA to complete their studies—who after migrating to Canada sponsored their wives.

8. This is done because according to our initial analysis, where we looked at them separately, these families did not differ from each other in terms of socioeconomic status (education, occupation, income, etc.) and internal family characteristics. Similarly, the differences in religion did not relate to either of these aspects. This may be perhaps over half the respondents were in their teens at the time of partition of India in 1947, and therefore, were exposed to various sociocultural similarities. Almost all of them manifested a similar degree of achievement orientation. Most of them who came to England, Canada and the USA in early or mid-sixties had pretty much similar educational and professional standing. The general life style of the family, patterns of decision-making, division of labour and the position of children in the family, did not show any visible difference. Also the families where the wives were foreign-born could not be differentiated from others in terms of socioeconomic status. However, they were found different with respect to their family behaviour. This latter difference could not be attributed to their religious affiliation *per se*, but rather to their greater exposure to the western culture as well as to their husbands' low traditional orientation—both these in turn relate to their length of stay in the western countries. Thus, instead of analysing this latter small group separately, we found it proper to study it along, with other families.

9. It may be noted that the data presented in Tables 4.1 and 4.2 are based on respondents' own assessment of the modes of participation in activities relating to family decisions and household chores. Since they were responding to white interviewers from a society where high value is placed upon husband–wife mutual sharing and jointness, we may expect some degree of bias in their answers. Especially, as shown by our observational data, the pattern of joint decision-making is a bit exaggerated.

10. These 13 decisions were weighted by 10 judges (five females and five males), randomly selected from the immigrant community, who were asked to indicate the importance of each decision on a five-point North-Hatt type scale. The theoretical range of scores on this scale was 1 to 5 (where higher scores indicate greater importance) but empirically the scores ranged from a minimum of 1.7 to a maximum of 4. The weighted scores for 13 decisions are as follows: buying a home, 3.6; children's discipline, 3.7; working of mother, 2.2; nature of fathers' jobs, 4.0; location of residence, 2.7; grocery shopping, 2.3; buying major appliances, 2.3; planning family budget, 3.0; amount and type of life insurance, 2.8; buying furniture, 2.1; going on or planning vacation, 1.7; buying clothes for children, 2.1; and buying a car, 3.1.

11. The decision with respect to the choice of a doctor was not asked in Saskatoon study.

12. A separate counting of those decision areas with an answer 'both husband and wife exactly the same' was done to obtain a measure of shared or joint decisions. After summing up the score of these decisions for each family, the total was divided by the number of families.

13. This exception is indicated in note six above.

14. The measure of role-orientation in accordance with sex-distinction is based on 'general cultural prescriptions' which define certain tasks or roles as 'masculine' and others 'feminine' etc. (see Blood and Wolfe 1960).

15. This is a very general conclusion and, in fact, emerged from some additional analysis of data—relating to various other aspects of the immigrant family, e.g., the extent to which it identifies with the back home and the Canadian culture as a whole. Part of these data relates to parental attitude towards dating and marriage of their children in the Canadian society, and children's attitudes towards parental authority and control, back home rituals and religious practices.

References

Ames, Michael M. and Joy Inglis. 1973–74. 'Conflict and Change in British Columbia Sikh Family Life', *B.C. Studies*, 22(Winter).

Bell, Norman W. 1976. *Dynamic Properties of Family Life: A Sociological Study of East York Families*. Toronto: Clark Institute of Psychiatry.

Blau, Peter M. 1956. 'Social Mobility and Interpersonal Relations', *American Sociological Review*, 21(June).

Blood, R. O. and D. M. Wolfe. 1960. *Husbands and Wives: The Dynamics of Married Living*. New York: The Free Press.

Bott, Elizabeth. 1971. *Family and Social Network*. London: Tavistock Publications.

Breton, Raymond. 1971. 'Institutional Completeness of Ethnic Communities and Personal Relations of Immigrants', in B. R. Blishen et al.: *Canadian Society: Sociological Perspectives*. Toronto: Macmillan of Canada.

Goode, William J. 1970. *World Revolution and Family Patterns*. Illinois: The Free Press.

Gore, M. S. 1968. *Urbanisation and Family Change*. Bombay: Popular Prakashan.

Information Canada. 1974. *1972 Immigration Statistics*. Ottawa.

Kapadia, K. M. 1966. *Marriage and Family in India*. Bombay: Oxford University Press.

Korson, Henry J. 1970. 'Career Constraints among Women Graduate Students in a Developing Society: West Pakistan', *Journal of Comparative Family Studies*, 1(1).

Kurian, George. 1974. *Socialisation of Children of Immigrants from India in Alberta*, unpublished manuscript.

McAllister, E. W. et al. 1973. 'The Adaptation of Women to Residential Mobility', *Journal of Marriage and the Family*, 35(May).

Mogey, John. 1955. 'Changes in Family Life Experienced by English Workers Moving from Slums to Housing Estates', *Marriage and Family Living*, 17(2).

Parsons, Talcott. 1953. 'Revised Analytical Approach to the Theory of Social Stratification', in R. Bendix and S. M. Lipset (eds.): *Class, Status and Power*. Illinois: The Free Press.

Pepanek, Hanna. 1971. 'Purdah in Pakistan: Seclusion and Modern Occupations for Women', *Journal of Marriage and the Family*, 33(August).

Porter, John. 1965. *The Vertical Mosaic*. Toronto: University of Toronto Press.

Ross, Aileen D. 1967. *The Hindu Family in its Urban Setting*. Toronto: University of Toronto Press.

Srivastava, Ram P. 1974. 'Family Organisation and Change among the Overseas Indians', in George Kurian (ed.): *The Family in India: A Regional View*. The Hague: Mouton and Co.

Turk, James L. and Norman W. Bell. 1972. 'Measuring Power in Families', *Journal of Marriage and the Family*, 34(May).

Turner, C. 1967. 'Conjugal Roles and Social Networks', *Human Relations*, 20(2).

Wakil, S. Parvez. 1974. 'The Immigrant Indo-Pakistani Family: A Case Study Research Note'. (A paper presented at the 8th World Congress of Sociology, Toronto, Ontario.)

———. 1976. *Women in Pakistan: A Socio-Ethnographic Study in a Muslim Society* (forthcoming).

Young, Michael and Peter Wilmott. 1972. *Family and Kinship in East London*. Harmondsworth, Middlesex: Penguin Books.

5

Contemporary Research on People of Indian Origin in Canada*

Norman Buchignani

The year 1988 marks the 84th year of Indian settlement in Canada. Once a small, isolated community in British Columbia, Indo-Canadians and their descendants now number at least 200,000, and may be as many as 250,000.[1] Indians are the largest component of peoples of South Asian origin in Canada, whose population at present is about 380,000.[2] They are presently one of Canada's most rapidly growing ethnocultural populations.[3]

I would like to take this opportunity to review the present status of academic research on Indians in Canada.[4] The discussion is divided into six parts. In the first, I briefly outline the historical development of research on Indians in Canada. The second part is devoted to research on the history of Indo-Canadians. Parts three and four focus on the analysis of immigration and contemporary Indo-Canadian life, respectively. Part five covers research done on social issues and inter-group relations. Part six deals briefly with Indo-Canadian and South Asian studies in Canada. These sections

*Originally published in Sociological Bulletin, Vol. 38, No. 1, March 1989, pp. 71–94.

are followed by a concluding assessment of the future prospects for research on Indians in Canada.

The Historical Development of Studies on Indians in Canada

Roughly 5,200 Indian immigrants arrived in British Columbia, Canada from 1904 to 1908.[5] Approximately 80–85 per cent were Sikhs, who had come either from Hong Kong or Punjab. Most of the rest were Muslim and Hindu Punjabis. In response to local anti-Asian feelings and the British government's concerns about the possible rise of 'seditious' activities among overseas Indians, the Canadian government banned Indian immigration in 1908.

There was little academic concern with this small Pacific coast community during the time when it was becoming established. The result is that whatever early literature we have on Indians is broadly of three kinds: folk discussions in newspapers and magazines, government reports and written commentaries by Indian immigrants about their plight in Canada. This literature is quite extensive,[6] but primarily useful as historical data rather than as studied analysis.

Indian immigration was virtually banned from 1908 to 1947.[7] After World War I, community life consequently stabilised, local racial hostility toward Sikhs decreased precipitously, and Indians vanished from the public spotlight. As a result, even secondary literature from the period 1919–47 is very sketchy. However, this period does mark the rise of some formal research—a handful of studies of immigrant adaptation (Ch'eng 1931, Das 1923 and Smith 1944) and of Indian immigration and Canadian politics (Morse 1935 and 1936, and Reid 1941). Work produced from 1947 to 1970 is not very substantial. During this period, Canadian racial immigration barriers were systematically dismantled, with the result that the Indian population of Canada increased from a few thousand to 67,000 in 1971. Early immigrants had been almost all Sikhs, but people arriving in the 1950s and 1960s came from an increasingly diverse range of ethnic and religious backgrounds. They soon began to establish new communities across the country. Most of these developments were completely ignored by the research community of the time. From this period we have only several studies of Sikh settlements in British Columbia (Button 1964, Lowes 1952, Mayer 1959 and Munday 1953) and a few others on Indian settlements elsewhere (Chawla 1971, Pannu 1970 and Pereira 1971).

In truth, there was nothing approaching an academic literature on Indians in Canada until the past decade. Since 1970, though, several factors have exponentially increased research activity in this area. One is the rise of public consciousness of Indian immigrants and issues concerning them. The overall Indo-Canadian population increased by more than four times between 1971 and 1981. This led to the rapid rise of Indian communities across the country where none had existed before and to dramatic increases in the size of those communities that were established earlier. Sikhs remained by far the largest Indian group (representing 120–130,000, or over one-half of all Indians in Canada today), and by 1980 substantial Sikh communities were established in virtually every city from British Columbia to Quebec.[8] Nevertheless, many new communities were formed by comparatively new immigrant groups such as Hindi-speaking (25,000) and Punjabi-speaking (6,000) North Indians, Gujaratis (20,000), Bengalis (5,000), Tamils (5,000) and Malayalees (3,000). Other communities were formed by immigrants with ultimate origins in India who came from Fiji (15,000), East Africa (30,000, chiefly Ismailis and Sikhs), South Africa (2,000), Guyana (25,000) and Trinidad (25,000). At present, small numbers of people in Canada represent every state and large ethnocultural or religious group in India, and virtually every outpost of the Indian diaspora.

Indian immigrants' settlement has generally proceeded very smoothly, due in no small part to the highly selective nature of this immigrant flow: about three-quarters of all post-World War II Indian immigrants have been highly educated and skilled. However, one immediate result of large scale Indian immigration in the 1970s and 1980s was the short-term rise of anti-Indian prejudice and discrimination, and the perception of Indian settlement in social problem terms.[9] Both were a significant impetus to research. So also was the rise of the Canadian policy of multiculturalism (established in 1971), programmes of which have thereafter continuously supported research, academic conferences and the like on Indians to Canada. A third factor was a dramatic increase in the number of Indo-Canadian social scientists and graduate students; I would estimate that well over half of the recent literature has been generated by such people. Today, there are about five hundred articles and books which in part or whole represent serious research on South Asians in Canada; of these, roughly 80 per cent concern Indians specifically. It is a literature which is now comparable in size with that on much larger Canadian ethnocultural populations such as Italians and Germans. At the same time, it is a body of research that suffers the obvious limitations and lack of unity of a new field. It is an amalgam of a wide variety of interests and disciplinary orientations, as illustrated in subsequent sections.

Historical Research on Indians in Canada

The historical literature on Indians in Canada is by far the most coherent and well-developed body of research dealing with this ethnocultural population. This is particularly true of formal chrono-logical history involving Indians. Such historical work began with Morse's (1935 and 1936) attempt to sort out the political and international consequences of early Sikh settlement. His work was greatly limited by his inability to reach sealed archival material in Canada, Britain and India. This deficiency was not rectified until the last 15 years, when more extensive research of the same sort was carried out by Andracki (1958), Bhatti (1974), Buchignani and Indra (1981a, 1985), Dodd (1972), Ferguson (1975), Johnson (1979, 1987), Lal (1976) and Ward (1973).[10] Much of this work deals with Canadian, British and Indian government reactions to Indians as immigrants, or with Sikh protests against the immigration restrictions imposed in 1908. The early rise of the *Ghadar* revolutionary move-ment among Sikhs in British Columbia (1912–14) had significant international political consequences in India, the United States and Southeast Asia. Recent research on *Ghadar* based on Canadian, American and Indian archival materials has greatly augmented our knowledge of this movement, as well as of relations between Canada, Britain and the British Indian government concerning Indians in Canada (Bose 1965, Buchignani and Indra 1981a, Deol 1969, Hilliker 1980, Josh 1970 and 1977–78, Mathur 1970, and Singh and Singh 1966).

The social history of Indians in Canada is considerably less developed. While it is now possible to piece together the minute sequence of events concerning, say, the 1908 ban on immigration, we know comparatively little about Indian family and community life in Canada during 1904–45. The key exception has been the work co-authored by Buchignani and Indra (1985), which developed a historical picture of the small, mostly male, British Columbia community based on oral history. In addition, Johnson (1987) has recently made a careful analysis of the demographic make up of the early Sikh community, which shows clearly the effects of a high rate of chain migration: virtually all were adult men, some 80 per cent of immigrants were from Doaba (mostly from Jullundar and Hoshiarpur), 85 per cent were Sikhs and over 80 per cent were Jats.

There are several other historical avenues which have not been well explored. One is the application of comparative sociological race relations theory to the situation of Indians during this historical era.[11] Moreover, Indians were then establishing themselves all around the world, where they always faced some form of racial prejudice and discrimination. There has been almost no integration of Canadian findings into worldwide historical Indian migration.[12] Also, Sikhs of that era showed a remarkable capacity for maintaining their ethnic and religious heritage, but rather little is known about how these people combatted acculturation (Dhami 1969).

Immigration and Migration

Most Indo-Canadians are immigrants who have come to Canada since 1972. Immigration and settlement are consequently key phenomena in the Indo-Canadian experience. A number of studies have tried to describe the complex process of immigration, settlement and consequent community-building (Adams 1977, Buchignani 1977b, Chadney 1984, Dossa 1985, Morah 1974, Moudgill 1977, Nasser-Bush 1973 and Pereira 1971). Even so, I know of no research directed specifically at immigration itself. Most settlement studies begin at the point when immigrants arrive in Canada. Motives for immigration are thus relatively well known, but not so the actual mechanisms of application, selection and migration. Chain migration has played an important role in Indian settlement, yet how it operates in India has not received the attention it deserves. No discussion whatever exists on secondary migration within Canada, save for a few incidental comments. Neither do we know what effects Indian immigration has on the source regions, villages and families from which immigrants come.[13] In addition, there is an enormous amount of visiting done between Canada and India. This process must profoundly affect the transmission and maintenance of Indian family values, inasmuch as marriages are arranged and family conflicts mediated through such links. People are also tied to social and political concerns in India through such visiting. All this remains unexplored. So do the effects of events in India upon Indian communities in Canada. A key case in point is the impact of the present turmoil in Punjab on Canadian Sikhs. Whereas it is clear that such events have resulted in a dramatic 're-traditionalisation' of Canadian Sikhs, much internal community factionalism and conflict, and a rupture of social ties with Hindu Indo-Canadians, none of this has yet been addressed by research.[14]

The Analysis of Contemporary Indian Canadian Life

Research on contemporary Indo-Canadian life has increased greatly over the last 10 years. In order to make the discussion more manageable, I have divided this large topic into three aspects: (a) Sociopsychological and individual level adaptation, (b) Family organisation and family adaptation, and (c) Community organisation and development.

Sociopsychological and Individual Level Adaptation

Rather little attention has been shown to the specifically psychological dimension of the Indo-Canadian experience. Indeed, Naidoo alone has been working consistently in this area. Much of her work has been on the personality makeup, motives and goals of Indian immigrant women (1980a, 1980b, 1984, 1987). She has also done a comparative study of Indian and 'Anglo-Saxon' Canadian women (1979). In addition to her work, Minde and Minde (1976) have demonstrated a high degree of maladjustment among Ugandan refugee children, a finding which is not in accord with most observations of Indian immigrant children. Beck (1982, 1987) has just begun work on symbolic association of adults to their family roles. Filteau (1980) has addressed the dynamics of love within the family, and Dusenbery has done important work on the symbolic and identity aspects of Sikh religiosity (1981, 1987a, 1987b).

I believe that work of this type is extremely important. Most of the ever-increasing studies of Indo-Canadian family life are based on rather ad hoc assumptions of the social psychology of individual family members; the same holds for the analysis of personal problems, such as the effect of discrimination, unemployment and family disorganisation on the individual. We need comparative data to Naidoo's on Indian men. Secondly, Indians are as culturally diverse as are all Europeans. Additional work must try to develop a greater understanding of the social psychological similarities and differences between Canada's many Indian communities.

Individual level attitudinal studies are somewhat more numerous. As mentioned below, much of the recent work on family and on education is based on survey data, and these surveys have been quite productive in identifying key Indian concerns about ethnocultural maintenance and adaptation; these studies are most conveniently discussed in the next sub-section.[15]

Family Organisation and Family Level Socioeconomic Adaptation

Despite their wide-ranging backgrounds, various Indian ethnocultural groups typically come to Canada with a number of common family experiences, with some variety of an extended or joint family, and with sharply defined family roles and statuses based on patriarchy, gerontocracy and the subordination of the individual to the interests of the family. Normative ideologies supporting these principles are also quite similar in various groups. Nevertheless, the structural changes in Indo-Canadian family organisation have been profound. Permanent extended family structure is rare in Canada—at least in the sense that it exists in India. Beginning with observations of Ames and Inglis (1973), a number of authors have reported a high prevalence of nuclear families in all groups (Adams et al. 1977, Buchignani 1977b, Chadney 1975, Moudgil 1977, Qureshi 1980, Sandhu 1980, C. Siddique 1977a and 1977b, M. Siddique 1974 and

1983, and Wakil 1974). Joint families are sometimes found among Sikhs (Chadney 1975 and 1984) and temporary extension was common in many communities when immigration rates were high and new immigrants lived for a while with their kin. Many families today contain one other family member who is not a part of the core nuclear family on a more or less permanent basis. Factors accounting for this shift to nuclear families are the limitation of available personnel as a result of immigration, and the individualisation of family member resources brought on through an integration into the Canadian economy; in short, there is little to be gained (particularly by the younger adults) by living in extended families.[16]

Many fundamental changes are also occurring in familial status and role relations. Authors report a high workforce participation rate for wives in all groups (Moudgil 1977, C. Siddique 1977a, Khosla 1980 and 1982, Ghosh 1983).[17] For no group (save for the most urban elite) might this have been common prior to immigration, and the economically-driven change has been one contributing factor in husband–wife conflict over responsibilities and authority. Indian husbands generally seem to try to maintain their traditional family status and role, even though they do not have the individual resources to maintain them (Quereshi 1980, M. Siddique 1974 and 1983). Women typically are expected to do virtually all housework and child rearing in addition to their work outside the home. Authority struggles between young men and women are often very sharp (Ghosh 1983: 95), and it is my impression that family violence and marital breakup among the young have been high. Unfortunately, little on this subject has been in print. However, studies of family decision-making (C. Siddique 1977a and 1977b, Ghosh 1981a, and M. Siddique 1974 and 1983) seem to indicate that changes towards more equitable decision-making are occurring, but that equality in this sphere is not a simple function of higher class background.

Changes in relations between parents and children appear to be even more profound, though research in this area is still limited. Parents of Indian groups seem generally to have high aspirations for their children, especially for their education and future economic success (Chawla 1971, Naidoo 1984). They also encourage their children to develop good relations with their peers. At the same time, parents typically wish to maintain some sociocultural aspects of their heritage in the second generation (Wakil et al. 1981). These relate primarily to family relations and marriage. There has been rather little formal research on parent–child relations from the child's point of view. Several studies have shown that in most groups children massively assimilate and strongly identify with their peers (Akoodie 1980, Buchignani 1977b, Chawla 1971, Sandhu 1980, and Wakil et al. 1981). Nevertheless, this has not come without some psychological and social difficulties stemming from social marginality (Akoodie 1980, and Minde and Minde 1976). This might possibly be a function of the degree to which parents try to impose 'Indian' behaviour on children, presumably under pressure of their ethnic group solidarity. We have almost no comparative research on this subject.

No traditional mainstream Indian ethnocultural group to my knowledge has a tradition of dating or of fully independent marital choice. What of those in Canada? Only Sikhs have been resident in Canada long enough for second generation patterns of marriage to become clearly evident.[18] Among Sikhs, dating by daughters is strongly discouraged; most marriages are formally arranged and the out marriage rate is very low; certainly, only a handful of Sikhs married non-Sikhs during the whole period 1904–70. The evidence that we have suggests that while parents in most other Indian ethnocultural groups are somewhat less conservative in their views about children, dating and marriage, they nevertheless usually wish their children to follow a fairly conventional path in such matters, as perhaps represented by the increasingly flexible standard set by emerging marriage practice in urban India which allows individual choice in selecting marriage mates, but ideally within a rather circumscribed set of potential partners of the same faith and ethnic origin, and with some parental input. In actual practice, it would seem that children are usually given more latitude than this, especially sons, and many professional class Indian parents do not even object to their children marrying non-Indians.[19] Different historical, class and cultural backgrounds clearly play a role, however, for research shows that while Sikhs have been very culturally conservative in this area, some diaspora groups like second generation Fijian Indians are unlikely to marry non-Indians extensively (Buchignani 1977b), while still others such as Ismailis encourage second generation assimilation, but seem to draw the line at out marriage (Dossa 1985, Fernando 1979 and Nasser-Bush 1973).

Marriage practices are obviously only one aspect of family level ethnocultural maintenance. Most community studies comment on the type and variety of adult cultural maintenance (cf. Chadney 1976 and Nasser-Bush 1973), but few attempts have been made to generalise on this (Buchignani 1980a). The general pattern seems to be one of near total material acculturation (save food), language maintenance in the home and private-level maintenance of religious observance.[20] The other great reservoir of 'traditional' culture among adults is chiefly ideological: family values and concerns remain strong (Beck 1982, Chadney 1975, Filteau 1980 and Quereshi 1980). Needless to say, whole areas of individual and family adaptation remain largely unchanged, including participation in politics (Wood 1978, 1981 and 1983) and the arts (Saidullah 1977 and Sugunasiri 1983). Insofar as children are concerned, there remains much work to be done to clarify the causes, details and limits of acculturation.

All studies confirm the high priority which Indian immigrants place on their children's education. Moreover, because the proportion of children of Indian origin in the schools increased rapidly in the 1970s, the literature on Indian Canadians' education is presently quite substantial. Studies now include one's own self concept and identity shift (Akoodie 1980 and Subramanian 1977b), psychological adjustment (Minde and Minde 1976) and attitudes towards Indians in schools (Ijaz 1980).

Research likewise confirms the central importance of economic settlement issues. Moreover, there is a general consensus that Indian immigrants usually rapidly achieve economic stability in Canada. Three factors seem to be relevant here (beyond immigrant enterprise): (a) relatively substantial class, linguistic and cultural backgrounds which give many Indo-Canadians an economic advantage over many other Canadians, (b) a relative absence of ethno-racial discrimination which allows these class resources to be effectively activated, and (c) the extensive use of familial economic pooling and kin-based financial mutual aid. Even those with comparatively few objective class resources usually do reasonably well economically. Surprisingly, though, I know of few studies oriented primarily towards economic issues (Buchignani 1987a: Ch. 4, Fernando 1979, Husaini 1981, Joy 1984). This is a great weakness in the literature, especially inasmuch as, general success aside, several key economic problems are faced by certain kinds of individuals and groups. For example, there are many structural barriers (such as certification requirements and the demand for Canadian job experience) to immigrant Indians becoming reestablished in their prior line of work, especially if they came by their work skills informally or were entirely Indian educated. Indo-Canadian male unemployment rates are very low, but such factors have resulted in considerable (unnecessary) underemployment and personal frustration. Also, Indian immigrant women lack the gender advantages of their male compatriots, have less substantial educational and occupational backgrounds than men and are constrained by the demands of housework and child rearing (Ghosh 1981a and 1981b). Women are thus at a severe disadvantage in securing rewarding work and often accept marginal or part-time jobs. Many Indians are concerned about possible occupational discrimination and this makes the need for more studies in this area even more pressing. Also it is well known that remittances and other financial links between Indo-Canadian families and their overseas kin are common, yet there have been no attempts to illuminate these links or to assess their impact on individuals and families concerned.

Community Organisation

Most Indian ethnocultural populations form informal communities— links between relatives and friends who share common ethnic, linguistic and religious roots. Informal community organisation of this kind (which has been investigated primarily through anthropological techniques) has been shown to be a powerful force for the maintenance of ethnic identity and values (Buchignani 1977b, Chadney 1984, Dossa 1985, Dusenbery 1981 and Mayer 1959). It also has served many useful functions for community members, especially new immigrants. These include psychological protection against marginality, social grounding in already existing social groups and access to information to Indian entrepreneurs and sometimes to a wide range of community institutions. Informal social boundaries between Indians of different backgrounds are generally quite sharply maintained, such that each ethnocultural group forms a somewhat discrete community. In the large cities there may be more than 20 of them.[21]

It has been generally observed that some Indian ethnocultural communities are more socially 'dense' and bounded than others; they are particularly strong when, like Sikhs, individuals possess a strong ethnic identity backed up by well-established community institutions (Buchignani 1980b and 1987b, Buchignani and Indra 1981b, Chadney 1984 and Dusenbery 1981). Lower-class origins and female gender can also socially constrain individuals to operate primarily in their own informal community, inasmuch as both attributes correlate with a comparative lack of bi-culturality and bi-linguality. At the same time, there appears to be considerable pan-Indian (that is, cross group) networking by the elite, though there seems to be little of it at the non-elite levels.[22]

Many questions remain about the informal community structure. Perhaps the most important one is whether ethnicity (that is, ethnic identity and ethnic affiliation) is its primary determinant at all.[23] Extensive chain migration has resulted on account of many people's informal community contacts being primarily kin. Are these therefore kin links or ethnic links? Also, in large cities the people with whom an Indo-Canadian could possibly maintain contact are far more numerous than those with whom one actually associates. Even so, the voluntaristic aspect of the maintenance of community ties also remains almost completely unexplored.

Outside of anthropological studies, interest in community organisation has been directed primarily towards formal community institutions—religious institutions (Dodd 1972, Dossa 1985 and Dusenbery 1981) and politics (Wood 1978, 1981 and 1983 and Stasiulis 1980). Our knowledge of Indian community institutions is still, however, weak. For example, what is the relationship between religious theology and organisational practice? It would appear that 'church-based' Indian religions like Sikhism (Dusenbery 1981) and Islam are far more easy to reestablish in Canada than community and individual-based religions such as Hinduism (Buchignani 1987a). Is this actually true? If so, what consequences does this have for ethnic maintenance? Also, while it is clear that the establishment of Hindu temples, Sikh *gurdwaras* and Muslim mosques have each brought together Indo-Canadians of rather diverse origins, little is known about how this institutional connection affects informal community organisation. Over the past 10 years the number of Indian Canadian formal ethnic group organisations and associations has increased; there may well be about 300 in existence at present. In addition to the representatives of these associations, most communities have a number of free-floating 'spokespersons' and 'leaders', whose constituency is either unclear or nonexistent. These people perform important brokerage roles between individuals and various provincial and federal branches of government concerned with cultural group maintenance and human rights. Some of these organisations perform valued functions in their communities, while others are associations in name only. Despite their ubiquitousness, almost no attention has been given to the structure of these organisations (Dusenbery 1981 and Stasiulis 1980). Neither do we know much about the role of community-based business and entrepreneurs, even though in large communities these are rather important.

Many aspects of sociocultural maintenance are clearly beyond the resources of individual families. Community organisations all across the country have accordingly taken up the task of teaching second generation individuals the key symbolic aspects of their parents' culture. These include language classes, religious instruction, and training in the arts (particularly dance). The prevalence, depth and effectiveness of such programmes are as yet completely unassessed.

Social Issues and Ethnic Relations

One ongoing weakness of the literature on Indians in Canada is that it is too much concerned with Indians and not enough concerned with Canada. Studies typically focus so closely on Indian individuals, families and communities that they are sociologically decontextualised. For example, in a study of family readjustment and change, it would be reasonable to expect that the author provides a Canadian family context as a basis of comparison, in addition to the Indian context of prior values which is usually supplied. Because so many Indo-Canadians are between two cultural worlds, a good understanding of their actions almost always requires this sort of dual contextualisation.

This is self-evident when one considers the question of Indians' relations with other Canadians. Relations between Indians and other Canadians are generally quite positive—certainly far more so than are relations between Indians and others in Britain. At the same time, many studies of majority group attitudes show that some Canadians characterise Indians as culturally and racially different (Berry et al. 1977, Henry 1978, Robson and Breems 1985 and Ubale 1977). Other studies show that Indians are likely to feel that they are at a risk of racial discrimination (Buchignani 1982, Buchignani and Indra 1981b,

Head 1981, Indra 1979b, J. B. Singh 1980, and Robson and Breems 1985).

Just about every community study has something to say about relations between Indians and the others. Even so, very little research has been carried out on actual, everyday interpersonal and inter-group relations between Indians and other Canadians (Buchignani 1980b, Buchignani and Indra 1981b). Analysis of relations between Indian Canadian communities (say, Gujaratis and Bengalis) is nonexistent. There has been only one controlled study of possible discrimination faced by Indian Canadians (Chandra 1973). We know little about intra-community prejudices and ethnocentrism. Whatever little work has been done in this area also suffers from not being well integrated into the world literature on ethnic and race relations. Lacking studies on discrimination, we can contribute nothing to easing Indian concerns about it. This lack of concern about intergroup relations extends back to questions of ethnicity involving the communities themselves. This is nowhere more evident than in the analysis of Indian ethnic identities. Current ethnic and race relations theory places great importance on identity formation and maintenance, superseding earlier perspectives which gave more emphasis to ethnic culture. As mentioned previously, Indian ethnic identities in Canada are extremely variable from group to group, even in their first generation. Their strength affects community solidarity, the development of community institutions and Indian Canadian relations with others. Even so, concerted research on the content and support for these identities is still minimal (Buchignani and Indra 1981a, Dusenbery 1981 and Subramanian 1977a).

Save for that related to education, social problems research on Indians remains very spotty. Social welfare and other social service workers dealing with individual and family problems have little literature to understand the cultural dimensions of the problems brought to them by Indian clients. This is especially true of intra-group social problems. There is almost no commentary on Indo-Canadian gender stratification, family violence, the dynamics of political and personal factionalism in South Asian communities, or on (admittedly rare) maladaptive Indian immigrant perspectives on government and social services. Male alcoholism is a significant problem in some communities, yet I have never seen it mentioned. I suspect filial piety and fear of community reactions to the public exposure of these social problems largely account for this void.

Indo-Canadian Research and South Asian Studies

In a disciplinary sense, Indo-Canadian studies have developed rather anomalously. Many studies (especially the more sophisticated ones) are primarily oriented towards the discipline of the author and to the theoretical literature within it. For example, a given author may use Sikh religious organisation in Vancouver in what is basically a contribution to the anthropological literature on ethnic identity and community organisation (cf. Dusenbery 1981). The major frame of reference of such work is therefore not Indo-Canadians. Alternatively, highly descriptive work rarely tends to be comparative, and therefore also does not efficiently build a unified literature on Indians in Canada. Someone writing on Sikhs in Montreal is unlikely to integrate his or her findings with others on Bengalis in Vancouver. Divergent methodologies also separate researchers. Sociological survey researchers discount data derived from anthropological fieldwork and vice versa; both neglect history or action-oriented (applied) research. To expect a homogeneous integration of so new a literature generated by such diverse people is unrealistic, yet an eventual unification of the discourse would do much to increase our understanding of Indians in Canada.

There is another dimension where Canadian Indian studies show an odd anomaly. This is in its total isolation from South Asian studies. Long association with the latter has convinced me that this isolation is at present largely a function of topical chauvinism among scholars of South Asia. South Asianists have treated Indo-Canadian studies as a mongrel cousin to 'real' research done on Indians in India. We who study Indians in Canada are by and large not Indianists (though there are some exceptions: Beck 1982 and 1987, and Srivastava 1975 and 1983). This was probably fortuitous, since it quickly oriented social scientists towards social issues of settlement and community development with many useful applied implications.

However, as this literature matures, it seems evident that there are certain topics which would be best addressed by researchers whose primary expertise is in India. These areas include the following:

1. Linguistic maintenance and change.
2. Religious adaptation.

3. The establishment of Indian artistic traditions in Canada.
4. The effects of immigration on source regions and villages in India.
5. Transnational kinship, ethnic, political and institutional links.
6. The analysis of kinship, caste and class.

Indo-Canadian studies is so new a field that it is unprofitable to conclude with a recapitulation of things not done. When I first surveyed the literature on Indians in Canada in 1977, the academic component of it was virtually limited to a few historical studies. This can no longer be said. A careful reading of the widely-dispersed literature now gives at least as good an understanding of Indo-Canadians as most ethnic populations of comparable size. Because the total literature is still small, every new study makes at least a descriptive contribution. As a consequence, our knowledge base continues to be in a state of rapid expansion. At the same time, the limitations of new birth are also consequential. The descriptive base of Indo-Canadian studies is clearly growing far more quickly than is its explanatory strength. The integration of studies with each other and the dialogue between researchers is still quite limited. I must admit that I do not see much substantial change in the near future for Indo-Canadian studies. The immediacy of the years of massive immigration and of Indians as a social issue is a thing of the past. So also are the days of very liberal research and conference funding. I believe that the foreseeable future will see a continued accumulation of findings and, hopefully, more synthetic and cross-societal analysis of the findings we have.

Notes

1. In all 148,109 people have immigrated to Canada directly from India between 1944 and the middle of 1987. In 1981, 24 per cent of all South Asians in Canada were Canadian born (Buchignani 1985: 8). If this (conservative) figure for Canadian born is included, this gives a total of 194,880. This total represents a significant undercount, for many people born in India have come to Canada via Britain, East Africa and elsewhere.

2. Most of those who are not of Indian origin are members of the Indian diaspora who can trace their roots back to India. They are from such diverse places as East Africa, Fiji, Mauritius, Jamaica, Guyana and Trinidad.

3. India was the third largest source of Canadian immigrants during 1971–81, supplying roughly 6.5 per cent of all immigrants during those years. Since then, it has always been among the top five source countries.

4. I have previously addressed this topic in a biographical survey of the total literature on South Asians in Canada as it stood a decade ago (Buchignani 1977a). Here I concentrate on more recent work. I should note that because of this diversity of various South Asian communities in Canada, wherein some come directly from India, some are native born and some have come from still other source countries, it is impossible to totally disregard the Indian diaspora here. Still, the concentration is primarily on those who were once Indian residents.

5. For details of this history, see references below.

6. For a full bibliography, see Buchignani (1977a).

7. Wives and children of legal Indian residents were allowed to immigrate from 1919 on.

8. This figure includes Sikhs born outside of India.

9. It should be noted that Canadians have never sharply differentiated their perceptions of Indians from their more general stereotype of 'East Indians', which includes all groups of South Asian origin. A strong determinant of this stereotype has been negative and unrepresentative mass media coverage of India (Indra 1979a and 1979b).

10. Buchignani and Indra's work (1985) probably represents the most general historical survey done to date.

11. Exceptions include Buchignani and Indra (1987), Ward (1973) and Buchignani and Indra (1981a).

12. As a case in point, a parallel set of Sikh communities established themselves along the American Pacific coast (see LaBrack and Leonard 1984, and LaBrack 1983) where they experienced quite similar race relations. However, no work has as yet compared Sikhs in Canada and the United States.

13. In the limited case of one diaspora community, Fijian Indians in Vancouver, I have shown (Buchignani 1979) that immigration produced a definite 'brain drain' of skilled working-class people.

14. Two rather journalistic books have been written about the key Canadian consequence of Punjab turmoil—the alleged bombing of an Air India plane near Ireland (Blaise 1987, Jiwa 1984).

15. More attitudinal research is addressed in the section involving ethnic and race relations further on in the article.

16. For a detailed analysis of how this operates in a Fijian Indian community, see Buchignani (1979 and 1987a).

17. M. Siddique (1983: 102) found a low workforce participation rate among Indians in a small professional class community in Saskatchewan, but this represents more of a class-specific phenomenon than an ethnic one. The 1981 census data shows that South Asian women's workforce participation rates were a bit higher than that for Canadians as a whole (Buchignani 1985: 25).

18. The typical adult Indian has only been in Canada about a dozen years, and few children have therefore come of age.

19. In contrast, there is often great reluctance to allow daughters to date, and there is a feeling that parents should play a more prominent role in their mate selection than for sons.

20. Indeed, I have recently argued (Buchignani 1987b) that even for Sikhs objective cultural patterns are primarily 'Canadian'.

21. In contrast, in cities and towns where Indians are relatively few in number there is far more extensive social contact between individuals of different ethnic and religious backgrounds. At the same time, Indians in Canada today are at least 97 per cent urban, and are heavily concentrated in Canada's larger cities, so that discrete communities following ethnic and religious lines are generally the rule.

22. Such elite, cross group social contacts were increasing rapidly even between Indian Sikhs and Hindus prior to 'Operation Blue Star', after which Hindu–Sikh social relations in Canada were almost completely ruptured.

23. See Buchignani 1987b.

References

Adams, B. et al. 1977. 'Ugandan Asians in Exile: Household and Kinship in the Resettlement Crisis', *Journal of Comparative Family Studies*, 8(2): 167–78.

Akoodie, M. A. 1980. *Immigrant Students: A Comparative Assessment of Ethnic Identity, Self-Concept and Locus of Control amongst West Indian, East Indian and Canadian Students*. DPhil dissertation. University of Toronto.

Ames, Michael M. and Joy Inglis. 1973. 'Conflict and Change in British Columbia Sikh Family Life', *B.C. Studies*, 20(Winter): 15–49.

Andracki, Stainslaw. 1958. *The Immigration of Orientals into Canada with Special Reference to Chinese*. PhD dissertation, Department of History, McGill University (reprinted in 1978, New York: Amo Press).

Beck, Brenda. 1982. 'Perceptions des relations parentales entre parent et enfant chez des immigrants au Canada: Variations selon qu'ils proviennent d'Inde, du Japon et de Hongrie', in K. V. Ujimoto and O. Hirabayashi (eds.): *Asian Canadians: Regional Perspectives*, pp. 207–21.

———. 1983. *Bread Crumbs or Yeast: Indo-Canadian Popular Culture and its Growth Potential*. University of British Columbia.

———. 1987. 'Bread Crumbs or Yeast: Indo-Canadian Popular Culture and its Growth Potential', in M. Israel (ed.): *The South Asian Diaspora in Canada*. Toronto: Multicultural History Society of Ontario, pp. 59–72.

Berry, John, et al. 1977. *Multiculturalism and Ethnic Attitudes in Canada*. Ottawa: Information Canada.

Bhatti, F. M. 1974. *East Indian Immigration into Canada: 1905–73*. PhD thesis, University of Surrey.

Blaise, Clark. 1987. *The Sorrow and the Terror: The Haunting Legacy of the Air India Disaster*. Markham Ontario: Viking Press.

Bose, Arun Coomer. 1965. 'Indian Nationalist Agitations in the United States and Canada till the Arrival of Haradayal in 1911', *Journal of Indian History*, 43: 227–39.

Buchignani, Norman. 1977a. 'A Review of the Historical and Sociological Literature on East Indians in Canada', *Canadian Ethnic Studies*, 9(1): 86–108.

Buchignani, Norman. 1977b. *Immigration, Establishment and the Management of Ethnic Identity.* PhD dissertation, Department of Sociology and Anthropology, Simon Fraser University (Vancouver).

——. 1979. 'The Effect of Canadian Immigration on the Political Economy of Fiji', in O. Mehmet (ed.): *Poverty and Social Change in Southeast Asia.* Ottawa: University of Ottawa Press, pp. 265–83.

——. 1980a. 'South Asians and the Ethnic Mosaic: An Overview', *Canadian Ethnic Studies*, 11(1): 48–68.

——. 1980b. 'The Social and Self Identities of Fijian Indians in Vancouver', *Urban Anthropology*, 9(1): 75–97.

——. 1982. *Perceptions of Racial Discrimination in Calgary: A Situation Report.* Ottawa: Multiculturalism Directorate. Secretary of State, p. 167.

——. 1985. *A Demographic Analysis of South Asians in Canada.* Ottawa: Secretary of State.

——. 1987a. *Fijian Indians in Vancouver: The Structural Determinants of a New Community.* New York: AMS Press.

——. 1987b. 'Conceptions of Sikh Culture in the Development of a Comparative Analysis of the Sikh Diaspora', in M. Israel and J. L. Connell (eds.): *Sikh Religion and History in the Twentieth Century.* Toronto: University of Toronto Press.

Buchignani, Norman and Doreen Marie Indra. 1981a. 'The Political Organisation of South Asians in Canada', in J. Dahlie and T. Fernando (eds.): *Ethnicity, Power and Politics in Canada.* Toronto: Methuen, pp. 202–32.

——. 1981b. 'Inter-Group Conflict and Community Solidarity: Sikhs and South Asian Fijians in Vancouver', *Canadian Journal of Anthropology*, 1(2): 149–57.

——. 1985. *Continuous Journey: A Social History of South Asians in Canada.* Toronto: McClelland and Stewart.

——. 1987. 'Key Issues in Canadian-Sikh Ethnic and Race Relations and their Implications for the Study of the Sikh Diaspora', in G. Barrier and V. Dusenbery (eds.): *The Sikh Diaspora.* Ann Arbor: University of Michigan Press.

Button, R. A. 1964. *Sikh Settlement in the Lower Mainland of B.C. (1904–1964).* BA graduating essay. Department of Geography, University of British Columbia.

Ch'eng, Tien-Fang. 1931. *Oriental Immigration in Canada.* Shanghai: Commercial Press.

Chadney, James G. 1975. 'The Joint Family as a Structure and Process', *Journal of Social Thought*, 1(1): 17–22.

——. 1976. *The Vancouver Sikhs: An Ethnic Community in Canada.* PhD dissertation, Michigan State University.

——. 1977. 'Demography, Ethnic Identity and Decision-Making: The Case of the Vancouver Sikhs', *Urban Anthropology*, 6(3): 187–204.

——. 1984. *The Sikhs of Vancouver.* New York: AMS Press.

Chandra, K. V. 1973. *Racial Discrimination in Canada.* San Francisco: R and E Research Associates.

Chawla, Saroj. 1971. *Indian Children in Toronto: A Study in Socialisation.* MA dissertation in Sociology, York University, Toronto.

Das, Rajani Kant. 1923. *Hindustani Workers on the Pacific Coast.* Berlin: Walter de Gruyter.

Deol, G. S. 1969. *The Role of the Ghadar Party in the Indian National Movement.* Jullundar: Sterling Publishers.

Dhami, Sadhu Singh. 1969. 'Discovering the New World', *Queen's Quarterly,* 76: 200–12.

Dodd, Balbinder Singh. 1972. *Social Change in Two Overseas Sikh Communities.* BA honours essay in Sociology, University of British Columbia.

Dossa, Parin. 1983. 'The Shi'a-Isma'ili Muslim Community in British Columbia', in Charles P. Anderson et al. (eds.): *Circle of Voices.* British Columbia: Oolichan Books, pp. 232–39.

———. 1985. *Ritual and Daily Life: Transmission and Interpretation of the Ismaili Tradition in Vancouver.* PhD dissertation, Department of Anthropology and Sociology, University of British Columbia.

Dusenbery, Verne A. 1981. 'Canadian Ideology and Public Policy: The Impact on Vancouver Sikh Ethnic and Religious Adaptation', *Canadian Ethnic Studies,* 8(3): 101–20.

———. 1987a. 'On the Moral Sensitivies of Sikhs in North America', in Owen Lynch and P. Kolenda (eds.): *Consuming Passions: Emotion and Feeling in Indian Culture.*

———. 1987b. 'The Sikh Person, the Khalsa Panth and Western Sikh Converts', in J. K. Lele et al. (eds.): *Boeings and Bullock Carts: Rethinking India's Restructuring.* Leiden: E. Brill.

Ferguson, Ted. 1975. *A White Man's Country: An Exercise in Canadian Prejudice.* Toronto: Macmillan.

Fernando, Tissa. 1979. 'East African Asians in Western Canada: The Ismaili Community', *New Community,* 7(3): 361–68.

Filteau, C. 1980. 'The Role of the Concept of Love in the Hindu Family Acculturation Process', in K. V. Ujimoto and O. Hirabayashi (eds.): *Visible Minorities and Multiculturalism.* Toronto: Butterworths, pp. 289–300.

Ghosh, Ratna. 1981a. 'Minority within a Minority: On Being South Asian and Female in Canada', in G. Kurian and R. Ghosh (eds.): *Women in the Family and the Economy.* Westport, Conn.: Greenwood Press, pp. 413–26.

———. 1981b. 'Social and Economic Integration of South Asian Women in Montreal, Canada', in G. Kurian and R. Ghosh (eds.): *Women in the Family and the Economy.* Westport, Conn.: Greenwood Press, pp. 59–71.

———. 1983. 'Sarees and the Maple Leaf: Indian Women in Canada', in G. Kurian and R. P. Srivastava (eds.): *Overseas Indians: A Study in Adaptation.* Delhi: Vikas Publishing House, pp. 90–99.

Head, Wilson. 1981. *Adaptation of Immigrants: Perceptions of Ethnic and Racial Discrimination.* Toronto: York University.

Henry, Frances. 1978. *The Dynamics of Racism in Toronto.* Ottawa: Secretary of State (mimeo).

Hilliker, J. F. 1980. 'The British Columbia Franchise and Canadian Relations with India in Wartime, 1939–1945', *B.C. Studies,* 46: 40–60.

Husaini, Zohra. 1981. *Social Networks: A Factor in Immigrant Economic Success.* PhD dissertation, Department of Sociology, University of Alberta.

Ijaz, Mian Ahmed. 1980. *Ethnic Attitudes of Elementary School Children Toward Blacks and East Indians, and the Effects of a Cultural Program on these Attitudes.* EdD dissertation in Educational Theory, University of Toronto.

Indra, Doreen. 1979a. *Ethnicity, Social Stratification and Opinion Formation: An Analysis of Ethnic Portrayal in the Vancouver Newspaper Press (1905–76).* PhD dissertation, Department of Sociology and Anthropology, Simon Fraser University.

———. 1979b. 'South Asian Stereotypes in the Vancouver Press', *Ethnic and Racial Studies*, 2(2): 164–89.

Jain, Prakash. 1984–85. *Class Analysis of Race Relations among Overseas Indians.* PhD dissertation, Department of Sociology and Anthropology. Carleton University.

Jiwa, Selim. 1984. *The Death of Air India Flight 182.* London: W.H. Allen.

Johnson, Hugh. 1979. *The Voyage of the Komagata Maru: The Sikh Challenge to Canada's Colour Bar.* Delhi: Oxford University Press.

———. 1987. 'Patterns of Sikh Migration to Canada, 1900–1960'. Paper presented at the Conference on 'Sikh Religion and History in the Twentieth Century'. University of Toronto.

Josh, Sohan Singh. 1970. *Baba Sohan Singh Bhakna: Life of the Founder of the Ghadar Party.* New Delhi: People's Publishing House.

———. 1977–78. *Hindustan Ghadar Party: A Short History.* New Delhi: People's Publishing House.

Joy, Annamma. 1984. 'Work and Ethnicity. The Case of the Sikhs in the Okanagan Valley of British Columbia', in Rabindra Kanungo (ed.): *South Asians in the Canadian Mosaic.* Montreal: Kala Bharati.

Khosla, Renu. 1980. *A Canadian Perspective on the Hindu Woman: A Study of Identity Transformation.* MA dissertation in Sociology, McMaster University.

———. 1982. 'The Changing Familial Role of South Asian Women in Canada: A Study in Identity Transformation', in K. V. Ujimoto and O. Hirabayashi (eds.): *Asian Canadians: Regional Perspectives*, pp. 178–84.

LaBrack, Bruce. 1983. 'The Reconstitution of Sikh Society in Rural California', in G. Kurian and R. P. Srivastava (eds.): *Overseas Indians: A Study in Adaptation.* Delhi: Vikas Publishing House, pp. 215–556.

LaBrack, Bruce and K. Leonard. 1984. 'Conflict and Compatibility in Punjabi and Mexican Immigrant Families in Rural California, 1915–65', *Journal of Marriage and the Family*, 46(3): 539–56.

Lal, B. 1976. *East Indians in British Columbia (1904–14): A Historical Study in Growth and Integration.* MA dissertation in History, University of British Columbia (Vancouver).

Lowes, George, H. 1952. *The Sikhs of British Columbia.* BA honours essay in history, University of British Columbia.

Mathur, Laxman Prasad. 1970. *Indian Revolutionary Movements in the United States 1922.* Delhi: S. Chand.

Mayer, Adrian. 1959. 'A Report on the East Indian Community in Vancouver'. Working paper, Institute of Social and Economic Research, University of British Columbia.

Minde, K. and R. Minde. 1976. 'Children of Immigrants: The Adjustment of Ugandan Asian Primary School Children in Canada', *Canadian Psychiatric Association Journal*, 21(6): 371–81.

Morah, Benson, C. 1974. *The Assimilation of Ugandan Asians in Calgary.* MA dissertation in Sociology, University of Calgary.

Morse, Eric W. 1935. *Immigration and Status of British East Indians in Canada: A Problem in Imperial Relations.* MA dissertation in History, Queen's University.

———. 1936. 'Some Aspects of the Komagatu Maru Affair', *Canadian Historical Association Annual Report*, pp. 100–108.

Moudgil, Ranvir. 1977. *From Stranger to Refugee: A Study of the Integration of Ugandan Asians in Canada.* PhD dissertation, State University of New York, Buffalo.

Munday, Jenifer G. 1953. *East Indians in British Columbia: A Community in Transition.* BA honours essay in Sociology, University of British Columbia (Vancouver).

Naidoo, Josephine C. 1979. 'Women of South Asia and Anglo-Saxon Origins in the Canadian Context: Self Perceptions, Socialisation, Achievement Aspirations', in C. S. Adam (ed.): *Sex Roles.* Montreal: Eden Press.

———. 1980a. 'The East Indian Women in Canadian Context: A Study in Social Psychology', in K. V. Ujimoto and O. Hirabayashi (eds.): *Visible Minorities and Multiculturalism.* Toronto: Butterworths, pp. 193–218.

———. 1980b. 'New Perspectives on South Asian Women', in N. Nyiri and T. Milan (eds.): *Unity in Diversity.* Waterloo: Wilfred Laurier University Press.

———. 1984. 'Contemporary South Asian Women in the Canadian Mosaic', in P. Caplan et al. (eds.). *Sex Roles II: Feminist Psychology in Transition.* Montreal: Eden Press.

———. 1987. 'Women of South Asian Origins: Status of Research, Problems, Future Issues', in M. Israel (ed.): *The South Asian Diaspora in Canada.* Toronto: The Multicultural History Society of Ontario, pp. 37–58.

Nasser-Bush, Merun H. 1973. *Differential Adjustment between Two Indian Immigrant Communities in Toronto: Sikhs and Ismailis.* PhD dissertation, University of Colorado.

Pannu, Gurdial Singh. 1970. 'Sikhs in Canada', *Sikh Review*, October: 33–34.

Pereira, Cecil Patrick. 1971. *East Indians in Winnipeg: A Study of the Consequences of Immigration for an Ethnic Group in Canada.* MA dissertation in Sociology, University of Manitoba.

Quereshi, R. B. 1980. 'The Family Model as a Blueprint for Social Interaction among Pakistani Canadians', in K. V. Ujimoto and O. Hirabayashi (eds.): *Asian Canadians and Multiculturalism*: 46–61.

Reid, Robie L. 1941. 'The Inside Story of the Komagatu Maru', *B.C. Historical Quarterly*, 5: 1–23.

Robson, R. A. H. and Brad Breems. 1985. *Ethnic Conflict in Vancouver.* Vancouver B.C. Civil Liberties Association.

Saidullah, Ahmad. 1977. 'A Critique of Indian Music', in A. Mukherjee (ed.): *East Indians: Myths and Reality.* Toronto: Indian Immigrant Aid and the Indian Students Association at the University of Toronto, pp. 317–23.

Sandhu, Sukdev Singh. 1980. 'The Second Generation: Culture and the East Indian Community in Nova Scotia'. *Ethnic Heritage Series*. Halifax: International Education Centre.

Siddique, C. 1977a. 'Changing Family Patterns: A Comparative Analysis of Immigrant Indian and Pakistani Families of Saskatoon', *Canadian Journal of Comparative Family Studies*, 8(2): 179–200.

————. 1977b. 'Structural Separation and Family Change: An Exploratory Study of the Immigrant Indian and Pakistani Families of Saskatoon, Canada', *International Review of Modern Sociology*, 7(1): 13–35.

Siddique, Muhammad. 1974. *Patterns of Familial Decision-making and Division of Labour: A Study of the Immigrant Indian and Pakistani Community of Saskatoon*. MA dissertation, University of Saskatchewan (Regina).

————. 1983. 'Changing Family Patterns: A Comparative Analysis of Immigrant Indian and Pakistani Families in Saskatoon, Canada', in G. Kurian and R. P. Srivastava (eds.): *Overseas Indians: A Study in Adaptation*. Delhi: Vikas Publishing House, pp. 100–27.

Singh, J. B. 1980. *Perceptions of Prejudice Experienced by International Students*. MA dissertation in Educational Theory, University of Toronto.

Singh, Kushwant and Satindra Singh. 1966. *Ghadar 1915: India's First Armed Revolution*. New Delhi: R and K Publishing House.

Smith, Marian W. 1944. 'Sikh Settlers in Canada', *Asia and the Americans*, 44(8): 359–64.

Srivastava, Ram P. 1975. 'Family Organisation and Change Among the Overseas Indians with Special Reference to Indian Immigrant Families of British Columbia, Canada', in G. Kurian (ed.): *Family in India: A Regional View*. The Hague: Mouton.

————. 1983. 'The Evolution of Adaptive Strategies: East Indians in Canada', in G. Kurian and R. P. Srivastava (eds.): *Overseas Indians: A Study in Adaptation*. Delhi: Vikas Publishing House.

Stasiulis, D. 1980. 'The Political Structuring of Ethnic Community Action: A Reformation', *Canadian Ethnic Studies*, 12(3): 18–44.

Subramanian, Indira A. 1977a. *Identity Shift: Post-Migration Changes in Identity among First Generation East Indian Immigrants in Toronto*. PhD dissertation, University of Toronto.

————. 1977b. *The East Indian Child in Toronto Schools: A Cultural Background and Psychological Profile*. Toronto: Toronto Boards of Education.

Sugunasiri, S. 1983. *The Search for Meaning: The Literature of South Asian Canadian Writers*. Ottawa: Secretary of State.

Ubale, Bhausaheb. 1977. *Equal Opportunity and Public Policy: A Report on Concerns of the South Asian Community Regarding their Place in the Canadian Mosaic*. Toronto: Indian Immigrant Aid Services.

Wakil, P. A. 1974. 'The Immigrant Indo-Pakistani Family: A Case Study'. Research note, 8th World Congress of Sociology, Toronto.

Wakil, S. P.; C. M. Siddique and F. A. Wakil. 1981. 'Between Two Cultures: A Study of Socialisation of Children of Immigrants', *Journal of Marriage and the Family*, November: 929–40.

Ward, William Peter. 1973. *White Canada Forever: British Columbia's Response to Orientals, 1858–1914*. PhD dissertation, Department of History, Queen's University.

Wood, John. 1978. 'East Indians and Canada's New Immigration Policy', *Canadian Public Policy*, 4(4): 547–67.

———. 1981 'A Visible Minority Votes: East Indian Electoral Behaviour in the Vancouver South Provincial and Federal Elections of 1979', in J. Dahlie and T. Fernando (eds.): *Ethnicity, Power and Politics in Canada*. Toronto: Methuen, pp. 177–201.

———. 1983. 'East Indians and Canada's New Immigration Policy', in G. Kurian and R. P. Srivastava (eds.): *Overseas Indians: A Study in Adaptation*. Delhi: Vikas Publishing House, pp. 3–29.

6

The Influence of Indian Islam on Fundamentalist Trends in Trinidad and Tobago*

Nasser Mustapha

The term 'fundamentalism' was originally applied to a Protestant movement in the United States of America. Irving (1982: 7), talking about New England, which was founded by the Puritans in the early 17th century, notes, 'These Puritans were English fundamentalists in their interpretation of the Holy Scriptures and they placed great emphasis on free enquiry. They initiated universal instruction in the western world so that each individual could understand the Bible by means of his own personal criteria'. According to Hess (1991: 408), fundamentalism represents a back to basics approach to religion, in the process resisting modernity and seeking to restore an original faith. The emphasis on returning to original sources, described by Hess as new old-time religion, usually arises from disillusionment with prevailing beliefs, practices and interpretations, an approach not usually favoured by mainstream churches. In fact, Hess indicates that in the United States, while the membership of mainstream Protestant denominations declined, that of the independent

---

*Originally published in *Sociological Bulletin*, Vol. 46, No. 2, September 1997, pp. 245–65.

fundamentalist sects rose sharply, and there was also a fundamentalist revival within Catholicism and Judaism.

Though not a new phenomenon, it is only recently that attention is being given to fundamentalist tendencies among Muslims. It was shortly after the Islamic Revolution of 1979 in Iran, culminating in the overthrow of the Shah's regime and the spread of anti-western sentiments among Muslims, that the term 'Islamic fundamentalism' came into vogue. In popular usage the term implies a reversion to the original teachings of Islam and carries overtones of fanaticism, intolerance and aggression. It also connotes resistance to the western culture and lifestyle (Hiro 1989: 3–20 and Sivan 1992: 11).

Muslims in various parts of the world are today attempting to assert themselves, coming into conflict with the established legal, political and economic systems. Furthermore, controversies are being raised over issues, seemingly trivial in the eyes of the public, such as dress, food and male–female relationships (Ali 1991: 21). Since Islamic fundamentalists encounter conflict with mainstream religious practices, they are in a sense similar to the Protestant Christian fundamentalists described above. However, Islamic fundamentalists are themselves ultraconservative, since they emphasise purity of doctrines and are suspicious of any form of religious innovation.

Much concern is being expressed nowadays over the rise of religious fundamentalism in various parts of the world. Even in the 'Land of Steelpan and Calypso', that is, Trinidad and Tobago, a group of extremist Muslims attempted unsuccessfully to overthrow the democratically elected government in July 1990 (Ryan 1991: 17). The reactions which this attempted coup elicited from the public in general and security officials in particular betrayed a lack of awareness of the various interpretations of Islam to be found in contemporary Trinidad and Tobago. There are hardly any works dealing with the Muslim migrants from India to the Caribbean islands (Smith 1963).

Trinidad and Tobago has a population of 1.2 million, 6 per cent of which are Muslims (Central Statistical Office 1990: 9). But whereas joint consideration of Hindus and Muslims may have sufficed in discussing the early East Indian[1] presence in the Caribbean (Clarke 1986, Klass 1961 and Niehoff and Niehoff 1960), recent developments in the region and in the world at large, however, point to the need for a separate and careful study of Muslims.

One often notices a tendency towards a monolithic view of Muslims, including the fundamentalists among them. This article intends to dispel such a notion by demonstrating the variety of Islamic fundamentalism that may co-exist in a religious community. Broadly, it is possible to distinguish between two types of reformist efforts in Islam. One is the aggressive and militant type, which is not only involved in proselytising activities, but also attempts to establish the political system of Islam and implement the *Shariah* (Islamic law). The other is the non-militant type which, though basically involved in the spread of Islam, nevertheless confines itself to theological matters. In both cases, the ultimate objective is to return to the original sources of Islam and hence can be described as fundamentalist.

This article represents a preliminary attempt to grasp the trends and influences shaping the Muslim communities in the Caribbean. It begins by tracing the origins of Islamic fundamentalism among East Indian Muslims in Trinidad and Tobago. Section I identifies the fundamentalist-styled movements in India and some of the numerous interpretations of Islam that developed here. What is striking is the diversity that emerged among the followers of Islam even during this early period, a manifestation of the cultural diversity of Indian society. In Section II, the attempts to reform Islamic thought are discussed. In Section III, the discussion shifts to Islam in Trinidad and Tobago. In Section IV, the conflicts and divisions among the Muslims in Trinidad and Tobago are analysed, and in Section V the origins of fundamentalist Islam in Trinidad are discussed, with the aim of showing the strong influence that India continues to exert upon these Muslims. In Section VI the historical development of Muslim organisations in Trinidad and Tobago is discussed, and Section VII concludes with some observations on the growing diversity of religious practices and interpretations of Islam in the Caribbean.

I

From AD 7th century onwards Islam spread rapidly from Arabia to various parts of the world. Contact with various cultures often led to the emergence of reinterpretations of the original teachings of the religion. Sporadic attempts to revert to the original form of Islam have met with varying degrees of success.

The formal introduction of Islam into India by an expedition led by Muhammad bin Qasim in AD 711 was not necessarily the first contact of Muslims with India (Herklots 1921: 4–5, Titus 1930: 12). There is a distinct possibility of such a contact as early as AD 664, only 32 years after the death of Muhammad. Through a series of conquests, particularly after the 11th century, Islam became a permanent element in Indian society. However, Titus (1930: 12) indicates that Indian religious thought influenced Muslims before Islam became established in India. In fact, Buddhist thought and 'wandering Indian monks' too, could have significantly influenced the development of tasawwuf (Islamic mysticism) which occurred mainly in Persia (Titus 1930: 13).

Islam as established by Muhammad in Arabia is a monotheistic system with its unique belief system, institutionalised rituals, commands and prohibitions. Reinterpretations under different sociocultural milieux are not unlikely, as confirmed by the evidence from India. The Sufi (the name derives from the word tasawwuf) subvariant of Islam, in particular, found a fertile ground in India where asceticism and mystical activities already had widespread acceptance.

Conversion to Islam, notwithstanding the tenacity of the indigenous culture and the loss of contact with the homeland of Islam, led to the emergence of several syncretic forms among Muslims in India. In south India, for example, magical practices were combined with Muslim rituals. Thurston (1909: 231) reports that in Madras tribal rituals were incorporated into Muslim marriages. Quranic verses were assumed to possess special powers of healing and warding off evil, and hence were written on pieces of article and stuck above doors and windows. With reference to north India, Herklots (1921: 7) observed that the Rajputs and Jats 'often supplement the orthodox ritual of Islam by Hindu marriage and death rites, follow Hindu rules of succession to real and personal property and particularly in times of trouble revere the local village deities'.

There was also a widespread belief that God can be better reached through some physical medium, and hence a system of saint and tomb worship evolved. Individuals with outstanding knowledge or allegedly superior powers came to be treated with awe and reverence by the masses. These 'saints' were perceived as being able to 'avert calamity, cure disease and procure children for the childless' (ibid.: 7–8). Upon the death of these saints, their tombs were often worshipped by subsequent generations.

In attempting to illustrate the close relationship between Hindus and Muslims (in this case Shias), Herklots reports that Hindus were involved in the procession of taziyas or tabuts, reminiscent of the martyrs Hassan and Hussein in the battle of Karbala, during the festival of Muharram. Samaroo (1988: 5) also documents the influence of Hindu religious rituals upon the form this festival assumes in India.

II

Periodically there have been deliberate attempts to re-establish the orthodox version of Islam in India. Generally these efforts advocated a return to the original sources of the religion: the Quran and the *Sunnah* (practice and sayings of Muhammad) and the rejection of all forms of religious innovation. Of course, there is no consensus among Muslims as to what constitutes an innovation.

The view held by Titus (1930: 12) that 1804 marked the birth of Islamic fundamentalism or puritanism (later called Wahhabism) in India is not totally accurate. The efforts of Shaikh Ahmad of Sirhind (1563–1624) appear to be one of the earliest attempts at reforming Islamic religious thought in India (the Wahhabi movement started in Arabia around the middle of the 18th century). Shaikh Ahmad, born in the early days of Akbar's rule, was noted for his strong resistance to government policies. He criticised the prevailing forms of Sufism and envisaged a return to the fundamentals of Islam. His ideas were said to have later influenced Aurangzeb, Akbar's great grandson, born four years after his death. He is referred to in the literature as *Mujaddid Alf-i-Thani*, 'Reformer of the Second Millennium'. Another influential individual was Shah Waliullah of Delhi. His major preoccupation was the reformation of religious thought and as a result his efforts resulted in limited practical reforms. He advocated an independent view of *Fiqh* (Islamic jurisprudence), as opposed to the four established schools of religious thought.

Among the militant and aggressive reformers were Sayyad Ahmad (1786–1831) and Shah Ismail Shahid (1779–1831). These two were actively engaged in reforming social affairs, becoming very influential on the north-western frontier. With reference to Sayyad Ahmad, Titus (1930: 47) says, 'The opponents of his sect,.the orthodox Maulvis and others spoke of them derisively as Wahhabis [puritans/fundamentalists]'. Maududi (1963: 27) also documents the continuing influence of these two individuals.

Around the beginning of the 19th century, Muslim influence began to decline in India, simultaneously with the growing dominance of the British. Initially, Muslims attempted a strong resistance to British influence by boycotting all British institutions. In fact, for many decades, Hindus were more advanced than Muslims in education (Titus 1930: 50). The appearance of Sayyad Ahmad led to a dramatic turn of events. His policies favoured cordial relationships with the wider society, including the British. He introduced several drastic social and educational reforms and established what can be described as the modernist approach to Islam.

In the latter part of the 19th century, Mirza Ghulam Ahmad of Qadian established another movement with strong modernist tendencies. His declaration of being a *mahdi* (reformer) and a prophet incurred the wrath of mainstream Muslims, who declared him an imposter and an agent of the British. His followers, referred to today as Qadianis and Ahmadis, are regarded as non-believers by orthodox Muslims. Thus, towards the end of the 19th century, Islam in India was characterised by marked inter-regional and intra-regional diversity. Some of the sub-variants of Islam in India are given here:

Hanafi Sunnis are those who follow Imam Abu Hanifa (699–767). This school appears to be the most accommodating and liberal of the four recognised schools of Islamic thought and is subscribed to by two-thirds of the Muslims in India and Pakistan (Titus 1930: 34). Several Sufi orders claim compatibility with this school of Islamic thought.

Sunnis with Wahhabi tendencies attempt to return to the original teachings of Islam as preached by Muhammad. Among them are the: *Ahl-i-Hadith* (People of the traditions of the Prophet), *Ahl-i-Quran* (People of the Quran), *Faraidiyah* (those who follow the obligatory aspects of the religion), and *Ghair Mukallid* (nonconformists or those who do not conform to anyone particular school of Muslim religious thought).

The *Shia Muslims* strongly favour hereditary leadership. The Shia sect originated in Arabia after the passing away of Muhammad, when some followers insisted that only members of the Prophet's family should succeed him in leadership. Shias are to be found in small numbers in various parts of India. Some Shias practice Sufism.

Modernist Muslims are less rigid in implementing religious rituals. By modifying the original Islamic teachings, they attempt to make them compatible with the dominant value system. Qadianis and Ahmadis would be included in this group. Some Sunnis with modernist tendencies can also be found among this section of Muslims.

III

Though evidence exists to indicate the presence of Muslims in Trinidad before the coming of East Indians to the Caribbean (Hamid 1978: 1, Quick 1990: 3–5), for the purposes of this article the discussion commences with the arrival of East Indians in the Caribbean. Muslims were among the first shipment of indentured immigrants to arrive in the Caribbean in 1845 (Jha 1973: 3 and Samaroo 1988: 1) The majority of Indian immigrants coming to the Caribbean were from the United Provinces (UP) and Bihar. According to the Census of 1901, in UP there were 85 per cent Hindus and 14 per cent Muslims, while in Bihar there were 92.7 per cent Hindus and 7.3 per cent Muslims. Sources also indicate that in 1891, among Trinidad Indians there were 85.9 per cent Hindus and 13.44 per cent Muslims. These figures correspond to the proportions found in UP around the same time. In these areas, Hanafis were in the majority, but Shias and Wahhabis were also found (Titus 1930: 33).

The Indians who came to the Caribbean tried to recapture their religion as they knew it back in India, and to establish it under the new and challenging circumstances. They viewed the wider Creole society (evolving from African and European elements) with suspicion. They resisted its influence by holding tenaciously to their Islamic heritage. With limited resources, simple mosques were constructed, which served as places of worship, community centres and *maktabs* (religious schools). Friday congregational prayers and the Urdu sermon used to be delivered in the *masjids* that were built. Community centres and *maktabs* became the focal points of festivities for the community. Pressures from the wider society and common ancestral ties led to a generally cordial relationship between Muslims and Hindus. Despite differences in religious beliefs and occasional disagreements, there was mutual respect for each other. For both the Hindus and Muslims, religion was crucial for their identity and the relationship between the two communities in the New World may have been even closer than in the motherland. According to Clarke (1986: 42), Muslims were more cohesive and less tolerant of Christianity than the Hindus. Being separated from their families back in India, religion served as a bond with their homeland during their supposedly temporary sojourn in this strange land. Religion gave their lives direction and a sense of completeness. With few books in their possession and not many educated persons among them, they tried to reconstruct their religious forms as closely as possible to the way they existed in India.

Khan (1987: 5) documents some aspects of Trinidad Muslim rituals that have been influenced by Hindu contact. These include the 'three-day' and 'forty-day' mourning functions (*mawlood* functions) and *neyaz* (an offering for the dead). Thus, reinterpretation of Islam under Hindu influence not only occurred in India but also in the New World. New elements were added which were perceived to be functional to their adherents under the circumstances. During the course of its evolution, the community reactivated and often modified various social events known in India. These provided opportunities for interaction among members of the community and served as important avenues for the socialisation of the younger generation. As is the case with Indians in Trinidad and Tobago generally, the close-knit family system, an integral part of a wider kinship network, also strengthened communal solidarity.

An important Indian survival, the Hosay festival (from the name of Hussein), could be traced to some of the early immigrants. As mentioned earlier, it is quite likely that some Shia Muslims of UP and Bihar could have been among the early immigrants in Trinidad. This group reconstructed this festival in its Indian form. It has since been significantly influenced by the local carnival and today has acquired a unique identity.

Indian syncretism of Islam with magical practices was also transported to the Caribbean. In several communities, individuals performed the 'medicine man' role. A well-known immigrant *maulvi* (a religious leader or learned person) performed this service in Barataria (near the capital, Port of Spain) for many years. Today, a few Indian-trained *maulanas* function as exorcists in south and central Trinidad. The *tabeej* (*taweez*) usually comprising some Arabic phrases inscribed on article, presumably verses from the Quran, would be worn as an armlet for warding off evil spirits. Services such as fortune-telling, healing of ailments, solving problems and detection of theft were also provided. During some life crises even today it is not uncommon for some Muslims to seek the services of a Hindu *pundit* (priest).

Sufism, another Indian Muslim survival, exists up to this day in Trinidad. The Sufi group, known locally as the *Halqa*, has its local leader who functions as the *pir* (spiritual guide) over his followers (*muridis*). The group is linked to a Grand Pir overseas and is engaged in mystical practices, which adopt an Indian form. The members of this group nevertheless claim to subscribe to the Hanafi school of thought.

The East Indian Muslims of Trinidad, despite minor theological differences, were largely united and maintained good relationships with their fellow Indians in order to successfully resist integration with the wider society. Smith (1963: 14) on the basis of studies conducted in Trinidad, concludes that 'To the present time, family organisation and organised religion have engaged the forces of assimilation and acculturation and won'.

IV

In contemporary Trinidad and Tobago, 95 per cent of the Muslims (who constitute 6 per cent of the total population) are East Indians. Muslims experience more conflict and tension among themselves than with other religious denominations in the society. The mere existence of about 17 organisations and over 100 mosques—often located very close to each other—on the island is adequate testimony of the conflicts and schisms occurring over the years. Though originally established by mainstream organisations, the majority of mosques are attended by persons of other orientations. Today, one can identify the following major interpretations among the East Indians of Trinidad and Tobago: the Traditionalists, the Tabligh Jamaat, the Wahhabi Sunnis, the Modernists and the Shias.

Traditionalists, by far the largest group, constitute about 50 per cent of the community, this proportion being a significant decrease from say 25 years ago. They claim to be Hanafi Sunnis and are theologically very similar to the movement founded by Ahmad Riza Khan (of Barelwi) in late 19th century India (Sanyal 1996). They subscribe to practices and observances such as *mawlood*, *tazeem*, three-day, forty-day and *neyaz*. Great emphasis is given to praying for the deceased; death anniversaries of saints are often observed. They look down upon Muslims who do not observe these traditions and call them Wahhabis or Deobandis. They are suspicious of interpretations of Islam which differ from their own, and censure foreign missionaries. They are highly insular and there is a notable lack of desire to propagate their faith.

The *Tabligh Jamaat* group is much smaller than the traditionalists (about 15 per cent of the community) but all its members are highly active. Mosques are the focal point of their programmes, though their members are marginalised in certain mosques. They also claim to be Hanafi Sunnis, but are in practice opposed to most of the traditions mentioned above, describing them as innovations. Their leaders, trained in India, have adopted a literal approach to the understanding of the sacred texts, giving great importance to emulating the model of the Prophet's life in minute detail. They isolate themselves, adopt a passive approach to social and political issues and avoid conflict with established authority. Nevertheless, their rigid stance on many issues often contributes to their unpopularity among both traditionalists and fundamentalists. Their efforts at spreading the message of their faith are confined to the Muslim community.

Wahhabi Sunnis constitute about 25 per cent of the community, a proportion which has grown significantly over the past two decades. They generally show high levels of religious commitment. Originally inspired by movements in the subcontinent and more recently by Middle Eastern and North American contact, they are often at odds with the traditionalists over their apparent overemphasis on ancestor traditions as opposed to the *faraaid* (obligatory) acts of worship. Many of the groups in this category actively engage in propagating their faith both among Muslims and non-Muslims. Generally, members of this group do not follow the rulings of any one of the four schools of thought (*mazhab*) and some find *ijtihad* (the exercise of judgement in the implementation of Islamic law) acceptable.

Modernists are the ones who claim to be Sunnis and many among these give modern interpretations of the texts. They come largely from the middle classes and wear western style clothes. The men avoid beards and the women seldom wear the *hijab* (veil). They place a high value on western education mainly because of the prestige it brings. They often frown upon the rigidity of both the fundamentalist Sunnis and Tabligh Jamaat, and are to a great extent indifferent to the practices of the traditionalists, confining Islamic rituals to weddings, funerals and special occasions.

Shias were reported among the early immigrants from India. It is only over the last 10 years that they have become organised into a separate group with their own mosque. The group is very small (less than one per cent of the community), has a foreign missionary and attempts, often unsuccessfully, to persuade other Muslims to join their fold. Their followers, largely of African descent, nevertheless find comfort and solace in the group, probably due to the solidarity existing within and their disenchantment with other groups.

Comparing Indian Islam to Middle Eastern Islam, Samaroo (1988: 7) observes 'In modern-day Trinidad and Guyana where there are substantial Muslim populations, there is much confusion, often conflict, between these two types of Islam'. Ryan (1991: 29) also shares similar views.

Conflicts arising from different interpretations of Islam are endemic among Trinidad Muslims. However, evidence shows that these different interpretations have come mainly through continuous contact with India. The influence of the Middle East on Trinidad Muslims would have only been significant in the last decade or so, and its influence is much less in comparison to the influence of Islam from India. As mentioned earlier, fundamentalist Islam appeared in India about two centuries before the Wahhabi movement in Arabia. In addition, many sub-variants of Islam evolved among the Muslims of India which inevitably manifested themselves in the New World. So significant is India to Trinidad Muslims, that there is a saying among the latter that 'the Quran was revealed in Arabia, recited in Egypt and practised in India'. After the 1977 Islamic Conference sponsored by the Arab-based Muslim World League (RABITA), the Anjuman Sunnat-ul-Jammat Association (ASJA) and its affiliating organisations were appointed as the representatives of traditional Indian Muslims who do not subscribe to the Middle Eastern Islam.

V

Sunni/Qadiani Conflict: Towards the end of the 19th century, bitter conflicts that developed in India between the followers of Mirza Ghulam Ahmad and orthodox Muslims came to the surface in Trinidad with the arrival of Maulana Durrani in Trinidad in 1921. Pressures from Syed Abdul Aziz and other local Muslims led to his departure in 1923. Durrani nevertheless persuaded a Trinidadian, Ameer Ali, to pursue studies at an Ahmadi institute in Lahore (Samaroo 1987: 30). Ameer Ali returned as probably the first formally qualified local *maulvi* in Trinidad. Gradually, Ameer Ali's interpretation intensified doctrinal conflicts which persist to this day. Ameer Ali adopted what was then seen as a modernist approach to religion (like encouraging free participation of women in religious activities). This did not go down well with the orthodox sections of the Muslim community and pressures from them forced Ameer Ali to form his own organisation called the Trinidad Muslim League (the

TML, named after the All India Muslim League). The TML was formed on 14 August 1947 (Pakistan Day) and has given its main mosque the name Jinnah Memorial Mosque (Rafeek 1954), after Muhammad Ali Jinnah, the founder of Pakistan. In the late 1960s, the TML became formally linked with the Ahmadi movement. Since 1976, however, the League has formally abandoned its earlier Ahmadi affiliation and declares itself to be *ghair mukallid* (nonconformist).

Beginnings of Wahhabism: The arrival of Nazeer Ahmad Simab in Trinidad in June 1935 probably represents the introduction of fundamentalist Islam in the country. He left his 'well-paying job' in the Punjab to come to Trinidad as a missionary on the advice of his group Khuddam-i-Islam (Servants of Islam). His ideas often led to conflicts with the local Muslim community, particularly with the ASJA. Through a retail store he financed his missionary work, which included taking classes, and bringing out numerous publications in Urdu and English. Local leaders such as Haji Ruknudeen, the *qazi* (literally, judge) of Trinidad labelled him and his followers as Wahhabis, not unlike the experiences of Sayyad Ahmad of India in the early 19th century.

Simab made significant contributions in the field of education, being instrumental in establishing the first non-Christian denominational school in the colony in 1942. He was also successful in having Captain Daniel, the then Deputy Director of Education in the colony, delete certain anti-Islamic statements from history textbooks (*see Muslim Standard*, December 1975: 8). Simab passed away in December 1942 and was buried in El Socorro, Trinidad. A few of his followers, some of whom are still alive today, expressed their familiarity with this interpretation of Islam when other fundamentalists later arrived on the scene.

Pasha: Another Indian missionary reported to have had the most significant impact on Trinidad Muslims was Syed Husein Saqqaf, also known as Pasha. He was originally from Madras and was assigned to the Islamic Missionaries Guild in the late 1960s. He strongly advocated that Muslims should return to the original sources of Islam, refrain from confining religion to the mosque and adopt it as a complete way of life. Pasha faced severe opposition from the local Muslims and his activities were outlawed by mainstream organisations, such as the ASJA and the Takveeat-ul-Islamic Association (TIA). They described him as a Wahhabi out to create disunity among the Muslims.

It is reported that in a youth camp held by the Islamic Missionaries Guild in December 1970, Pasha came into conflict with Hisham Badran (a Jordanian) because of the latter's liberal interpretation of Islam. Pasha attracted some educated persons from various parts of Trinidad and trained them intensively in reading Arabic, in Quranic studies, and familiarised them with the *hadith* (sayings of Muhammad) and the *sirah* (life history of Muhammad). Pasha introduced to Trinidad books written by Maulana Maududi, founder of the Jamaat-i-Islami party, a religiopolitical movement with branches in India and Pakistan. Thousands of copies of *Towards understanding Islam* have been printed locally and are used as the basic text in Islamic classes. The followers of Pasha themselves started small courses in various parts of the country and made attempts at religious propagation. After his departure in 1974, they continued to meet on a regular basis to study Islam.

Tabligh Jamaat: This group, founded in India by Muhammad Ilyas, advocates a rigid system of routine adherence to the fundamentals of Islam. Members read a restricted range of books, refrain from polemics and adopt a mechanical, literal and often dogmatic approach to religion. Among all the fundamentalist efforts in Trinidad, the Tabligh Jamaat has the strongest connections with India. Several of its members still attend four-month training programmes in India. Also, many Trinidadians have obtained scholarships to pursue Islamic studies at the Dar-ul-Ulum Institute in Bangalore. Some have returned qualified as *maulanas* (scholars) and one person as a *mufti* (a religious jurist). On his return to these shores, Mufti Shabil Ali established a Dar-ul-Ulum in Central Trinidad, patterned on the institute in India. The curriculum and methods of instruction (though now through the medium of the English language) have not changed much. Even its use of the compounds as classrooms in the isolated rural community of Cunupia, reminds one of India.

The Tabligh Jamaat strongly opposes western sartorial styles for both males and females. It favours the use of many Urdu expressions instead of English ones. This group today has a significant international influence, especially among the Indian diaspora groups.

Islamic Trust: In mid-1975 Abdul Wahid Hamid, an Indo-Trinidadian historian, formed the Islamic Trust in which he was joined by the former associates of Pasha. His interpretation of Islam was similar to Pasha's, although his methodology was somewhat different. Hamid, however, had never met Pasha. For fear of being perceived as divisive, founders of the trust never intended to form a separate Muslim organisation, but functioned as a service bureau and as 'catalysts' in the Muslim community. The trust established a reference library and a bookshop and held classes at various venues throughout the country. It published numerous books and brought out a monthly magazine called *Muslim standard*. The trust forcefully expressed itself over a number of social and political issues, leading the then prime minister of Trinidad and Tobago, Dr Eric Williams, to comment that the Muslims had become aggressive in their missionary activity (Hamid 1978: 4). The publication was eventually banned from mosques controlled by mainstream organisations, mainly on account of its scathing criticisms of Kamaluddin Mohammed, a minister and leader of the traditional Muslim community. The Nur-e-Islam Mosque Board, of which Mohammed was the Chairman, issued a statement in the *Trinidad Guardian* stating that the *Muslim Standard* was the product of 'a few recalcitrant young Muslims' and does not represent the views of the Muslim community.

Hamid nevertheless considered himself part of the traditional Muslim community. He taught history at the ASJA (the country's largest Muslim organisation) Boys' College, held Arabic classes at various ASJA mosques and schools and even delivered a article on the invitation of ASJA at its Teachers Conference in late 1976.

Since Pasha's time, the group had attracted many persons of African descent to Islam. In February 1977 the Afro-American leader of the Islamic Party in North America (IPNA), Muzaffar-ud-Din Hamid, came to Trinidad as a guest of ASJA. Muzaffar-ud-Din delivered public lectures at various venues including the ASJA Boys' College and the ASJA mosque in Port of Spain. He then held several private meetings with the associates of the trust (as they preferred to be called) and discussed the constitution of the IPNA with them. He pointed out that the trust was merely functioning as a 'reformist group' rather than as a 'revolutionary' one and that social change was proceeding at too slow and gradual a pace with their methods of functioning. Instead of concentrating their efforts on reforming a 'decadent Muslim community', they were urged to work towards the establishment of a new Islamic society. This brought about a split, with the majority of the African members leaving the trust and forming the Islamic Party of the Caribbean.

The Islamic Party acquired a large building in Laventille, a depressed suburb of the capital (Port of Spain), which was used both as a mosque and living quarters for its members. In 1982, this group eventually joined forces with two other Afro-based groups to form the Jamaat-ul-Muslimeen (the group which attempted to overthrow the elected government in July 1990). The trust, considerably weakened by this turn of events, nevertheless continued its work. In late 1977, Abdul Wahid returned to London and continued to write and publish his views of Islam.

Evolving out of the Islamic Trust was the Islamic Dawah Movement, a more formalised body with registered members and a constitution. A number of other smaller groups evolved from the trust, including the Muslim Youth Brigade, the North-Eastern Muslim Youths, and Iqra Productions (Ali 1991: 29). A handful of trust associates, probably inspired by events in Iran, adopted the Shiite interpretation of Islam. They sometimes pray at the regular mosques, but operate in isolation from other Muslims. A few Shiites are said to be linked to the Jamaat-ul-Muslimeen.

VI

Ali (1991), in a thesis outlining the historical development of Muslim organisations in Trinidad and Tobago, observes that there are two federated groups of Muslim organisations: the Muslim Coordinating Council (MCC) and the United Islamic Organisations (UIO). The MCC consists of three better established groups incorporated by acts of parliament, that is, the ASJA, the TIA and the TML, whereas the UIO is made up of 13 smaller and recently established groups, not having the same legal status as incorporated bodies. The 13 UIO groups are: Dar-ul-Ulum, Iqra Productions, Islamic Dawah Movement, Islamic Funeral Services Trust, Islamic Missionaries Guild, Islamic Trust, Islamic Resource Society, Islamic Housing Cooperative, Muslim Credit Union, Muslim Youth Brigade, North Eastern Muslim Youth, Tobago Muslim Association and The University of the West Indies Islamic Society. The Jamaat-ul-Muslimeen has left the UIO while the Majlis-ul-Ulama is no longer functional. Compared to the UIO groups, the MCC is conservative and has cordial relations with the state. Its groups have (or had, as is the case with the TIA) larger memberships and their leadership consists of middle-class businessmen or professionals. They own most of the property in the Muslim community, mainly schools and mosques. The rank and file of these groups do not generally display high levels of commitment.

The ASJA and TIA are Hanafis, but the TML is *ghair mukallid*. The majority of the members of the MCC groups are East Indians. The traditional women's garb, the *hijab*, is worn by a relatively small percentage of their followers and polygamy is generally unacceptable among them.

The TIA, founded in 1927, is the oldest of the three organisations, with five primary schools and three mosques under its control. This group has been largely inactive over the years (Kasule 1986: 11), but has been recently attempting to resurface with some success. Both the ASJA and the TML were originally part of the TIA (Samaroo 1987: 9).

The ASJA was founded in 1936, when differences occurred over the then leader of the TIA, Moulvi Ameer Ali, who was described by some members as an Ahmadi. ASJA has since grown into the largest and most influential Muslim organisation in Trinidad and Tobago. It represents the orthodox, conservative Hanafi Muslims and supports practices such as *mawlood* (celebration of the Prophet's birthday). ASJA has always maintained a strong link with India and Pakistan, mainly through scholars such as Maulana Ansari and Maulana Siddiqi. Over the years some members of ASJA have been associated with the local Sufi Halqa.

In 1947, Ameer Ali and his followers left the TIA and formed the TML. The group had been ostracised for a number of years by the Trinidad Muslims, mainly due to its Ahmadi affiliations. Since 1976, the Council of the TML voted in favour of severing links with the Ahmadi movement. To this day, the TML represents the *ghair mukallids* or nonconformists. Over the years the TML has been the most liberal of the Muslim groups in the country (with the exception of the Ahmadi Anjuman which evolved more recently). It strongly encourages women to seek education and to participate at all levels of the organisation. It has five schools under its control and has an impressive record of achievements in the field of education (see Table 6.1).

The TML does not confine itself to any one of the four recognised schools of Islamic law and believes in the exercise of *ijtihad*, nor does it subscribe to some of the traditional practices sanctioned by the ASJA but the relationship between them is nevertheless very cordial. Both orientations, namely, *ahmadiyah* and *ghair mukallid*, found within the TML over the years, are of Indian origin.

Groups that constitute the UIO are generally more fundamentalist in orientation and have often been critical of established institutions.

Table 6.1: Muslim Organisations in Trinidad and Tobago

Organisation	Per cent*	Official Orientation	Current Orientation
Muslim Co-ordinating Council (MCC)			
ASJA	35	Hanafi Sunni	Traditionalist/Modernist
TIA	10	Non-sectarian	Traditionalist/Modernist
TML	15	Ghair-Mukallid	Non-conformist/Modernist
United Islamic Organisations (UIO)			
Tabligh/Dar-ul-Ulum	15	Hanafi Sunni	Hanafi Sunni
Islamic Missionaries Guild MCU	5	Wahhabi	Wahhabi/Traditionalist
(Outside MCC)	7	Open	Sunni with Wahhabi tendencies
IDM/IRS	5	Wahhabi	Wahhabi
Others**	8	Wahhabi/Open	Wahhabi/Traditionalist

* The figures are approximate and based upon unstructured interviews, documentary evidence and attendance at various programmes.
** Includes North Eastern Muslim Youth, Muslim Youth Brigade, Islamic Housing Cooperative, Islamic Funeral Services Trust, Iqra Productions, Islamic Trust, Tobago Muslim Association, and UWI Islamic Society.

These groups have smaller memberships (with the exception of the Muslim Credit Union) drawn mainly from the youth. Apart from the Islamic Missionaries Guild and Dar-ul-Ulum, these groups do not own much property and most members display high levels of religious commitment. Members do not generally subscribe to certain traditional practices of the ASJA and the TIA.

Though the UIO groups have agreed to 'co-operate on the basis of righteousness', much diversity exists among them with respect to interpretation of religion. Unique among them is the Dar-ul-Ulum Institute (mentioned earlier), which is rigidly Hanafi in its orientation, but differs from the ASJA or TIA Hanafis. The Islamic Dawah Movement, North-Eastern Muslim Youths, Muslim Youth Brigade and Iqra Productions have all evolved from the Islamic Trust and are similar in their interpretation of religious matters. They can be classified as Wahhabis (as defined earlier). The Islamic Missionaries Guild, though evolving from the ASJA, is officially Wahhabi but contains vestiges of traditionalism. The UWI Islamic Society is a transient student body and does not have a clear ideological position.

The Islamic Funeral Services Trust, Islamic Housing Co-operative, Iqra Productions and the Muslim Credit Union are service oriented groups that cater to all Muslims. The Tobago Muslim Association contains both Wahhabi and traditionalist elements. Finally, the Majlis-al-Ulama, a forum for Islamic scholars to discuss matters affecting the community has not been functional lately.

The Jamaat-ul-Muslimeen, an organisation consisting of over 90 per cent Afro-Trinidadian members is a Wahhabi institution. Its militant, aggressive and uncompromising approach puts it apart from all the other groups. In fact, although the Jamaat-ul-Muslimeen has found acceptability as an orthodox Muslim body, its involvement in the attempted coup of July 1990 has been vociferously condemned by all local Muslim groups outlined above, including the 'more radical' UIO groups (Ryan 1991: 68). In fact, this group was forced to resign from the UIO in March 1994. It operates independently of all other Muslim organisations. Some former members of the Jamaat-ul-Muslimeen have formed the Islamic Resource Society, the IRS, which joined the UIO in 1995 and the Islamic Housing Co-operative in 1996.

VII

As we have seen, Indian interpretations of Islam continue to exert a significant influence upon the Muslims, belonging to both traditional and fundamentalist groups in Trinidad and Tobago. Though the influence of the Middle East has been growing over the past decade, it is still not as strong as the Indian influence.

Close and continuous contact of East Indian Muslims has contributed to the growing diversity of religious practices and interpretations in Islam. Furthermore, even the conflicts that characterise interpretations of Islam in India have been carried over to the Caribbean. The visits of a number of missionaries from India and Pakistan have contributed significantly to the emergence of numerous schisms and fissions among the local Muslim groups. Among the two major groups of Muslim organisations in Trinidad and Tobago, the UIO is more fundamentalist. The fundamentalist groups are weaker in both membership and control of resources, but are more active in proselytising activities. They are more vociferous on matters that affect Muslims and are more likely to come into conflict with established authority. Their women generally wear traditional Muslim garb (the *hijab*) and free mixing of the sexes is not encouraged. They generally demonstrate equality of the sexes, with the exception of the Tabligh movement in which there is a tendency to relegate women to an inferior, domesticated status. Though all fundamentalist groups regard polygamy as permissible on account of its religious sanction, it is widely practised only among members of the Afro-based Jamaat-ul-Muslimeen and the India-based Tabligh movement.

Contacts between Trinidad Muslims and the Middle East have increased over the past decade mainly through the influence of Arab-trained scholars. About 20 youngsters left these shores to pursue studies at universities in Saudi Arabia; some of them have already qualified. In comparison, approximately four times that number went to India on scholarships to pursue Islamic studies at Bangalore, Deoband and Aligarh. India still constitutes the preferred destination of the majority of Islamic scholars from Trinidad and Tobago.

Note

1. The term 'East Indian' refers to migrants from India. It is popularly used in the local literature for differentiating their group from other 'Indians' in the West, such as 'West Indians' and 'American Indians'.

References

Akhtar, K. B. and A. H. Sakr. 1982. *Islamic Fundamentalism*. Cedar Rapids, Iowa: Igram Press.

Ali, F. 1991. *A Historical Development of Muslim Organisations in Trinidad and Tobago*. Caribbean Studies, BA dissertation, The University of the West Indies, St. Augustine.

Central Statistical Office. 1990. *Population and Housing Census 1990*. Port of Spain, Trinidad and Tobago: Government Printery.

Clarke, C. G. 1986. *East Indians in a West Indian Town*. London: Allen and Unwin.

Hamid, A. W. 1978. 'Muslims in the West Indies'. Paper presented to the Muslim Minorities Seminar, Islamic Council of Europe.

Herklots, G. A. 1921. *Islam in India*. London: Kurzon Press.

Hess. B.; E. Markson and P. Stein. 1991. *Sociology*. New York: Macmillan.

Hiro, D. 1989. *Holy Wars: The Rise of Islamic Fundamentalism*. New York: Routledge.

Irving, T. B. 1982. 'Foreword', in K. B. Akhtar and A. H. Sakr: *Islamic Fundamentalism*. Iowa: Igram Press, pp. 7–14.

Jha, J. C. 1973. 'The Indian Heritage in Trinidad', in J. La Guerre (ed.): *From Calcutta to Caroni*. Trinidad: Longman Caribbean, pp. 3–22.

Kasule, O. H. 1986. 'Muslims in Trinidad and Tobago', *Journal of the Institute of Muslim Minority Affairs*, 7(1): 195–224.

Khan, F. 1987. 'Islam as a Social Force in the Caribbean'. Paper presented in the Conference of the History Teachers Association of Trinidad and Tobago, June 1987.

Klass, M. 1961. *East Indians in Trinidad*. New York: Columbia University Press.

Maududi. S. A. A. 1963. *A Short History of the Revivalist Movement in Islam*. Lahore: Islamic Publications.

Muslim Standard. 1975. 3(December): 10–11.

Niehoff, A. and J. Niehoff. 1960. *East Indians in the West Indies*. Milwaukee: Milwaukee Public Museum Publications in Anthropology, No. 6.

Quick, A. H. 1990. *Deeper Roots: Muslims in the Caribbean Before Columbus to the Present*. Nassau, Bahamas: AICCLA.

Rafeek, M. 1954. *A History of Islam and Muslims in Trinidad*. Trinidad Muslim League Inc. (Commemorative Brochure).

Rizvi, G. A. A. 1965. *Muslim Revivalist Movements in Northern India*. Aligarh: Aligarh Muslim University.

Ryan, S. 1991. *The Muslimeen Grab for Power: Race, Religion and Revolution in Trinidad and Tobago*. Port of Spain, Trinidad and Tobago: Inprint Caribbean Ltd.

Samaroo, B. 1987. 'The Indian Connection: The Influence of Indian Thought and Ideas on East Indians in the Caribbean', in D. Dabydeen and B. Samaroo: *India in the Caribbean*. London: Hansib Publishing Ltd., pp. 25–59.

———. 1988. 'Early African and East Indian Muslims in Trinidad and Tobago'. Paper presented at a Conference on Indo-Caribbean History and Culture, University of Warwick, May 1988.

Sanyal, U. 1996. *Devotional Islam and Politics in British India: Ahmad Riza Khan Barelwi and his Movement 1870–1920*. Delhi: Oxford University Press.

Sivan, E. 1992. 'Radical Islam', in A. Giddens (ed.): *Human Societies*. Cambridge: Polity Press.

Smith, R. J. 1963. *Muslim East Indians in Trinidad: Retention of Ethnic Identity under Acculturative Conditions*. Unpublished PhD dissertation, University of Pennsylvania.

Thurston, M. 1909. *Castes and Tribes of Southern India* (in 7 Vols.). Madras: Christian Literature Society.

Titus, M. T. 1930. *Islam in India and Pakistan*. Madras: Christian Literature Society.

7

The Dynamics of Language in Indian Diaspora: The Case of Bhojpuri/Hindi in Trinidad*

N. Jayaram

Indian diaspora is a complex and heterogeneous phenomenon: In terms of the history of their emigration; their regional, religious, social, economic and educational backgrounds; the politicoeconomic context in which they have developed over time; and the sociocultural experiences they have undergone, the Indian communities in diaspora vary considerably. Expectedly then, the status of the languages which the different diasporic communities carried as part of their sociocultural baggage is highly variable. They have experienced attrition and disappeared altogether, or they have survived in extremely limited spheres of life, or they have been modified and retained, or they continue to exist and are in contact with their ancestral roots, or they have been sought to be revived and revitalised with varying degrees of success.

*Originally published in *Sociological Bulletin*, Vol. 49, No. 1, March 2000, pp. 41–62.

*The information and insights presented in this article were gathered during the author's sojourn as Visiting Professor of Indian Studies at The University of the West Indies, St. Augustine, Trinidad, in 1994–96. The assistance and affection received from Dr Brinsley Samaroo are gratefully acknowledged. Thanks are also due to the anonymous referee for her/his useful comments.

Thus, the Estate Tamils in Sri Lanka, the Sikh Punjabis in England, and the Hindu Gujaratis in the United States of America have retained their ancestral language, whereas the Indians in Jamaica have lost all their ancestral languages. In Mauritius, Fiji and Surinam, Indic languages are still spoken. A local dialect of Bhojpuri is used in all informal spheres and standard Hindi in religious and cultural domains. In Fiji and Mauritius, standard Hindi is even officially recognised. In Guyana and Trinidad, Bhojpuri is used in folk songs and Standard Hindi in religious services and ceremonies. In all these countries, the *lingua franca* is the dominant local language(s)— Sinhalese in Sri Lanka, English in England and the United States of America, Creole French or Creole English in Mauritius, Fijian or English in Fiji, Creole Dutch in Surinam, and Creole English in Guyana and Trinidad.

What accounts for the differential dynamics of language in Indian diaspora? In the literature on Indian diaspora, there is neither an empirically cogent sociological answer to this question nor a theoretically sound sociolinguistic formulation about it. Such an answer or formulation, no doubt, can only come out of extant comparative studies of the history and status of Indian languages among different diasporic communities. Before such comparative studies can be embarked upon, however, we need benchmark sociohistorical surveys of the dynamics of language among the different diasporic communities.

Surprisingly enough, the dynamics of language has hardly attracted the attention of anthropologists and sociologists working on Indian diaspora.[1] The focus of a few sociolinguists who have dealt with this subject is understandably circumscribed by the concerns of their discipline: The effect of Creole and to a lesser extent of Standard Hindi on Mauritian Bhojpuri (Domingue 1971), the formal changes in Trinidad Hindi as a result of language adaptation (Durbin 1973), the koine formation in the Indian speech community in Guyana (Gambhir 1981), the sociolinguistic structure and process in Mauritian Bhojpuri (Gambhir 1986) and Fiji Hindustani (Siegel 1975), the linguistic adaptations of Fiji Indians (Moag 1979), the Sarnami as a living language in Surinam (Damsteegt 1988), the morphology of Trinidad Bhojpuri (Mohan 1978) and the death of that language (Mohan and Zador 1986), and the relationship between language and socioeconomic and cultural factors in a Trinidad village (Sperl 1980).

This article analyses the dynamics of language among diasporic Indians in Trinidad. It traces the linguistic element in the sociocultural baggage brought by their ancestors during the indenture era; it examines the metamorphosis and attrition that this element experienced in the course of over 150 years of their presence in this country; and it documents the efforts at reviving and rejuvenating the linguistic element of their cultural heritage and reflects on the prospects thereof.

Diglossia and the Evolution of Trinidad Bhojpuri

Between 1845 and 1917, 143,939 Indians were brought into Trinidad under the scheme of indentured labour, of which only 33,294 (or 23.13 per cent) eventually returned to India (Laurence 1971: 26 and 57). There is no official record of the languages and dialects which they brought with them. It is now difficult to determine the numerical strength of emigrants from each district and the language and dialect spoken by them. Nevertheless, considering the region from which an overwhelming majority of the Indians were recruited—namely, the western part of Bihar, the eastern part of the then United Provinces and the southern (or Ranchi) plateau of Chota Nagpur—it is justifiably presumed by linguists that most of these immigrants 'must have been native speakers of the various dialects of Bhojpuri'[2] (Mohan 1978: 8). This is further confirmed by 'the striking similarities between the Bhojpuri widely spoken in Trinidad (in comparison with other Indic languages) and the different varieties of Bhojpuri spoken in India' (ibid.: 11).

Besides the dialects of Bhojpuri, the emigrants brought other languages and dialects. The small groups of recruits from outside the Bhojpuri-speaking areas brought with them Avadhi, Magahi and Maithili. Mohan claims that 'there is anecdotal evidence that these languages were once spoken in Trinidad, as well as languages from further afield, such as Bengali, Nepali, and Telugu' (ibid.: 11). The immigrants hailing from the Madras Presidency (forming about 10 per cent) brought with them south Indian languages, most notably, Tamil.

The linguistic confusion resulting from a multiplicity of languages and dialects among the immigrant Indians was often remarked by observers.[3] For instance, Reverend W. H. Gamble (1866: 33), a British missionary, noted:

> The Bengalis speak Hindustani and Bengali, while the inhabitants of the Madras Presidency speak Tamil, a totally different language. When these people meet in Trinidad, it strikes me as somewhat strange that they have to point to water and rice, and ask each other what they call it in their language. So totally different are the languages, the Hindustani and the Tamil, that English has to become the medium of communication.

How Reverend Gamble's forecast eventually became true we will see later. Initially, however, the languages brought by the Indians were preserved. According to Tinker (1993: 211), this was due to the persistence of the Indians in speaking their mother tongue among themselves. This was also assisted by the lack of educational facilities for their children, which would have forced them to learn an alien language in school. Even when educational facilities first became available, most Indian parents kept their children away from school for various reasons, not excluding the fear of conversion to Christianity (Singh 1985: 48–49).

At the outset, the exigencies of plantation life made two linguistic demands on the Indian immigrants: first, they were required to develop a language for communication among themselves, a *lingua franca* as it were. And second, they had to develop the ability to communicate with the authorities and in the market, which meant acquiring a more or less intelligible English patois and adopting Creole English as their link-language. About the latter, Tinker (1993: 211–12) observes that 'the plantation Indian learned to regard language as a means of protecting himself—making himself understood, when this was needed, and making himself hard to understand when that would serve him'.

The development of a *lingua franca* for internal communication was not easy, despite the fact that those hailing from the Bhojpuri-speaking areas of north India formed the numerical core of the Indian community. Even the Bhojpuri brought to Trinidad was not homogeneous, and it reflected the dialectal variations of the parts from which the speakers came.[4] In due course, however, through a process of koineisation (that is, levelling) of different dialects, a new variant of Bhojpuri was evolved as a reasonably homogeneous *lingua franca* on the sugar plantations.[5] This variant is called by linguists as 'Trinidad Bhojpuri' (see Mohan 1978, Mohan and Zador 1986) and by historians, following plantation and colonial officials, as 'Plantation Hindustani' (see Tinker 1993: 208).[6]

According to Gambhir (1986: 193), the process of dialect-levelling was almost automatic as the various dialects and languages of the immigrants more or less represented 'a linguistic continuum of the western to the eastern dialects in India in such a way that there were minimal differences between any two geographically adjacent dialects'. This process was boosted by the 'psychological and emotional unity' provided by the perception of the speakers of the various north Indian linguistic systems as forms of Hindi or Hindustani.

In the opinion of sociolinguists, Trinidad Bhojpuri is a linguistic system by itself (see Mohan 1978, Gambhir 1986). It is governed by linguistic rules like any other natural language. That it is a compromise between different speakers, or that it is a simplified version of Indian Bhojpuri, does not make it linguistically less different. Some of 'the competing linguistic alterants from the second stage' may, no doubt, persist in the speech of some people. These are only redolent of the multidialectal origin of Trinidad Bhojpuri (Gambhir 1986).

·   The evolution of Trinidad Bhojpuri as a distinct language has not been documented, and 'it is extremely difficult to reconstruct' (Mohan 1978: 12). It may be surmised, that with every succeeding generation, the relatively greater impact of peer groups as compared to that of parents in the matter of language use must have contributed to the increasing homogenisation of Trinidad Bhojpuri. That is, there must have developed 'a single system [of language] incorporating residual dialectal variation rather than persisting as a series of distinct dialects' (Mohan 1978: 13). By the time the Indians had settled down as an agricultural community in the last decades of the 19th century, Trinidad Bhojpuri had become their ethnic language. Thus, in his 1914 Report on Trinidad, J. McNeill could observe that 'soon after arrival all immigrants learn Plantation Hindustani' (quoted in Tinker 1993: 211).

Although Trinidad Bhojpuri evolved as a language different from the ancestral languages, it never became a 'native language'. This was due to the fact that with the expansion of education, the younger generation, especially those in urban areas, gradually adopted Creole English and/or Standard English as the native language. According to a sociolinguistic profile prepared by Sealey (1983: Intro–2) on the basis of 1970 census data, currently the Indo-Trinidadians 'share with the rest of the population...varieties of Trinidadian Creole English as the major L1 and language of daily communication'. This community-wide language shift over the decades has meant that Trinidad Bhojpuri is a dying language (see Durbin 1973, Mahabir and Mahabir 1990: 3, and Mohan and Zador 1986).

Using Roger Bell's sociolinguistics formula, Sealey (1983: TB–1–2) arrives at the following profile of Trinidad Bhojpuri: 'A dialect of "mainland" Bhojpuri', 'a Tolerated Language', 'spoken as an L1 by less than 3 per cent of the population' and 'used as a language of restricted internal communication', Trinidad Bhojpuri monolinguals are generally over 75 years of age, and Trinidad Bhojpuri and Trinidad English bilinguals (including semi-speakers) are generally in the age group of 55–75 years. The fluent speakers of that language are Hindus who have remained fairly isolated in rural areas.

The few native speakers of Trinidad Bhojpuri use it among their restricted friends or kin circle. It is reportedly used by the elders in the presence of strangers or children when they discuss something confidential or when they wish to exclude them from conversation. The same is said to be true of the very few elderly persons in the 'Madrassi' settlements in rural areas, who still speak Tamil, and the elderly Muslims who speak Urdu.

Missionaries and the Introduction of Standard Hindi

The process of dialect-levelling and the emergence of Trinidad Bhojpuri was spontaneous and unconscious, and it was determined by the exigencies of plantation life. Not surprisingly, the speakers of this language did not even give a name to it and observers called it 'Plantation Hindustani'. Parallel to this was the conscious effort of the Canadian Presbyterian Mission at introducing Standard Hindi in Trinidad. The credit for this goes primarily to the doyen of that Mission in Trinidad, namely, Reverend John Morton of Bridgewater, Nova Scotia in Canada.

Reverend Morton came to Trinidad in 1868 and established a Mission to work almost exclusively among what were then called the

'East Indians'. He at once appreciated the need to use the native language of Indians for propagating Christianity among them.[7] The native language which he found best suited for his work was 'the Hindi dialect'.[8] By the end of 1870, he notes in his diary, 'I have now familiarised myself with the Hindi and use it or the Urdu, according as the person to whom I speak may be a Hindu or a Mussalman'. In December 1871, he was granted a government license 'to practice as a sworn Interpreter of the English and Hindustani languages in this colony' (Morton 1916: 66 and 67).

In the early days of the Mission, its members had to learn Hindi so that they could communicate with the newly arriving immigrants from India. The first regular church of the Canadian Presbyterian Mission was the 'Susamachar Church' in San Fernando. In this Church religious service was given in Hindi. As of August 1871, there was only one complete copy of 'the Hindi Scriptures' in Trinidad, and that was Reverend Morton's own. In January 1872, there arrived from Calcutta boxes of books containing Bibles, and tracts and catechisms in Hindi. In 1872, Reverend Morton began translating and preparing hymns, assisted by Reverend Andrew Gayadeen. A little book containing 30 hymns thus produced was printed (in Halifax, Canada) in 'the Hindustani language, employing Roman character' (Morton 1916: 110 and 111).

Considerations of economy of time and money soon made the Mission think of starting a Hindi printing press of its own. First, Morton purchased 'all the East Indian's type' and got press-work done in Port of Spain. Then he bought a hand-press and moved the plant to Tunapuna and started his own press. At this first Hindi press in Trinidad were printed, in 1903, thousands of copies of *Prarthna Mala* (The Garland of 'Prayers), the Hindi hymn book, which came to be used at all Hindi services not only in Trinidad but in far away Jamaica too. Also brought out from this press were copies of 'a simple catechism' adapted to 'the Hindi using the Nagari character'. At this press Morton also translated, printed and published 'for the Government all their Hindustani notices and circulars' (Morton 1916: 425, 432 and 433).

In March 1905, Morton began printing four pages of Hindi in those copies of *The Trinidad Presbyterian* which circulated among the 'East Indians'. Morton also brought out the 'International Sabbath School Lessons' in Hindi with a simple commentary in English. This publication went a long way in systematising the teaching of Hindi in the Sunday School, allying it closely to the religious instruction in the day schools (Morton 1916: 432).

Thus, under the stewardship of Reverend John Morton, the Canadian Presbyterian Mission played a pioneering role in introducing and propagating Standard Hindi in Trinidad. Though the Mission continued to use Hindi for its activities right through the first half of 20th century, gradually the initiative was lost and Standard Hindi experienced attrition even among the Presbyterians. According to Niehoff and Niehoff (1960: 149 and 151), who observed the situation in the late 1950s, the Mission gave up the emphasis on Hindi as its administrators found that 'the young Indians no longer have any interest in it'. In fact, their field work revealed that 'except for the very old, they [the Presbyterians] show very little interest in maintaining Hindi as a spoken language and it is very rarely heard in Christian homes' (ibid.: 151).

At a Thanksgiving ceremony in a Presbyterian household in LaRomaine in south Trinidad in December 1995, the author heard an octogenarian lady recite what she called a *bhajan* in Hindi, and freely translate it into English for the benefit of those (i.e., nearly the entire audience?) who did *not* understand the original. She lamented on the loss of Hindi among her Presbyterian brethren. The religious service that evening was carried out exclusively in English, and the hymn book (*Hymns and choruses*, published by the Presbyterian Church in Trinidad) circulated among the members of the audience, consisted of five *bhajans* in Hindi printed in Roman characters.

Attrition of Trinidad Bhojpuri and Standard Hindi

By all accounts then, the spontaneously evolved Trinidad Bhojpuri and the deliberately developed Standard Hindi did not survive for more than a century in Trinidad. If at all they are still spoken fluently, it is almost exclusively by the very elderly in rural areas, and as such there is no speech community of these ethnic languages left among the Indo-Trinidadians anymore.[9] Whatever has survived is mostly in their folksongs and in their lexicon of kitchen and food, and to some extent in their kinship terminology. The only systematic ethnic use of Hindi in contemporary Trinidad is to be found in the religious realm among the Hindus.

The attrition[10] of native languages among diasporic Indians in Trinidad, and the attrition of the *lingua franca* which was spontaneously evolved (Trinidad Bhojpuri) and deliberately developed (Standard Hindi) by them are intriguing to scholars engaged in the study of Indian diaspora. This is particularly so considering that the diasporic Indians are the single largest ethnic community in Trinidad (forming 40.3 per cent of the population, according to 1990 Census), and considering that other elements of culture (e.g., religion and food habits) and social organisation (e.g., marriage and family) have been reconstituted relatively successfully (see Klass 1961, Vertovec 1992). What explains this linguistic attrition among diasporic Indians in Trinidad?

To begin with, throughout the period of indenture, and later too, the life of the immigrant Indians was witnessed by the patterns of their ancestral culture being ignored, ridiculed or suppressed by the carriers of the dominant culture of the colony. Their economic exploitation was matched by cultural subjection, and there was continuous pressure on them to Creolise. That the Indians did not allow the total obliteration of their 'Indianness' under these conditions is indeed surprising. Though with some loss (including their language), the Indians still retain more of their own cultural identity than their African counterparts (see Tinker 1993: 208).

Although through a process of koineisation the Indians evolved Trinidad Bhojpuri or Plantation Hindustani as a *lingua franca*, 'few recognise it as a language distinct from rather than derivative of Standard Hindi'. The lexical similarity (notwithstanding the morphological and grammatical differences) between the two languages resulted in this language being viewed as a 'corrupted' variety of Standard Hindi (Mohan 1978: 2). The speakers of Trinidad Bhojpuri themselves referred to it as 'broken Hindi' or 'bad-Hindi' (Sealey 1983: TB–2). Some even refer to it disparagingly as '*chamar* Hindi (low-caste Hindi) or *gaoo bolee* (village speech)' (Mahabir and Mahabir 1990: 3).

The Trinidad Bhojpuri speakers used Standard Hindi as their index of comparison. Standard Hindi was viewed as 'Good Hindi' or 'Proper Hindi' (Mahabir and Mahabir 1990: 3). They heard this Hindi spoken in Hindi films, which have a wide audience in Trinidad, and by the few expatriate residents (i.e., Indian nationals) there (Sealey

1983: TB–2). In other words, the native speakers of Trinidad Bhojpuri themselves had feelings of inferiority about that language. This, according to Mohan (1978: 2), is 'partly responsible for the failure of its speakers to transmit this language to younger generations of Trinidad Indians'.

Significantly, right from the beginning, the Canadian Presbyterian Mission adopted Standard Hindi, and not Trinidad Bhojpuri, as its language of religious propagation. Whether the Mission too had a poor image of Trinidad Bhojpuri ('the language of the heathens') vis-à-vis Standard Hindi ('the language of the civilised'), is difficult to say. Be that as it may, the Mission's efforts did not ensure the survival of Standard Hindi. As noted earlier, even before a century after its establishment, the Mission almost entirely switched over to English.

From the point of view of the larger community of Indians, the identification of Standard Hindi with the Canadian Presbyterian Mission was perhaps what subdued its chances of developing as a second language in the country. The use of Standard Hindi by the Mission was suspected by many a Hindu and Muslim alike as a stratagem for their conversion to Christianity. In Seepersad Naipaul's (father of V. S. Naipaul) perceptive work of fiction, *The Adventures of Gurudeva and Other Stories,* depicting the life of Indians in rural Trinidad in the 1940s, Sohun (the school teacher) tells Gurudeva (the protagonist): 'In school you never were keen on Hindi. Your father felt that teaching you Hindi was only a ruse on my part to teach you the Bible. He preferred his sons to grow up as ignorant Hindus rather than as intelligent Christians' (1976: 91–92).

There is no gainsaying the fact that when educational advancement was unthinkable for the indentured immigrants, the doors of English education were opened for the children of those Indians who got converted to Christianity, more so to Presbyterianism. Along with this came the prospects of employment in the emerging modern sector, including the cherished professions of medicine and law. Such an education also meant exposure to Christianity and to a new outlook on life. One element of their culture which English-educated Indians sacrificed as part of the process of modernisation was their ethnic language.

English, and literacy in English, carried high prestige in the colonial period.[11] As a language of education, English became a *sine qua non* of upward mobility in the colonial social order. Sperl (1980), who studied the language shift towards Trinidad Creole English in an Indian village in Trinidad, concluded that this shift reflects the acculturation to wider society and the decreasing meaningfulness of 'guiding principles' which are rooted in tradition and religion. The later part of her conclusion is, however, certainly contestable (see Vertovec 1992).

Not only has there been a shift towards Trinidad Creole English as the first language, and even as the mother tongue, among the diasporic Indians, but also there has been a pronounced strain towards monolingualism in that language. This is explained by the fact that their native language has no use whatsoever in commerce and administration. Trinidad Creole English is the first language of most Trinidadians and Standard English is the official language of the country.[12] Trinidad Creole English (at primary level) and Standard English (at secondary level and beyond) are used in education. From the utilitarian point of view, those who study an additional language, invariably choose Spanish or French.

Retention and Survival of Linguistic Heritage

According to Berko-Gleason (1982: 21), 'the traditional linguistic subsystems (phonology, morphology, syntax and vocabulary) may suffer differential loss in attrition, since they are learned separately'. It is important to note that both Trinidad Bhojpuri and Standard Hindi were predominantly a part of the oral culture and the script was basically confined to the religious literati—the pandits among the Hindus and the ministers among the Presbyterians. This accounts for both the general attrition of these two languages among the Indians and the survival and retention of some elements of their native languages.

Thus, Hindi is still used in liturgy and Bhojpuri has been retained in folk songs. The survival of Bhojpuri or Hindi (and even Tamil) words in the spheres of food, domestic worship and kinship relations, is also to be understood in this light (Winford 1972: 13–14).[13] The polite routines and routinised sequences, which are taught/learnt explicitly, have been similarly retained.[14] These expressions have little intellectual or referential content, but serve sociocultural purposes. Similarly, numbers, songs and emotionally laden words like curses or swearwords have survived.[15]

Language retention is also an age-related phenomenon. It was mentioned earlier that Trinidad Bhojpuri monolinguals are generally over 75 years of age, and Trinidad Bhojpuri and Trinidad Creole English bilinguals (including semi-speakers) are mostly in the age group of 55–75 years. The same could be said about the retention of Standard Hindi. The elders retained their first language mainly because they did not know English.[16] They did not develop as a bilingual community. With the younger and newer generations becoming increasingly proficient in English, their incipient bilingualism gave way to monolingualism in English. If language survival is noticeable at all among the young Indo-Trinidadians today, it is only at the lexical and idiomatic levels (Mahabir and Mahabir 1990: 3).

There is a gender dimension in language retention. The social organisation which the Indian settlers reconstituted in Trinidad was pronouncedly patriarchal, resembling that of their ancestral land. In the post-indenture period, men had the major share of interactions in the outside world where English (Creole or Standard) was the ruling language. While the role of woman was not entirely confined to the family, the responsibility for running the household and the socialisation of children was primarily hers. Not surprisingly, it is in the spheres of kitchen and food, and household and kinship that the survival of the lexical and idiomatic elements of Trinidad Bhojpuri and Hindi are most pronounced.

Ethnicity and Linguistic Revival

In Seepersad Naipaul's fiction referred to earlier, there are perceptive observations about the linguistic situation among Indians in rural Trinidad in the 1940s. A few characters in this novel speak Hindi: 'In nearly half a century's residence in the island Boodhoo still spoke nothing but Hindi,...he being India-born'. Some characters speak 'mongrel Hindi'—'a sort of patois Hindi which, spoken elsewhere but in Trinidad, would be unmeaning gibberish'. Though he himself is a pretender speaking Standard Hindi, Gurudeva, the protagonist of the novel, bemoans the fact 'that not two in a hundred knew their mother tongue' and he exhorts the village youth to regard it as 'their duty to learn Hindi' (1976: 64, 38 and 106).

Seepersad Naipaul's portrayal of the Indian community in rural Trinidad reveals the realisation among some Indians as early as the 1940s that with their community shifting to English their linguistic heritage was facing extinction. The celebration, in 1945, of the centenary of their arrival in Trinidad, and the introduction of adult suffrage in 1946, gave the ethnic self-perception of Indo-Trinidadians a boost. This combined with increasing contact with visiting religious personages from India triggered off a concerted effort at cultural revival and rejuvenation among them. As part of this general movement, Standard Hindi, not Trinidad Bhojpuri, was sought to be revived.

It is true that an ethnic group is not necessarily coterminous with a linguistic or speech community. But, there is no gainsaying that in a multiethnic polity characterised by cultural contentions, language could become an important element of ethnic identity. Thus, the efforts at revival of Hindi and its propagation, which began in the 1950s, could be viewed as a conscious reaction by sections of the Indo-Trinidadians against the loss of their distinctive cultural heritage through linguistic attrition. Several organisations and individuals, religious and/or cultural in orientation, played a role in this.

The Sanatan Dharma Maha Sabha (established in 1952), the major religious body representing the Hindu population, the Arya Pratinidhi Sabha (incorporated in 1943) and other Hindu religious bodies took an interest in Hindi[17] as a liturgical language of the Hindus.[18] Pandits went to India to study Hindi and learn scriptures like *Bhagwad Gita*, *Ramayana*, *Srimad Bhagavta*, *Shiva Purana*, *Vishnu Purana*, etc. Hindi has now become a religious requisite of the pandit class. Many leading pandits of Trinidad, both in the Sanatan Dharma Maha Sabha and the Arya Pratinidhi Sabha are Hindi graduates. Hindi is taught in *mandirs* (temples) under the jurisdiction of the Sanatan Dharma Maha Sabha, and as part of the radio programme '*Dharm Shiksha*' (Religious Education) for school children sponsored by it.

Although the cultural aspect is not ignored, the Hindi orientation of the Hindu organisations is primarily religious in nature. However, Hindi, unlike Sanskrit which has become essentially a sacral language, has far wider sociocultural potential. The recognition of this fact was behind the establishment, in 1952, of the Hindi Education Board under the sponsorship of the then High Commissioner of India, Anand Mohan Sahay. The Board had as its objective the teaching of Hindi and elements of Indian culture in villages. It offered Hindi courses at three levels—*Prarambhik* (Beginner), Junior and Senior (equivalent to India's lower secondary). Books published by the Dakshin Bharath Hindi Prachar Sabha, Madras (now Chennai), were used as approved text books.

Till 1957 the Board functioned under the able directorship of Edward Joseph Pillai.[19] He was replaced by Induthai Kelar, who was deputed by the Government of India. Under her directorship about 650 students passed the Board examination. After her departure from Trinidad, the Board slackened in its activities and the number of students began dwindling steadily. The propagation of Hindi was resumed after the arrival, in 1966, of Hari Shankar Adesh as a Secretary at the High Commission of India in Port of Spain. Because of his efforts several classes were restarted, seminars were held and a cultural camp was organised. In the last Board examination, held in 1970, 251 Hindi students were successful.

Though the propagation of Hindi was resumed under the leadership of Adesh, the Board continued to be embroiled with internal differences about the scope of its activities. Some wanted the Board to confine itself exclusively to teaching Hindi and conducting examinations. Others wanted the scope of the Board to be extended to include fine arts too. The infighting within the Board aggravated to such an extent that it even became difficult to convene a General Body meeting. Eventually, the Board became defunct.

As if in anticipation of the void about to be created by the collapse of the Hindi Education Board, Adesh had founded the Bharatiya Vidya Sansthaan in November 1966. This organisation sought the all round development of Indian culture, including the teaching of Indian languages (Hindi, Sanskrit and Urdu), music (both vocal and instrumental) and performing arts (like dance and drama). The Sansthaan has made considerable contribution to the revival and propagation of Hindi in Trinidad. Starting with a few students, the Sansthaan has established more than 30 schools spread all over the country. It prepares students for the Hindi examinations conducted by the University of London, the Rashtra Bhasha Prachar Samithi (Wardha) and the Bharatiya Vidya Bhavan (Mumbai). Starting from March 1968, the Sansthaan has been publishing a monthly magazine called *Jyothi*. One of the former pupils and a notable activist of the Sansthaan, Kamla Ramlakhan, has written a two-part Hindi language text book—*Hindi Prabhaat* (Dawn of Hindi)—keeping in mind the sociocultural background of the Trinidad learners.[20] Incidentally, it is the Sansthaan which has sought to popularise *Namaste* as a form of greeting among Hindus, whose culturally rooted mode of greeting has been *Sitaram* (Panday 1993).

The Hindu bias in the propagation of Hindi by the Sanatan Dharma Maha Sabha and the Bharatiya Vidya Sansthaan hardly needs to be emphasised. Contrasted with this is the pronouncedly less religious orientation of the Hindi Nidhi (Hindi Foundation of Trinidad and Tobago), established in 1986 to propagate Hindi in Trinidad. The Nidhi has brought out a few Hindi textbooks for beginners, and it sponsors the teaching of Hindi in schools and the *Hindi Sikhen* (Let us learn Hindi) programme on the radio. It had organised an International Hindi Conference at Couva in central Trinidad in April 1992 and in collaboration with The University of the West Indies, St. Augustine, it organised the Fifth World Hindi Conference in April 1996.

It is appropriate here to mention the keen interest that the Government of India has evinced in the revival and propagation of Hindi in Trinidad, as also in some other countries with a substantial proportion of population of Indian origin. The initiative taken by the High Commission of India in the establishment and working of the now defunct Hindi Education Board has been referred to earlier. The Commission had started free evening classes in Hindi in 1985 which, after being suspended for some years, were restarted in 1992. It also observes Hindi Divas on January 14 every year.

The Government of India has been providing scholarships to Trinidadians for studying Hindi in India. The Indian Council for Cultural Relations has been offering the services of two Hindi Professors—one at the St. Augustine campus of The University of the West Indies (since 1989), and the other at the National Institute of Higher Education and Research in Science and Technology in Port of Spain (since 1987).

Also important to note here is the sudden spurt in the use of Hindi in the audiovisual media in recent years. Before 1993, Indian cultural programmes hardly got a few hours of broadcast time on the radio. Now there are three radio stations broadcasting Indo-Trinidadian and Hindi programmes, and two exclusively so.

They also carry a few advertisements in Hindi. In 1995, two of them offered Hindi lessons—*Hindi Sikhen* (Let us learn Hindi) anchored by V. R. Jagannathan on WABC's FM 103 and *Hindi Mein Bath Chith* (Conversation in Hindi) anchored by Sumita Broomes on Radio ICN. Hindi films and film-based programmes, and cultural programmes using Hindi in varying degrees are regularly telecast by the local television stations. Cinema halls regularly screen Hindi movies, whose audience has reportedly grown over the years. Also, the innumerable cultural organisations and associations often use Hindi in varying doses.

Prospects of Hindi as an Ethnic Language

It is more than 40 years now that concerted efforts have been on at reviving Hindi in Trinidad and propagating that language among Indo-Trinidadians. What has been the outcome of these efforts? What are the prospects of Hindi becoming an ethnic language of Indo-Trinidadians, and of Indo-Trinidadians becoming a distinct speech community and bilingual (in English and Hindi)? The growth of interest in Hindi in the recent past and the increasing observability of Hindi in the audiovisual media may suggest that the prospects are bright. However, a sociological review of the historical experience of language attrition and revival among Indo-Trinidadians does not allow one to be sanguine. The development of a speech community is a complex and long drawn sociolinguistic process, and more so in an ethnic group in diaspora which has experienced language attrition.

First is the problem of the interface between Hindi and Hinduism. Certainly, there is no intrinsic linkage between language and religion. When conscious efforts are made to introduce a language or revive it, however, language can hardly be religiously neutral. One may recall here that the Canadian Presbyterian Mission carefully chose Standard Hindi, and not Trinidad Bhojpuri, as its liturgical language. This move kept many a Hindu away from Standard Hindi in the colonial era. It was in a way ironical that when the Christian Missionaries were getting their scriptural materials translated into

Hindi, the Hindu religious leaders were using English translations of their scriptures.

Successful efforts at propagating Hindi today are associated with Hindu religious bodies or organisations leaning towards Hinduism in one form or other. Whereas for the Hindu pandits Hindi is a sacral language, for the Presbyterian ministers it has long since been replaced by English, and for the Muslim mullahs Arabic rather than Hindi or Urdu is the sacral language.[21] Any effort at propagating Hindi is expected to be articulated by groups which have an element of religious agenda, with its own consequences. The excessive emphasis on the sacral nature of Hindi and its identification with Hinduism is, therefore, likely to alienate non-Hindus from learning it, let alone adopting it as an ethnic language.

The emphasis on *Shudh* (Pure or Standard) variety on the part of most propagators of Hindi, including the Indian and India-trained teachers, is an impediment to the revival of Hindi in the diaspora. As Sperl (1980: 9) has observed, 'language loyalty movements among Indians in Trinidad attempt to counter the language shift towards Creole/English by promoting not Trinidad Hindi, the ordinary local vernacular, but Standard Hindi as spoken in India'. For Indo-Trinidadians learning Standard Hindi is as good as learning an alien language. In fact, most of those who have learnt Standard Hindi become diffident, and even apologetic, when they have to use that language in interacting with Indian nationals.[22]

How to interpret the burst of Hindi in the audiovisual media over the last few years? One must remember that Hindi movies and Hindi film music have always been popular among Indo-Trinidadians. Hindi movies portray what Indo-Trinidadians perceive as the society and culture of their ancestral land. They even seem to subconsciously identify themselves with the dynamics of family and folk culture depicted in the Hindi movies. The impact of Hindi film music, both songs and dance, on what Indo-Trinidadians call 'the Indian culture' in Trinidad is pronounced, as witnessed in such extremely popular programmes as *Mastana Bahar* and 'Indian Cultural Pageant'.[23]

What the average Indo-Trinidadian is interested in is Hindi *movies*, and not Hindi *per se*. Hindi movies screened in Trinidad invariably carry English subtitles and a few popular Hindi movies have even been dubbed into English. In their Sunday magazine section, the two prominent dailies often include supplements—*Tamasha* (*Sunday Express*) and *Savera* (*The Sunday Guardian*)—containing news and articles in English from Bollywood, the Indian equivalent of Hollywood. The average Hindi moviegoer's familiarity hardly exceeds a few routine phrases or popular expressions and a few lines of film lyrics.

Similarly, most Indo-Trinidadians listen to Hindi songs without understanding them.[24] These songs may be characterised by soothing melodies, lilting tunes or fast beats. Their appeal may be in the emotions or sentiments they seem to convey or in their easy adaptability to dance. Reviewing Mani Ratnam's film 'Bombay', Joannah Bharose wrote in *Trinidad Guardian* (7 September 1995), 'I could not understand a word of Hindi or Arabic but the music sounded great'. Similarly, columnist Omatie Lyder declared in *Daily Express* (6 May 1995):

> For years I have listened to Indian singers and sung along with them. It never mattered to me that I couldn't translate a verse of Kishore Kumar's or Lata Mangeshkar's songs. Not understanding them didn't take away the joy of listening. The same can be said of my fascination with Latin music.

The interest in Hindi songs sans their meaning can result in piquant situations with songs being sung in wrong situations. The author has heard a funeral song sung at a farewell function and a love song with sexual innuendoes sung at a Thanksgiving party.

Considering the nature of Trinidadian ethnic politics in general and the politics of culture in particular, the increasing observability of Hindi in the audiovisual media appears to be an attempt by sections of Indo-Trinidadians to occupy the keenly contested cultural space in the country. In ethnic terms this 'culturalisation of politics' (see Jain 1997: 351) is significant considering the Indo-Trinidadian perception that 'national culture' in Trinidad is almost exclusively identified with the Creole culture of Afro-Trinidadians. Substantively too, the Hindi programmes (mostly film-based) offer ready-made material to fill the available broadcast/telecast time. Shrewd entrepreneurs are always alert to exploit the situation to their advantage.

In the ethnic politics of Trinidad, the Hindi question has often acquired a political colour. According to John La Guerre, in the post-colonial suffrage situation, 'Hindi and the institutions associated with Hindi...were seen as centres of resistance against the newly independent government and also as centres for opposition resistance'. Viewed in this light, the first International Hindi Conference held in Trinidad in April 1992 appeared to him to be a celebration, of 'not really a language, but the presence of the Indians on the social and political stage of Trinidad and Tobago' (*Daily Express*, 20 April 1992).

In view of the ethnic tag attached to Hindi, anybody explicitly advocating its introduction in schools during the early decades of independence would have been accused of advancing an ethnic cause. Campbell's (1992: 84) following commentary is indicative of this:

...the biggest surprise in terms of Indian demands for something which would benefit Indians alone came from Hans Hanoomansingh in December 1970, when he called for a full debate on the teaching of Hindi and Urdu in Indian schools. Nothing had been heard in Parliament about this since the PNM[25] first came to power. Hanoomansingh never got his debate; and there is no indication that the majority of the Indian parliamentarians would have supported him.

Even today nobody dares to raise the cause of Hindi without being apologetic about it. In his speech at the flag raising ceremony to officially signal the launching of the Fifth World Hindi Conference, Foreign Affairs Minister Ralph Maraj was constrained to assure that there was nothing to fear from sections of the national community seeking to rediscover their roots, since Trinidad and Tobago is a cosmopolitan country. He even expressed a desire to see the Afro-Trinidadians teach their ancestral languages (*Daily Express*, 17 February 1996).

Conclusion

The revival of Hindi in Trinidad and the prospect of it becoming an ethnic language of Indo-Trinidadians is thus apparently enigmatic. The basic material requirements for the revival and development of Hindi are there: The Indo-Trinidadians form 40.3 per cent (1990 census) of the population; organisations such as Bharatiya Vidya Sansthaan (established in 1966) and Hindi Nidhi (Hindi Foundation of Trinidad and Tobago, established in 1986) provide the institutional base and direction; the Indian Council for Cultural Relations and the High Commission of India extend academic support and guidance;

Hinduism, the religion of the majority of Indo-Trinidadians, uses Hindi in liturgy as well as in popular religion; and the audiovisual media give exposure to the language in high density.

However, what is lacking is functionality. Hindi is seldom sought to be used in interpersonal communication in everyday life within the community. Even the few who have learnt the language feel diffident to use it in speech. The possibility of Hindi being used in economic transactions or in administration is extremely remote as these involve inter-ethnic group interactions. Moreover, since ethnicity has evolved even without language providing the emotional glue, and in view of the likely identification of Hindi with Hinduism, there is not much use of Hindi as an ethnic binder either.

Thus, in the light of the general domination of Trinidad Creole English and Standard English in the wider society, and in the absence of economic motivation or the administrative necessity for learning Hindi, the prospect of Hindi becoming the ethnic language of Indo-Trinidadians and their becoming bilingual does not appear to be bright. Hindi will certainly take deep roots as a sacral language of the Hindus and it will be widely tapped and used in the cultural domain. Motivated by divergent reasons, some Indo-Trinidadians will continue to learn Hindi with varying degrees of commitment and competence. In brief, while Hindi may develop as a language among Indo-Trinidadians, Indo-Trinidadians are not likely to become a distinctive speech community.

Notes

1. There is not a single reference on this theme in the Special number of *Sociological Bulletin* on 'Indians Abroad', guest-edited by Sharma (1989); Jain's (1993) survey of literature on Indian diaspora lists only one study on this subject.

2. Bhojpuri is the westernmost member of the Magadhan family of Indo-Aryan languages spoken in northeastern India (see Grierson 1919: 125–26).

3. The virtual babel of Indian tongues was, however, welcomed by the plantocracy: 'The proprietors or managers of sugar estates purposely choose men speaking three or four separate and distinct languages not understood by each other, in order to prevent combination in cases of disturbances among them', observed Baptist missionary Reverend Bronkhurst (1888: 18).

4. In her study, Mohan (1978: 12 and 35) found 'evidence of this initial diglossia in the pockets of variation in present-day Trinidad Bhojpuri where the formal options correspond to features which are functionally equivalent in the

different dialects of Indian Bhojpuri'. She noticed 'the lexicon and the Present/ Optative forms of the copula' to be the aspects manifesting 'the highest degree of dialectal variation (due to differences between the Indian parent varieties rather than to Creole contact)'.

5. Unlike in British Guiana and Trinidad, where Bhojpuri formed the basis for dialect-levelling, in Surinam (Dutch Guiana) the evolution of Sarnami was largely influenced by Avadhi (Damsteegt 1988).

6. Long after Grierson (1919) classified Bhojpuri as a Magadhan language rather than as an eastern variety of Hindi as was previously assumed, there is a tendency among some scholars to mistake it (as also some other languages/ dialects) as a dialect of Hindi. For instance, Tinker (1993: 53) refers to Bhojpuri (the language spoken by people of Shahabad) as 'a form of Hindi'. Similar misrepresentation is also noticed with reference to south Indian languages. For instance, 'the Malabar language' (Malayalam?) is identified as Tamil (ibid.: 77).

7. In British Guiana, Reverend William English had pleaded with the Wesleyan Methodist Missionary Society in London to 'send a missionary to us who is able to speak the language of India'. This resulted in Reverend J. E. S. Williams, who had worked with Tamils in Ceylon (Sri Lanka), being sent to British Guiana in 1852 (Ruhomon 1947: 207).

8. Reverend Morton uses the word 'Hindui' as including the Urdu dialect (Morton 1916: 67).

9. Mohan (1978: iii), who studied the morphology of Trinidad Bhojpuri in 1970s, notes: 'Ajie, my grandmother, who taught me this dying language from my earliest childhood in solitary defiance of convention, and, more recently, helped me to decipher and transcribe all my recorded data'.

10. Following Freed (1982: 1) we may broadly define language attrition as the loss of any language or any portion of a language by an individual or a speech community. It may refer to the declining use of mother tongue skills by those in bilingual situations or among ethnic minorities in (some) language contact situations where one language, for political or social reasons, comes to replace another. Mohan and Zador (1986: 293) refer to 'a community-wide shift to a new native language, in such a way that the community of native speakers ceases to be self-renewing, and/or the speakers cease to be native' as language death.

11. Significantly, in the 1940s the Franchise Commission had proposed that universal adult suffrage should be restricted only to those who were competent in the English language.

12. Trinidad Creole English (Trini) and Standard (Trinidadian) English are lexically related. They coexist 'not as discrete codes but as a continuum of speech forms exploited according to the communicative intent of members of the speech community' (Sealey 1983: 4). For a more general theoretical statement on 'cultural continuum', see Drummond (1980).

13. See the dictionaries compiled by Mahabir and Mahabir (1990) and Sookhoo (1985). It is noteworthy that in compiling A Dictionary of Common Trinidad Hindi, Mahabir and Mahabir have relied on 'purely oral' sources and have not consulted any existing Hindi-English dictionary or glossary. Sookhoo's Hindi–English dictionary, which cannot claim such an originality of sources, has in addition, however, proverbs and 110 pithy sayings. A Dictionary of Hindi Names has been compiled by Orie (1994).

14. Polite routines such as *Sitaram* (Greetings) and *Kaisen hai* (How are you?), and routinised sequences such as *Shabas, beta!* (Bravo, son!) and *Wha-wha* (exclamation) are still in use in Trinidad.

15. Sometimes an expression used by a public figure becomes a catchword: For instance, the expression *Nemackharaam* (ingrate) used by Basdeo Panday (the then Leader of Opposition in Parliament and now the Prime Minister of Trinidad and Tobago) in 1986 to refer to some of his erstwhile cabinet colleagues in the then National Alliance for Reconstruction government has become so popular that even people of non-Indian descent use it now.

16. For instance, Sookhoo's (1985: iii) 'ajie' could not speak English. She told stories in Hindi, and someone had to say *Han* at the end of each sentence.

17. Visiting Hindu missionaries from India such as Pandit Hariprasad Sharma (in 1914) and Pandit Kunj Beharry Tiwary (in 1917) had commented on the loss of native language among Indians and its adverse impact on Hinduism. The arrival of Pandit Jaimini Mehta (1928) marked a milestone in the development of Hindi as he assisted in the establishment of a Hindi school in Marabella. Also, even before their establishment/incorporation, the Hindu organisations had been in the vanguard of the effort to retain or revive Hindi. According to Forbes (1984: 156), 'whereas many Sanatanist Hindi schools were extremely ephemeral, the Arya Samaj schools were maintained, during the 1930s and early 1940s, in a semi-institutional manner...'.

18. Sanskrit is the sacred liturgical language of Brahmanic Hinduism in India. Traditionally, Brahmans, the priestly caste group, held a monopoly over it. In Indian diaspora, however, it is Hindi which has taken the place of Sanskrit, from which it is derived, in Hindu liturgy. The credit for rendering the famous Hindu epic *Ramayana* into Avadhi–Hindi, so that laypersons can understand it, goes to Goswami Tulsidas, whose *Ramacharita Manas* is a popular religious text among the Hindus in Trinidad.

19. Forbes (1984: 157–58) highlights the point that Pillai was a 'Madrassi' and a Christian, and Hindi was not his parents' native tongue nor did it have direct cultural import for him. 'His interest in the language was motivated by broader cultural nationalism, similar to that of Swami Dayananda, the Arya Samaj founder, who learned Hindi late in life because he recognised it to be the language of Indian unification'.

20. Ramlakhan also has to her credit *Smaran*, a compilation of Hindi Bhajans in Nagari script with transliteration in Roman alphabets and translation in English. Incidentally, in his collection of poetry in Hindi written by people of Indian origin abroad, Pandey (1985) has included the poems of two Trinidadians, both of whose mother tongue is English. They are Karmchand Ganesh, teacher at the Bharatiya Vidya Sansthaan, and Tara Vishnudayal Singh.

21. About 13 per cent of the indentured immigrants who came from India were Muslims. According to the 1990 census, Muslims constitute 5.8 per cent of the population of Trinidad and Tobago. Like Trinidad Bhojpuri, Urdu, a language which most Muslims spoke, has faced attrition. There are a few elderly Muslims who can converse in Urdu. Observations made about language attrition, retention and survival will thus hold good for the rest of the Muslim population. Currently, under the auspices of the Anjuman Sunnatul Jamaat Association (the major organisation representing the Indo-Trinidadian Muslims), the Haji

Ruknuddeen Institute of Islamic Studies, offers a course in Arabic, *not* Urdu, as part of a Diploma in Islamic Learning.

22. Tinker (1993: 211) refers to an instance in British Guiana in the colonial era: 'When the allegation was made in Demerara that the interpreters of the Immigration Department could not speak Hindustani, the Agent-General defended the proficiency of his staff, though he admitted that they spoke a "literary" form of the language'. He quotes the following communication (dated 14 March 1883) from Robert Mitchell, Immigration Agent-General, British Guiana, to the Governor, 'I remember Sir Richard Temple [Lieutenant–Governor of Bengal] addressing a Bengali return immigrant at the Transit Depot in Calcutta in his native tongue, which he spoke fluently, and the man asked me in Creole French what His Honour had said'.

23. That this impact is not necessarily positive has been stressed by some Indo-Trinidadian commentators. Maharaj (1995: 31–32) speculates that the Indo-Trinidadians would be more creative if they had not started imitating the packaged Hindi film culture and music. He bemoans that Indo-Trinidadian drama has become almost extinct, and at ceremonies like *matikor, barahi, chathi* and weddings, folksongs are, by and large, replaced by loud speakers providing film music.

24. It is interesting to note that a key objective of Hindi Nidhi's newly designed Hindi courses for beginners is to help them 'comprehend dialogues and songs from Hindi films' and 'read and understand Ramayana' (Hindi Nidhi's advertisement in *Trinidad Guardian*, 8 September 1995).

25. The People's National Movement (PNM) is the political party founded by Dr Eric Williams in 1955. It has always been perceived, not only by Indo-Trinidadians but also by Afro-Trinidadians, as a party mainly representing the interests of Afro-Trinidadians.

References

Berko-Gleason, Jean. 1982. 'Insights from Child Language Acquisition for Second Language Loss', in Richard D. Lambert and Barbara F. Freed (eds.): *The Loss of Language Skills*. Rowley, Mass.: Newbury House Publishers, pp. 13–23.

Bronkhurst, Reverend H. V. P. 1888. *Among the Hindus and Creoles of British Guiana*. London: T. Woolmer.

Campbell, Carl. 1992. *Colony and Nation: A Short History of Education in Trinidad and Tobago, 1834–1986*. Kingston, Jamaica: Ian Randle Publishers.

Damsteegt, Theo. 1988. 'Sarnami: A Living Language', in R. K. Barz and J. Siegel (eds.): *Language Transplanted: The Development of Overseas Hindi*. Wiesbaden: Harrassowitz.

Domingue, Nicole Zuber. 1971. *Bhojpuri and Creole in Mauritius: A Study of Linguistic Interference and its Consequences in Regard to Synchronic Variation and Language Change*. Unpublished PhD dissertation, University of Texas (Austin).

Drummond, Lee. 1980. 'The Cultural Continuum: A Theory of Intersystems', *Man*(NS), 15: 352–74.

Durbin, Mridula Adenwala. 1973. 'Formal Changes in Trinidad Hindi as a Result of Language Adaptation', *American Anthropologist*, 75(5): 1290–304.

Forbes, Richard H. 1984. *Arya Samaj in Trinidad: A Historical Study of Hindu Organisational Process in Acculturative Conditions*. Unpublished PhD dissertation, University of Miami (Florida).

Freed, Barbara F. 1982. 'Language Loss: Current Thoughts and Future Directions', in Richard D. Lambert and Barbara F. Freed (eds.): *The Loss of Language Skills*. Rowley, Mass.: Newbury House Publishers, pp. 1–5.

Gambhir, Surendra K. 1981. *The East Indian Speech Community in Guyana: A Sociolinguistic Study with Special Reference to Koine Formation*. Unpublished PhD dissertation, University of Pennsylvania (Philadelphia).

———. 1986. 'Mauritian Bhojpuri: An International Perspective on Historical and Sociolinguistic Processes', in U. Bissoondoyal and S. B. C. Servansing (eds.): *Indian Labour Migration*. Moka, Mauritius: Mahatma Gandhi Institute, pp. 189–206.

Gamble, Reverend W. H. 1866. *Trinidad, Historical and Descriptive: Being a Narrative of Nine Years' Residence in the Island*. London: Yates and Alexander.

Grierson, George A. 1919. *Linguistic Survey of India* (Vol. I, Part 1). Calcutta: Government of India.

Jain, Ravindra K. 1993. *Indian Communities Abroad: Themes and Literature*. New Delhi: Manohar.

———. 1997. 'A Civilisational Theory of Indian Diaspora and its Global Implications', *The Eastern Anthropologist*, 50(3–4): 347–55.

Klass, Morton. 1961. *East Indians in Trinidad: A Study of Cultural Persistence*. Prospect Heights, Illinois: Waveland Press.

Laurence, K. O. 1971. *Immigration into the West Indies in the 19th Century* (Chapters in Caribbean history 3). Aylesbury, Bucks, UK: Ginn and Co.

Mahabir, Kumar and Sita Mahabir. 1990. *A Dictionary of Common Trinidad Hindi*. El Dorado, Trinidad: Chakra Publishing Co.

Maharaj, Ashram B. 1995. 'Impact of Indian Movies', in *The Indian Review* (Commemorating the Sesquicentenary of the Arrival of Indians to Trinidad, 1845–1995). Couva, Trinidad: Indian Review Committee, pp. 31–32.

Moag, Rodney F. 1979. 'The Linguistic Adaptations of the Fiji Indians', in Vijay Mishra (ed.): *Rama's Banishment: A Centenary Tribute to the Fiji Indians, 1879–1979*. Auckland: Heinemann Educational Books, pp. 112–38.

Mohan, Peggy Ramesar. 1978. *Trinidad Bhojpuri: A Morphological Study*. Unpublished PhD dissertation, The University of Michigan (Ann Arbor).

Mohan, Peggy and Paul Zador. 1986. 'Discontinuity in a Life Cycle: The Death of Trinidad Bhojpuri', *Language*, 62: 291–319.

Morton, Sarah E. (ed.). 1916. *John Morton of Trinidad: Pioneer Missionary of the Presbyterian Church in Canada to the East Indians in the British West Indies (Journals, letters and papers)*. Toronto: Westminster Company.

Naipaul, Seepersad. 1976. *The Adventures of Gurudeva and Other Stories*. London: Andre Deutsch. (First published in 1943 as *Gurudeva and Other Indian Tales*).

Niehoff, Arthur and Juanita Niehoff. 1960. *East Indians in the West Indies*. Milwaukee, Wisconsin: Milwaukee Public Museum.

Orie, Siddartha L. 1994. *A Dictionary of Hindi Names: Towards a New Consciousness*. Freeport. Trinidad and Tobago: Hem Publications.

Panday, Trilochan. 1993. 'Trinidad mein Hindi' (in Hindi), *Gagananchal* (Indian Council for Cultural Relations, New Delhi), 16(4): 109–22.

Pandey, Raj Kishore (ed.). 1985. *Videsh Ke Hindi Kavi* (in Hindi). Hyderabad: Hindi Prachar Sabha.

Ruhomon, Peter. 1947. *Centenary History of the East Indians in British Guiana, 1838–1938*. George Town: The Daily Chronicle.

Sealey, W. (in collaboration with P. Aquing). 1983. 'A Sociolinguistic Profile of Trinidad', Paper presented for the Caribbean Lexicography Project, June (Mimeo).

Sharma, S. L. (ed.). 1989. *Sociological Bulletin*: Special Number on Indians Abroad, 38(1).

Siegel, Jeffrey. 1975. 'Fiji Hindustani', *Working Papers in Linguistics* (Honolulu: University of Hawaii), 7(3): 127–44.

Singh, Kelvin. 1985. 'Indians and the Larger Society', in John La Guerre (ed.): *Calcutta to Caroni*. St. Augustine, Trinidad and Tobago: Extra Mural Studies Unit, The University of the West Indies, pp. 33–60.

Sookhoo, James R. 1985. *Hindi-English Dictionary: Build Your Hindi Vocabulary Through English*. St. Augustine, Trinidad: Trinidad Industrial Laboratories Research Ltd.

Sperl, Savitri Rambissoon. 1980. *From Indians to Trinidadians: A Study of the Relationship Between Language Behaviour, Socio-Economic and Cultural Factors in a Trinidad Village*. Unpublished MPhil dissertation, University of York (Toronto).

Tinker, Hugh. 1993. *A New System of Slavery: The Export of Indian Labour Overseas, 1830–1920*. London: Hansib Publishing Limited.

Vertovec, Steven. 1992. *Hindu Trinidad: Religion, Ethnicity, and Socio-economic Change*. London and Basingstoke: Macmillan.

Winford, Donald. 1972. *A Sociolinguistic Description of Two Communities in Trinidad*. Unpublished PhD dissertation, University of York (Toronto).

8

Race Relations, Ethnicity, Class and Culture: A Comparison of Indians in Trinidad and Malaysia*

Ravindra K. Jain

The purpose of this article is twofold: (a) to provide a comparative analysis of the situation of Indians in two widely different national settings, namely, Malaysia and Trinidad; and (b) to explore the interplay and the relative significance of such factors as race relations, ethnicity, class and culture in defining the varying identity of the Indians in the two countries. In particular, the article seeks to answer the following questions:

1. Why is it that a *race relations* framework is utilisable in Trinidad whereas *ethnicity* defines and locates the situation of Indians in Malaysia?
2. What are the factors which enable the Indian identity to be retained and activated in Trinidad and Malaysia? How may one juxtapose the variables of race, ethnicity and culture to arrive at the definition of Indian identity in 'plural' contexts?

*Originally published in *Sociological Bulletin*, Vol. 38, No. 1, March 1989, pp. 57–70.

3. What is the substantive status of defining the Indian community as a 'middle-class' in Trinidadian towns and as 'proletarians' on Malaysian plantations? Does the class structure
   prove to be the determining framework of Indian identity
   overseas or do the variables of race relations and ethnicity take
   priority?

Race Relations

We agree with Rex (1973) that there were three elements which were
necessary and sufficient to characterise a situation as a race relations
situation: (a) a situation of abnormally harsh exploitation, coercion
or competition between groups; (b) an individual in these groups
could not simply choose to move himself or his children from one
group to another and (c) that the system should be justified in terms
of some sort of deterministic theory, usually of a biological sort.

The construction of a race relations situation in Trinidad neces-
sitates our viewing the racial system there from a dual perspective:
(a) from the Indian (i.e., East Indian in the context of the West Indies)
perspective, and (b) from the Creole point of view.

West Indies scholars are agreed that from the Indian point of view,
a category distinction is made between 'Kirwal' (a Bhojpuri corrup-
tion of 'Creole') and 'coolie'. The former is used by the East Indians
to refer to all African and African-descent influenced population in
Trinidad. The latter, in turn, are recognised by the former through
the pejorative category term 'coolie'. This category distinction refers
to the history of population settlement in Trinidad: the import of
African slaves from 1777 onwards and their emancipation in 1833
and the import of indentured labourers from India from 1848
onwards, and their constituting nearly half the population of the
island by the 1980s. This category distinction has had all the
attributes of racial antipathy and bitterness and has been the main
obstacle in the struggle for Afro-Indian solidarity in Trinidad and
Tobago (cf. Ryan 1966, Samaroo 1985).

However, the Indian perspective has been distinct from as well as
subsumed into a more powerful and enduring West Indian racial
framework based on the sociocultural evaluation of gradations of
colour according to the polar contrast as well as intermixture between

'whites' and 'blacks'. In the West Indies perspective, the term *Creole* has the connotation of the original Spanish term *Criollo* as 'born in, native to, committed to the area of living' and it is used in relation to both white and black, free and slave. In a structural–historical framework such as that provided by Rex, the category-term *Creole* in this perspective refers particularly to freed slaves, the offspring of mixed marriages and 'poor whites', namely, a 'group in colonial society (which) is the germ of a new society developing in the womb of the old' (Rex 1978: 24).

There are two characteristics of the *Creole* model which should be noted at the outset. The East Indian group is not accommodated in this model; they are aliens and in an almost literal sense 'outcaste' from the model. The consciousness and summation of history of the people of the West Indies severely exclude people of the Indian origin from this model. Since this is ideologically the more powerful, transnational (Caribbean) model in Trinidad and Tobago it explains why all *Creole* and white authors (cf. Braithwaite 1975, Brereton 1981 and Williams 1964) have given such short shrift to the demographically dominant East Indian group in the population of Trinidad and Tobago and of Guyana (cf. remarks to this effect by Smith 1984: Ch. 7). A second characteristic of this model is that it answers to the imperatives of acculturation as contrasted with interculturation (on this see later), namely, it provided to the *Creoles* what has been called the 'Afro-Saxon' model of mobility. If during the Black Power movement of the 1970s Eric Williams was criticised and an (abortive) effort made to somehow seek alliance between the African and the East Indian groups, what was being run down was this 'white-mask' aspect of the *Creole* model.

The East Indians of Trinidad and the Relevance of Race

Strictly speaking, then, the identity of the East Indian group in Trinidad is not expressed in terms of the racially-grounded framework of the *Creole* model.

To recapitulate, the Indian model expresses the distinction and antipathy between the Africans and East Indians while the Creole model, which is expressive of the truly colour-based status distinctions in Trinidadian society, should be seen primarily in terms of the white-black antipathy from which the East Indians are excluded. However, the demographic and historical coexistence of Africans and East Indians in Trinidad society for more than two generations has given rise to a process of 'interculturation' (cf. Jain 1986) between the Indian and the *Creole* models. That, primarily, is the reason why the East Indian-*Creole* relations in this society may be seen as a corollary of 'race relations' rather than merely of 'ethnicity', that is, the non-antagonistic co-existence of two structurally disparate cultural groups. The caste system of the East Indian group, is strictly speaking ideologically a hierarchical system contrasted with systems of individualism and equality such as the western class system (Dumont 1970: 239–58). However, through contamination with the *Creole* model, the hierarchical 'caste' ideology of the Indian model has been transformed into a 'racist' ideology. This transformation has come about through a process of interculturation and is manifest concretely in the 'racial' endogamy of the East Indian group: 'caste having "passed" into race' (cf. Jain 1988: 137). To be sure, this has happened largely due to the segmentary potential of the caste system itself having interpenetrated the 'racial' system without its colour connotation. But in this process the biological and ancestry aspects of East Indian identity are emphasised and the progeny of mixed African and East Indian unions are designated as '*dougla*' which literally means 'bastard' in Hindi.

In other words, we can say that in the macro-framework of Trinidadian (or even Caribbean) society the identity of the East Indian group shows an alignment between culture and race, namely, the Indian derived culture of hierarchy and the West Indian model of a racial system. In that sense there is a straddling between race and ethnicity in the identity formation of the East Indian group. In postulating this we disagree with Van den Berghe's distinction (1967) between 'race' and 'ethnic group' where the former refers to 'a group that is socially defined on the basis of physical criteria' and the latter as 'socially defined...on the basis of cultural criteria'. It seems, on the other hand, more reasonable to go along with Smith (1984: 28):

> It is always necessary to distinguish first the biological stocks within a population on the basis of the relevant objective physical criteria; and then, secondly, to record and analyse the folk classification and criteria

that relate to race, to ethnicity, and the other biological conditions, paying special attention to their relationship.

The former distinctions may or may not be emically significant; hence everything depends on the people's folk classification. This, as we have seen, yields the two models: (a) Indian, and (b) *Creole*, in Trinidad. Secondly, whether or not the importance of ethnicity or race is paramount will depend on whether or not the three indicators of race relations enunciated by Rex obtain in a particular situation. Of crucial relevance is criterion '(a)', namely, the existence of antagonistic relationships. By this test we are justified in locating the East Indian group in Trinidad within the framework of race relations rather than ethnicity *per se*.

Ethnicity in Malaysia

Despite the fact that, in a manner of speaking, both Trinidad and Malaysia are 'plural societies', there are crucial differences between the macro-structures of the two countries having a remarkable bearing on the identity of the Indian group in them. Let us first note some of the factual contrasts as a necessary input for discerning structural differences.

The situation of overseas Indians in Trinidad is, in many crucial respects, different from that of Indians in Malaysia. The obvious difference of geographical distance in the case of the former and of proximity from India in the case of the latter may be noted at the outset. Second, whereas Indians in Malaysia constitute a mere 10 per cent of the population, they are as much as half of the total population of Trinidad and Tobago. Third, whereas the majority of the recruits for Trinidad came from north India, the Malayan recruits were largely south Indians, mainly Tamils. Fourth, immigrant Indians were introduced in Trinidad to work on the seasonal crop of sugarcane as indentured labourers, whereas in Malaysia after initial experimentation with large-scale sugarcane and coffee planting with indentured Indian labour (1840–1910), the bulk of Indian labourers was recruited to work for the perennial crop of rubber under the 'Kangany system' from 1910 to 1938. The latter was markedly different from the former system in many respects: indenture implied an *individual contract* for a period of three to five years but the Kangany system was essentially geared to indefinite employment in the rubber estate sector on the basis of a *gang member's* loyalty to and supervision under a recruiter–foreman (Kangany), usually from the same village or region in India as the labourer himself. Family, kin and caste ties were preserved and respected much more in the Kangany system than under indenture. Similarly, patron–client ties between the Kangany and his recruits—even when they left one estate and took up employment on another under pressure of 'crimping' during periods of high demand for labour—were an enduring feature of the latter system. In broad terms, therefore, the system of recruitment and settlement of immigrant Indian labour as it obtained in Trinidad and as was eventually established in Malaya could be distinguished as 'individualistic' in the former and 'communal' in the latter. Paradoxical as it may seem, in sociocultural rather than politico-economic terms the indentured recruit in Trinidad had greater occupational freedom than his Kangany-recruited counterpart in Malaya. Combined with the facts that in Malaya there was an indigenous peasantry (the rural Malays) while the remaining Crown Lands were progressively cornered by the large European-owned plantations under the highly profitable perennial crop of rubber, Indians in Malaya did not become peasants (for exceptions, cf. Jain 1966 and 1969). In Trinidad, on the other hand, the lack of an indigenous peasantry in a 'settlement society' (Jain 1986), the exigencies of seasonal rather than the perennial crop of sugarcane and the imperative to cut costs following an early depression in sugar prices (1884)—all conspired to create favourable conditions for the contract-expired or 'free' Indian recruits to take up peasantry.

In terms of the macro-structure of Malaysia, the location of the Indian group and its identity maintenance is clearly influenced by the lack of a 'colour–caste' system. Second, in particular reference to Indians in Malaysia, two of the three indicators of race relations are absent, namely, (a) there isn't a situation of abnormally harsh exploitation, coercion or competition between groups, and (b) the system is not justified in terms of a deterministic theory of a biological sort. I realise that there is room for disagreement here. Authors like Stenson (1980) have isolated race, class and colonialism as forming the trinity of a framework within which the historical experience of Malaysian Indians should be interpreted and a similar argument is bound to be advanced by proponents of a 'plantation mode of production' thesis (cf. Beckford 1972). However, we wish to counter these latter perspectives by appeal to methodological arguments. First, a comparative analysis shows the cultural system of race relations such as found in Trinidad to be absent in Malaysia. For example, even though Freedman (1960) went on to speak of the emergence of Malays, Indians and Chinese as 'structural blocks' in post-independence Malaysia, he was careful to note that the plural society in Malaysia does not consist of 'ethnic blocks', as Furnivall seemed to imply, but consists of 'ethnic categories within which small groups emerged to form social ties inside and across ethnic boundaries' (cf. also Husin Ali 1984: 14). Second, and positively, the Indians' plantation experience in Malaysia has been characterised by an 'enclave' situation of their life-chances and expectations (Jain 1988). Unlike in Trinidad, they have looked upon themselves as an appendage to south India and on Malaysian plantations have been effectively isolated and insulated from the wider currents of society. Finally, the variable of culture, as we shall see in a later section, has taken predominance over that of class and, therefore, emically we are not justified in positing 'a class for itself' emerging out of what is ostensibly and clearly a 'class in itself' on Malaysian plantations (Jain 1984).

Caste as Culture

I begin with the vicissitudes experienced by Indians in Malaysia and Trinidad as regards the traditional institution of social distinction and inequality in India, the caste system. To be able to appreciate the Indian caste system in dynamic terms it is useful to view it as a segmentary structure, that is, recognising its potential for fission and fusion in ascribing identities and positions to individuals, categories and groups according to context. Among south Indians resident on rubber plantations in Malaysia, *jati* exists as a framework for ascribed identity and distinction on various levels of the segmentary scale. For carrying out traditionally ascribed functions those of priests, drummers, washermen etc., for example, a distinction and hierarchy is maintained between the non-Brahman and Adi Dravida (roughly, ritually 'clean' and 'unclean' castes, respectively). It is a fact, for

Malaysia as a whole, that Brahmans did not migrate to work as estate labourers and are, therefore, conspicuous by their absence in labour-lines. Marital ties, increasingly but yet thinly, are formed right across the board of the caste structure (for example, there are reported cases of marriages between Adi-Dravida men and non-Brahman women, cf. Rajoo 1985), but there are two especially dense points of distribution: the Vanniar as a subcategory of the non-Brahman but in itself a 'fusion' of several endogamous non-Brahman *jati* of Tamil Nadu and the 'kindred-around-Kangany' or 'micro-caste' given the traditional preference for cross-cousin marriage among south Indians. The Vanniar level is located in the middle ranges of the segmentary caste structure and the 'micro-caste' at the lower end. This system of caste stratification is cut across by the common status of labour-line residents as wage labourers on the plantation, but only imperfectly. The system of Kangany recruitment and supervision and the formation of 'kindreds-around-Kanganies' among both the non-Brahman and the Adi-Dravida had led to the marginal retention of caste, by and large, in marriage, in the distribution of informal power and social control and even in the settlement pattern of a typical large European-owned rubber estate in Malaysia.

It is significant to note that the particular articulation of the labour-line residents' caste identities and their common identity as a 'plantation proletariat' found cultural expression in the 1950s and 1960s in and through collective mobilisation as 'Tamilians', that is, a sub-ethnic categorisation. I am not here concerned with the historical origins, manifestations and organisational vehicles in south India and Malaysia of this populist ideology; but its salient features were: (a) It cuts across castes without being specifically anti-caste but by being anti-Brahman; thus its target of attack conveniently were the Brahmans who were existentially not part of the 'lived in' experience of estate workers; (b) it was derived from India, hearkened back to another mythical target for Malaysian Indians, the southern Indians' rebellion against the dominant north Indians; and (c) it marginally reflected the knowledge and the overall structural significance of sub-ethnicity in this population of Malaysian Indians. It was a 'false consciousness' (that is, counter-factual to their potential 'class' consciousness as plantation proletariat) which functioned to legitimise symbolically their particular station in life as an Indian plantation proletariat in Malaysia.

Unlike in Malaysia, the recruitment and settlement of Indian immigrants to Trinidad from 1845 to 1917 as individual labourers struck a deathblow to caste as the traditional functional system of social stratification in the new setting. Neither the recruitment procedures, nor the long journey and least of all the patterns of life and labour on the sugar estates, were favourable to the recreation of mutually interdependent and clearly hierarchised functioning groups to which the immigrants belonged in rural north India. The historical delineation of this change has been done *ad nauseam* in Caribbean scholarship; the anthropological contributors to this topic also usually sketch in the historical background before reporting their field-data of the 1950s and 1960s. By comparing various anthropological reports on caste among overseas Indian communities (including those from the Caribbean areas) and placing them in relation to research on caste in South Asia, Mayer (1967: 18) draws out an empirical generalisation:

> ... within the pan-Indian sphere, there is a continuum of situations: at one end may be placed the Pathan pattern, in which the ideological elements of Hindu caste are at a minimum; and at the other end are overseas Indian communities, in which caste's structural characteristics are of less importance than is a caste ideology which is then applied to relations within the new society.

With some theoretical reservations about being able to distinguish sharply between 'structural characteristics' (for which better read 'structural-functional') and 'ideology', I take this view to be a succinct statement of the nature of significance of Hindu caste in the Caribbean. It can serve as a point of departure for our exploration of the culture of caste in shaping the experiences of stratification and mobility for the East Indian population in Trinidad. Let me note at the outset that the 'disintegration' thesis for caste in overseas Indian communities to which I subscribe for Trinidad is sometimes associated with an effort to mark out historically specific phases of 'deinstitutionalisation' and 'reinstitutionalisation' (Sharma n.d.). I believe such a view to be theoretically mistaken since destructuration and restructuration are coeval social processes. Mayor's conclusion about the endurance of a caste ideology in overseas Indian populations provides a corrective. In following up the implications of caste ideology for the case at hand we shall also explore a phenomenon to which the Malaysian case has already alerted us, namely, that this ideology and its fragmented structured manifestations can bear an altogether different practical relationship with Hinduism than reported for India.

In a situation like that of Indians in Trinidad what obtains of caste as a segmentary structure? It is worth emphasising that a conceptualisation of caste in segmentary terms does not predispose us to a sociology of groups but is geared more to a relational perspective among individual, categorical and also, potentially, group or quasi-group identities, as well as coalitions of agents.

Whereas in the case of Trinidad Indians, the functions of caste groups—internal cohesion (e.g., largely through endogamy), interdependence (e.g., through *jajmani* relationships) and hierarchy (through a precise attribution of ritual purity and pollution)—are largely removed, caste ideology of inclusion and exclusion operates at a high level of segmentation, incorporating the similarly-circumstanced non-Indian population, namely, the *Creole*.

Following the implications of the segmentary caste model for the *internal* structure of the East Indian population in Trinidad it may fairly accurately be said that there are no distinct levels above the *jati* of the individual. The north Indian hierarchical classification between the *dwija* (the twice-born) and the rest is not operational, nor for that matter, the fourfold *varna* scheme. Although attempts have been made by scholars to provide statistical models of endogamous and exogamous marriages in East Indian communities using the criteria of *jati* and *varna* which identities, with varying frequencies, the investigators claim are known to individual agents, none of these is anywhere near being mechanical models. The distinction between these two types of models closely follows Levi-Strauss (1963: 277–345) including the proposition that models of frequency-distribution in class societies practising homogamy and hypergamy remain statistical rather than mechanical ones. There remains a 'bonus of esteem' for members of the highest caste, that is, the Brahman, and a corresponding heritage of social obloquy for those of the lowest caste, that is, the Chamar. The former is centrally associated with the Brahmans' continuing role as high priests of Hinduism in Trinidad representing a structural transformation over their corresponding status in north India. As to the latter, when a person is abused as being 'Chamar', the reference is to his or her 'nation', a Caribbean designation more ethnic and racist than caste, and certainly not translatable directly as *jati*. There is a lingering folk form of earth-worship among the Chamar (personal communication from Steven Vertovec), but that seems to me to be related to a particular sectarian symbolisation of land possession by families who call themselves Chamar, rather than a symbolic representation of *jati* identity. That hierarchical distinctions of relative purity and impurity between the Chamar and the higher castes—including the Brahman—are completely obliterated is more than amply borne out by free exchange of labour and of food and drinks among members of teams for agricultural operations (*guayap* groups) reported for rural Trinidad as early as 1890s (Johnson 1972: 57) and, again, as recently as the 1960s. Klass (1961) gives the name *hur* for this arrangement and Schwartz (1967: 130–37) provides details. It is noteworthy that such mutual cooperation in manual labour tasks—especially for house construction—still takes place irrespective of caste even among largely urban and suburban East Indians.

The disintegration of caste as a functional system and the attempted transformation and incorporation of race at the higher margins of its segmentary structure were two conditions—internal and external respectively—for the East Indian population in Trinidad delimiting the social space for positions defining stratification and mobility in the new setting. In the initial stages, the repository of symbolic capital for this population was Indian culture. The bases for economic and social capital presented themselves in the material or embodied forms of owning land and house and the diversification of occupations on the one hand, and opportunities for education on the other. Profits in the form of institutionalised relative socio-economic positions were to be derived through symbolic struggles.

Class Variables

We have portrayed the institution of caste among Indians in Malaysia and Trinidad as a cultural variable. The reason for so doing, and not discussing caste as an aspect of social stratification, is that in the overseas Indian situation the ideological rather than the structural functional dimension of caste takes precedence (see e.g., the quote from Mayer in the previous section). Furthermore, caste 'passes' into ethnicity in Malaysia and into race in Trinidad. And, again, precisely due to the function of caste as a cultural variable in the context of ethnicity and race relations cutting across socioeconomic strata in Malaysia and Trinidad, respectively, we are alerted to the possibility that social stratification—comprising the dimensions of class, status and power—may not be the determinant framework of Indian identity in the overseas context. More specifically, through a sociohistorical sketch of the Indian community in Trinidad and Malaysia (see, Jain 1988) we have shown that the typification of the Indian community as a 'middleclass' in Trinidad towns and as 'proletarians' on Malaysian estates is sociologically inaccurate. Nor, for that matter, in a context of change can the Trinidad Indians be regarded as proletarians and the Malaysian Indians (contrary to rhetoric) present themselves as a burgeoning middle class. As Smith (1984) has shown in his extended review 'Culture, race and class in the Commonwealth Caribbean', neither the dichotomous class distinctions nor the trichotomous class-cum-colour divisions of these plural societies provide a sound analytical framework of their structure and dynamics. To be sure, the class structure of these societies deserves to be taken into account as an important variable, but in so doing we shall have to reckon with the historical colonial situation and end up with a long list of strata (cf. Rex 1978: 29–30) which are not based solely on the relations of these groups to the means of production. As Rex (1982: 208) has recently recognised with regard to racially divided societies,

> ... the sociology of stratification in colonial societies is as yet far from subtle enough to be able to distinguish the differences in class and status which coincide with the colour distinction. One point worth noting is that this distinction on colour lines occurs between groups of men who have something like the same economic position and cannot therefore be derivative from relation to the means of production.

What is true of class and colour based societies is undoubtedly true for societies based on ethnic distinctions also.

Conclusion

In an important article comparing culture and ethnicity in Guyana and Fiji, Jayawardena (1980: 448) stated, 'I have explored three main factors in the production of ethnicity: class, social status and power. Political processes arising from these fields of action transform ethnic identity into that self-conscious phenomenon one may term "ethnicity"'. What Jayawardena never discusses is why in Guyana the collective interests of class, status and power should generate or be associated with 'ethnic identity' in the first place, since in his argument 'ethnicity' evidently presupposes the former in order to exist. The answer to this conundrum lies in the obvious fact that identity is closely related to culture. The mutual dependence of race and culture in Trinidad and of ethnicity and culture in Malaysia is crucial in defining the collective identity of Indians in the two countries. This correlation also explains why religion is a strong diacritic of identity maintenance among Indians in Trinidad and language the prime indicator of ethnic and sub-ethnic identities among Indians in Malaysia.

References

Beckford, George L. 1972. *Persistent Poverty*. New York: Oxford University Press.

Braithwaite, L. 1975. *Social Stratification in Trinidad*. Jamaica: The University of the West Indies.

Brereton, B. 1981. *A History of Modern Trinidad, 1783–1962*. London: Heinemann.

Dumont, Louis. 1970. *Homo Hierarchicus: The Caste System and its Implications*. London: Weidenfeld and Nicolson.

Freedman, M. 1960. 'The Growth of Plural Society in Malaya', *Pacific Affairs*, 33: 158–68.

Husin Ali. (ed.). 1984. *Ethnicity, Class and Development in Malaysia*. Kuala Lumpur: Persatuan Sains Sosial Malaysia.

Jain, R. K. 1966. *Ramnathpuram Experiment: Paradigm of an Estate-Farm-Factory Community in Malaya*. Maitland, Australia: Mercury Press.

———. 1969. 'Kampong Padre: A Tamil Settlement Near Bagan Serai, Perak', *Journal of the Malaysian Branch Royal Asiatic Society*, 36 (Part 1, May 1963).

———. 1984. 'Caste, Estate and Class: The Dynamics of Social Stratification Among Indian Malaysians', *South East Asian Perspectives*, 1(1): 153–64.

———. 1986. 'The East Indian Culture in a Caribbean Context', *India International Centre Quarterly*. 13(2): 153–64.

———. 1988. 'Overseas Indians in Malaysia and the Caribbean: Comparative Notes', *Immigrants and Minorities*, 7(1): 123–43.

Jayawardena, C. 1980. 'Culture and Ethnicity in Guyana and Fiji', *Man* (n.s.), 15: 430–50.

Johnson, Howard. 1972. 'The Origins and Early Development of Cane Farming in Trinidad, 1881–1900', *The Journal of Caribbean History*, 5(November): 46–74.

Klass, Morton. 1961. *East Indians in Trinidad: A Study of Cultural Persistence.* New York: Columbia University Press.

Levi-Strauss, C. 1963. *Structural Anthropology.* New York and London: Basic Books.

Mayer, A. C. 1967. 'Introduction', in B. M. Schwartz (ed.): *Caste in Overseas Indian Communities.* San Francisco: Chandler, pp. 1–20.

Rajoo, Rengasamy. 1985. *Politics, Ethnicity and Strategies of Adaptation in an Urban Indian Squatter Settlement in Peninsular Malaysia.* PhD dissertation, Department of Indian Studies, University of Malaysia.

Rex, John. 1973. *Race, Colonialism and the City.* London: Routledge and Kegan Paul.

———. 1978. 'Introduction', in *Race and Class in Post-Colonial Societies.* Paris: UNESCO, pp. 11–52.

———. 1982. 'Conclusion: Racism and the Structure of Colonial Societies', in R. Ross (ed.): *Racism and Colonialism.* The Hague: Martins Nijhoff, pp. 199–218.

Ryan, Selwyn. 1966. 'The Struggle for Afro-Indian Solidarity in Trinidad and Tobago', *Trinidad and Tobago Index*, 1(4): 3–28.

Samaroo, B. 1985. 'Politics and Afro-Indian Relations in Trinidad', in J. La Guerre (ed.): *Calcutta to Caroni.* St. Augustine, Trinidad: The University of the West Indies, pp. 77–94.

Schwartz, B. M. 1967. 'The Failure of Caste in Trinidad', in B. M. Schwartz (ed.): *Caste in Overseas Indian Communities.* San Francisco: Chandler, pp. 117–48.

Sharma, K. N. (n.d.). 'Changing Forms of East Indian Marriage and Family in the Caribbean' (Mimeographed).

Smith, M. G. 1984. *Culture, Race and Class in the Commonwealth Caribbean.* Jamaica: The University of the West Indies.

Stenson, Michael. 1980. *Class, Race and Colonialism in West Malaysia: The Indian Case.* St. Lucia: University of Queensland Press.

Van den Berghe, Pierre. 1967. *Race and Racism: Comparative Perspective.* New York: John Wiley and Sons.

Williams, E. E. 1964. *History of the People of Trinidad and Tobago.* London: Andre Deutsch.

9

The Uneven 'Inclusion' of Indian Immigrants in Mauritius*

S. R. Mehta

In this article I am interested in looking at the 'inclusion' of Indian immigrants in the sociocultural and politicoeconomic set-up of Mauritius. For this purpose, I will follow Alexander's multidimensional model of 'inclusion' which focuses on core solidarity, ethnic out-groups and social differentiation within a multiethnic society.

The 'Inclusion' Model

Some of the basic elements of the 'inclusion' model are: solidarity, core solidarity group, ethnic out-group, terminal community and inclusion. Solidarity refers to the subjective feelings of integration that individuals experience for members of their social group. Solidarity problems differ from those of economics, politics and culture, according to Alexander among others (Alexander 1978, Parsons 1967 and 1971, and Shils 1975). A core solidarity group is the pivotal group of the society both historically and politically. With territorial

*Originally published in *Sociological Bulletin*, Vol. 38, No. 1, March 1989, pp. 141–54.

expansion or immigration, new ethnic groups are encountered which are called ethnic out-groups (Weber 1977). Terminal community refers to the widest solidarity group with which individuals feel significant integration. 'Inclusion' refers to felt solidarity and not simply to behavioural participation. To the extent that individuals are felt to be full members of the 'terminal' community, they have been, to that degree 'included' (Alexander 1980).

'Inclusion' can be measured by the degree to which the 'terminal community' has become more civil and less primordial. Primordial refers to the natural ties such as race, religion, kinship, language and territory (Geertz 1973 and Shils 1975). People feel direct emotional bonds if they share any of these traits. Generally, these ties are few. Sex, kinship, age and territory have been observed to be the main axes for solidarity identification in a simpler society. On the other hand, civil ties are more mediated and less emotional, more abstract and self consciously constructed and their emergence can be seen as a process of differentiation, similar to economic, political and religious differentiation, significant in modernisation theory.

The transition from primordial to civil solidarity is significantly related to economic and political transformation, characterising the modernisation process. Civil solidarity, apart from being influenced by various social, cultural, economic and political processes of development, is further enhanced by factors such as more efficient transformation and communication, increased geographical and cultural mobility, urbanisation, secular education, mass and elite occupational mobility, intermarriage and increasingly consensual civil ritualisation (Goode 1963, Lipset and Bendix 1960, and Shils and Young 1975).

Civil integration is generally unevenly attained since some of the highly differentiated institutions may at some later point in time tend to act as focussed solidarities opposing any further development. Further, civil integration is uneven as every national society has a historical core which will show primordial traits to a certain extent, despite a highly differentiated political framework (Alexander 1980).

In the aforementioned backdrop, Alexander sets his model of 'the Internal and External Axes of Inclusion'. Ethnicity has been defined as the real or perceived primordial qualities that accrue to a group by virtue of a shared racial, religious or national origin, including in the latter category linguistic and other cultural attributes associated with a common territorial ancestry (Schermerhorn 1970). 'Inclusion' of an ethnic out-group depends on two factors: (a) the external or environmental factor, which refers to the structure of the society that surrounds the core group; this includes the economic, political, integrative and religious systems of society; the more differentiated these systems are, the more inclusion becomes a legitimate possibility; and (b) the internal or volitional factor, which refers to the relationship between the primordial qualities of the core group and out-groups. To the degree that primordial complementarity exists between core group and out-group, members of the core group will tend to regard 'inclusion' of the out-group as a desirable possibility. Although both external and internal factors can be measured behaviourally, yet their most significant dimension is subjective and phenomenological. As such, to the degree that the social structure is differentiated and primordiality is complementary, the felt boundaries of the 'terminal' community will become more expansive and civil. Analytically, each factor can be examined by keeping the other constant to demonstrate the extent of solidarity from primordial to civil social order (Alexander 1980).

Mauritius

History

Ill de Maurice is called the pearl of the Indian Ocean. It represents an island community in an area of 720 square miles, measuring 38 miles by 28 miles. The island was first discovered by the Portuguese around 1509, but they did not make any settlement. Later on, it was named 'Mauritius' after the name of Prince Maurice of Holland, who occupied it in 1598. The Dutch, after taking possession of this country, introduced sugarcane plantation from Java. Because of the non-cooperative and vindictive attitude of the slaves who became violent and refused to work, the Dutch lost interest in the island and moved over to Capetown in South Africa. However, they returned around 1664 as they did not find it profitable to continue in South Africa and remained in Mauritius until 1710. Reunion Island, close to Mauritius, was already a French territory. The French took possession of the island in 1715 and many of the planters from the Reunion Island came over to settle here.

Mahe' de Labourdonnais (1735–47) was the founder of the French island. He utilised the slaves during his regime in developing agriculture, ship building, road construction, sugarcane plantation and in setting up industries. The runaway slaves were hunted and put to hard work. A large number of experienced labourers, skilled artisans and good technicians were also brought from India. Their contribution to the development of the island was substantial.

The British conquered this island in 1810. Some 800 Indian convicts were also brought in during the early period of their rule. Sugarcane production on the island increased and there was a regular flow of Indians into the island because of their hardworking nature right from 1834 to 1923. The Indian population went on increasing in proportion to the total 'general population'.

Both the Franco Mauritians (white planters) and the British (rulers) had joined in their efforts to suppress the immigrant Indians. The labour supply on the sugar estates was through the British and the Indians had to fight for their existence and welfare through the enactment of labour laws. The French had imposed their language on the Indians and had East India Company not intervened there would have been complete Franco phononising of Indians. Hinduism would have given way to Christianity and English language would not have found a place (Varma 1973).

The arrival of Mahatma Gandhi in the early part of 1901, just for a fortnight, and his speeches provided a turning point in the history of participation of Indian immigrants in the politics of Mauritius. The granting of limited franchise by the British had not improved the conditions of Indians. The coloured people, opposed to the white conservative group, had to seek the support of Indians to strengthen their democratic demands. They sought the support of Indians who helped tilt the political balance in their favour.

Mani Lall Doctor, inspired by Gandhi, took up the mission of improving the unhygienic living conditions of the Indians and aroused their political consciousness. The efforts of Mani Lall Doctor were carried forward by many persons of Indian origin including Dr Ramgoolam whose struggle figures as an outstanding event in the liberation of this nation. Inspired by the Arya Samaj Movement, which reached Mauritius in 1910, Dr Ramgoolam organised the oppressed labourers against the onslaughts of the planters and pushed forward the freedom movement. He fought for a new constitution which was obtained in 1947. In the first popular elections in 1948, he as a leader of the labour party defeated the 'Parti Mauricien', the new political organ of the conservatives. In 1964 elections, he accommodated the opposition in an All-Party Government. With his clear vision, love for the masses, reaction against imbalance, inequality and injustice, he got independence for the country in 1968 (Varma 1975).

Population

The present population of this tiny island is nearly one million, with an average density of 1,180 persons per square mile, thus making it one of the thickly populated countries of the world. Its population has more than doubled during the last three or four decades, the rate of growth being over three per cent a year during the 1950s. This was generally attributed to a high birth rate and declining death rate over the years. Improved health, medical facilities and eradication of Malaria resulted in bringing death rates down to 7.4 in 1974. On the other hand, the birth rate declined from 40.2 in 1962 to 22.7 in 1973 but it moved to 27.1 in 1974. This resulted in the increase of younger persons in the population. Mauritius has almost an equal proportion of males (50.06 per cent) and females (49.94 per cent) in its population. The distribution of population in urban and rural sectors is 44.14 per cent and 55.86 per cent respectively (Mehta 1981).

Mauritius is a multiethnic community. It is inhabited by the Hindus who constitute the majority group (60.33 per cent) and the Muslims who are 13.77 per cent of the total population. These two groups together constitute 74 per cent of the total population and are known as Indo-Mauritians. Their forefathers had come from India as indentured labourers. The older generation among them still speaks Bhojpuri, Telugu, Tamil or Marathi, and they understand Hindi or Urdu. In the recent past, there have been lots of efforts to promote these oriental languages. All the four *varnas* of the Hindu caste system exist whereas the Muslims are represented by various sects. Apart from Indo-Mauritians, the next important ethnic group is that of 'general population' comprising of European white settlers, African Creoles and Mixed Creoles, who constitute nearly 24.46 per cent of the total population. They are Christians and a majority of them are Catholics. They speak either French or Creole (local dialect which is broken French but includes words from Bhojpuri, Urdu, Tamil, Telugu, etc.). The Sino-Mauritians or the Chinese represent a very small proportion of the Mauritian population (1.44 per cent) but they constitute an important group because of their hold on trade and commerce. Most corner shops catering to the daily consumer needs of the people are owned by the Chinese. They are mostly of the Christian faith while some of them continue to remain Buddhists.

In short, the population of Mauritius represents a panorama of cultures from Asia, Africa and Europe with borrowing of ideas and cultural traits taking place among different cultural groups. Despite the acculturating influences of one ethnic group over the other during the last two centuries, the ethnic groups have by and large maintained their identity, language, religion and cultural systems (Mehta 1981).

Economy

The highlight of the Mauritius economy is the monocrop of sugar. Of the total land area (460,800 acres), more than half (272,500 acres) has been classified as agricultural land of which sugar cane cultivation alone accounts for 92 per cent. Sugar contributes nearly 90 per cent of the total export earnings, absorbs one-third of the total labour force and constitutes more than 50 per cent of the GNP. Before Independence, Mauritius had a stagnant economy. Population growth was upsetting the increase in national income. But during the 1970s, its economy showed positive signs of growth and development. As a result of record sugar crops and sustained high sugar prices during the early 1970s, the other sectors of development especially construction, trade and manufacturing industries received a boost.

The per capita income at current prices in 1976 was Rs 4,278. This need not be taken as indicative of a high level of living, as income disparities have been observed to be wide among different segments of the population. Nearly three-fourths of the sugar proceeds accrue from 21 sugar estates both for planting and milling operations (20 of these sugar estates are in the private sector and only one is in the public sector). The remaining one-fourth is owned by nearly 31,000 owners and tenant planters who mostly belong to the Hindu ethnic stock. The sugar estates in the private sector are owned exclusively by European white settlers. Nearly 16 per cent of the total labour force aged 15 and above is classified as unemployed and the majority of them (40 per cent) have been observed to be in the 15–24 years age group. Most of the unemployed have completed their primary or secondary education and are generally reluctant to work as labourers in agriculture. This sets the limit to the absorption of youth in the plantation economy (*Mauritius Economic Review* 1976).

After sugar, the next important crop is tea, with an annual production of 4 to 4.5 million kilograms. Rice cultivation is included in the diversified agricultural programme. The other crops cultivated on a limited scale include tobacco, maize, groundnuts, potatoes, tomatoes, other vegetables and pulses. There is an increasing interest among the villagers to grow vegetables in the front or back yards of their homesteads. Apart from agriculture, another occupation of the rural population is livestock breeding. There are nearly 25,000 cowherds on the island. The cattle breeding meets the meat and milk requirements of the people only partially. Largely these consumption articles are imported. It holds good even for fishing as the annual catch over the last few years has gone down due to over exploitation of the sea by the Japanese and others.

To supplement the agricultural sector, the manufacturing industries have been promoted by the Government. Until 1960, the only important industry was sugar. But as a consequence of incentives provided by the Government for import substitution, as many as 102 industries were established, the important ones being manufacture of furniture, aluminium and plastic goods, tuna fishing, canning, repairing shops and fertilizers. The Export Processing Zone Act of 1970 further provided incentives for manufacturing industries, and it was reported that by 1974 nearly 9,000 jobs were created in 36 industries under this Zone. These industries included electronics, toys, ready made garments as well as diamond cutting and polishing. Besides industries, tourism is another developing industry in Mauritius. In 1974 the inflow of tourists as compared to pre-independence period had increased fourfold. As a consequence of expansion of agriculture and industry on the island, the service sector of the economy also increased considerably (*Mauritian Economic Review* 1976).

The Uneven 'Inclusion' of the Indian Immigrants: Sociocultural Differentiation and Integration

The core solidarity group in the context of this island is that of European settlers or planters who had complete inclusion of black Creoles and mixed Creoles within their fold through the religious system of Christianity. The value orientations of the blacks and mixed Creoles also reflected European ideas, beliefs and cultural traits. The ethnic out-groups were the Indo-Mauritians (Hindus and Muslims) and the Sino-Mauritians (Chinese). On account of their conversion to Christianity, many of the Chinese had acquired value orientations of the white settlers, but nevertheless, they had held on strongly to some of their social institutions such as the family and other groups, associations, etc. The numerically dominant ethnic out-group of the Hindus (60.33 per cent) together with a notable proportion of the Muslims (13.77 per cent) as against 24.6 per cent of the 'general population' provide an interesting profile of the uneven civil solidarity on the island.

Keeping the internal axis of 'inclusion' model constant, let us first analyse the external factors including economic, political, social and religious systems of the Mauritian society.

Mauritius still has the typical plantation economy and its monocrop of sugar. It is characterised by large scale enterprises. The capital investment and its return are concentrated in a few hands that might have acquired land at a relatively cheap price. Of the 21 sugar estates having sophisticated sugar mills, as many as 20 are owned by the private sector (European white settlers), whereas one is being managed by the public sector. It is observed that in 1974, out of the total area under sugar, as much as 56 per cent of it was cultivated by 21 sugar estates whereas 44 per cent was cultivated by 29,539 owner planters and 1,512 metayers (tenant cultivators). They were able to acquire land due to the policy of Morcellament which allowed parcelling of land to tillers with a view to retaining them on the sugar estates, following the banning of slavery. But these landowners and tenants have land-holding of less than five arpents (Arpent is a French measure for land-holding, it is slightly more than an acre) and the majority of them are having land-holdings of less than one acre. Even the average cane fields per *arpent* in the case of sugar estates or mill planters is three times more than that of owner-tenant planters.

This skewed distribution of land-holdings between the mill planters and owner-tenant planters speaks of wide disparities between the two. However, as a consequence of land ownership, these owner-tenant cultivators who primarily are Hindus have emerged as a middle class in the agricultural differentiation process. The majority of agricultural labourers also belong to the Hindu stock whereas in the coastal villages one observes a large number of black Creoles and mixed Creoles as fishermen. The Muslims in the countryside are either self-employed, traders or 'Banyans' (middlemen) in the fishing trade.

Despite the efforts of the government to promote industries, one finds a very limited entrepreneurship among the Indo-Mauritians. The industrial sector continues to be dominated by European multinationals or by the Chinese entrepreneurs. The trade and commerce again are in the hands of European multinationals and Chinese. A few of the Indo-Mauritians are in trade and commerce, majority of them being Hindu Sindhis and Muslim Gujaratis. Both are later immigrants to Mauritius. Most of the Muslims are located in urban centres and employed as skilled workers or self-employed technicians. The educated Indo-Mauritians do not find entry into the private sector dominated by European mill planters and multinationals. They are, by and large, absorbed by the bureaucracy because of the Hindu dominated political structure.

In the economic differentiation brought about by modernisation in agriculture and industry, we find the uneven 'inclusion' of Indo-Mauritians into different sectors of the economy. The educated youth, especially among the Hindus, refuse to work as labourers on the sugar estates. Instead, they prefer to work as technicians or skilled workers in the industries. The nature of work discourages them, but more importantly they have a built-in psychological resistance to work as labourers on sugar estates because of their history of bondage or exploitation during the colonial days.

Political emancipation appears to have fostered greater homogeneity among the core and ethnic out-groups on the island. Political struggle of Indo-Mauritians, who over a span of time had acquired a majority status under the leadership of Dr Ramgoolam, succeeded at last in winning universal suffrage. This resulted in the Independence of the country in 1968.

All along after independence, in the general elections, left-of-centre groups headed by the Indo-Mauritians especially the Hindus have been at the helm of affairs of the political setup, while the extreme fascist and left forces have found their places mainly in the opposition benches. In a few instances, there have been alliances among various political parties because of political differentiation process, but the national leadership has so far remained with the Hindus. During the 1976 elections, of the 70 seats the Mauritius Movement Militant (MMM) won 30 seats whereas the Labour Party in alliance with the Comited Action Musulman (CAM) got only 25 seats. The Parti Mauritian Social Democrate (PMSD), a party of the conservative forces, got seven seats. The nominated seats were shared as follows: three by Labour Party, one by PMSD and four by MMM. All other parties based on communal, religious or kinship bases were wiped out completely. Caste or kinship factors played an important part in this election. Despite MMM getting a majority, it could not form a government and the Labour Party ruled the country again in alliance with the conservative group of PMSD.

The political emancipation has helped in the emergence of local leadership and initiative. The elections to village councils gave a further fillip to the rise of local leadership. Political differentiation provided a constitutional framework which has promoted and encouraged the participation of all eligible members of different ethnic groups and this makes the move towards civil solidarity quite an achievement for the Mauritian society.

The social integrative dimension in the traditional or pre-industrial stage in Mauritius was largely characterised by the predominance of kin orientation and religious pluralism. With the onset of modernisation and industrialisation things have changed, leading to migration from rural to urban areas and weakening of the joint family system. All this has resulted in the loss of direct control of elders over the youth. This encouraged growth of personal choice and love as a basis of courtship and marriage. Consequently, the importance of marriage arranged by elders received a setback. This has raised the status of women who feel less dependent now on their husbands and are consulted more often on all important family matters. The spread of education among women has given them more opportunity to move out and take up jobs and positions in social life. New work situations and job opportunities have provided a platform for intermixing of different ethnic or religious groups and this has helped them to acquire more rational value orientations. These trends may be indicative of movement towards civil solidarity but these are visible more in urban than in rural areas. Even in the urban centres, inter-community or inter-ethnic marriages are not much pronounced. However, due to well established legal integrative mechanisms on the island, registered marriages are preferred to the traditional marriages for purposes of inheritance, etc. But in the case of Hindus and Muslims, they seem to be keen that their traditional marriages should also have sanctity equal to that of registered marriages. However, in many cases, both types of marriages are being performed. This type of liberal attitude towards marriage and family, together with a secular outlook, to a limited extent, has weakened both the institutions of family and marriage. In addition it has promoted many vices, such as teenage pregnancy, higher incidence of unwed mothers, prostitution, etc. Of late, Indo-Mauritians are getting conscious of these evils and with greater awareness and knowledge of their ethnic cultures, they are tending to show conservatism towards such undesirable aspects of social life. These reverse trends towards cultural identity hamper the 'inclusion' process towards civil solidarity.

However, it has been observed that religion continues to have a deep influence on the way of life of the people. In the early years of Indo-Mauritians' immigration to the island, many of them were converted to Christianity, but it did not happen with the later immigrants who were largely drawn from better socioeconomic backgrounds. Arya Samaj movement also helped halt conversion to Christianity. The Indo-Mauritians thus have been keen to maintain their religious exclusivism.

Turning to the internal axis with its focus on race, territory, kinship, language and religion, we find more evidence of uneven 'inclusion' of the ethnic out-groups into the Mauritian society. On the dimension of race, European settlers whether drawn from Holland, France or Britain, belonged to the white Caucasian stock, which facilitated their 'inclusion' into the core solidarity without any difficulty. Even the mixed Creoles of finely graded white to black colour, because of their religious affiliation, were included in this stock of 'general population' in Mauritius. The yellow Mongoloid racial stock of Chinese, in most cases, because of religious affiliation to Christianity are also included in the core solidarity. However, the Indo-Mauritians, belonging to the brown racial stock from India (both the Hindus and the Muslims), maintain their identity as such and do not merge into the core solidarity on this primordial tie. Territory as a primordial tie does not have much application in the context of Mauritius as almost all the groups moved into the island either from Europe, Africa or Asia. There does not appear concentration of any particular ethnic stock in a geographical area or region except that the Muslims are having some concentration in the urban centres while the Hindus in the rural areas. However, the road networks and communication facilities are so good that for all practical purposes it becomes difficult to differentiate the rural from urban areas.

Among the Indo-Mauritians and also among the Sino-Mauritians, caste and kinship ties are highly pronounced. The extended kinship ties have influenced family formation among the Indo- and Sino-Mauritians. Caste and sect have restricted the scope of mate selection for purposes of marriage among the Hindus and the Muslims. They have also played an increasingly important role in influencing the voting behaviour of Indo-Mauritians and their social interactional patterns both inside and outside the bureaucratic organisations. These primordial ties have thus set limits to the 'inclusion' process. On the dimension of kinship, the civil solidarity is a distant proposition.

Language as a primordial tie shows a greater degree of complementarity between the core solidarity and the ethnic out-groups. As a result of resentment shown by the Indo-Mauritians during the freedom struggle against the imposition of French language, special efforts have been made by the government in the post-independence period to promote oriental languages such as Hindi, Urdu, Tamil, Telugu, Marathi, Gujarati, Chinese, etc. But in spite of these efforts, French language permeates and mediates the Mauritian society. Although the official language of the government is English, one does not find a single newspaper in that language. All the newspapers, including political party bulletins are printed in the French language. The spoken language all over the island is Creole, a broken form of French which has words from other Indian regional languages. It is reported that at the time of British takeover of the island from the French, the British were committed not to disturb the language of the people. This led to the perpetuation of French and its sister 'Creole' on the island with the result that it is now a cementing force for Mauritians as a civil society. On this dimension, the Indo-Mauritians are included almost completely into the core solidarity group and the spoken 'Creole' language is the only commonly shared cultural trait by all.

Religion appears to be a key factor in influencing their way of life. It is essential to point out that religion has been included in both the external and internal axis of 'inclusion' model. However, in the case of external axis the thrust is on the religious institutional system while in the case of internal axis the focus is on religious life style. People of all the faiths on the island are more religious than their counterparts elsewhere. The attendance at the churches is generally quite impressive. The religious festivals of the Hindus or the Muslims or those of the Chinese are observed with great pomp and show. In fact, it is a nation of festivities and festivals. There is a grand admixture of faith and recreation observed in these festivities. Old folks have reverence and respect for the various deities and they perform the religious rites with sanctity, the young folks appear to enjoy the recreational aspects more than the religious ones.

There is increasingly more interaction within a religious group than between different religious groups. Religion thus prompts people to maintain their cultural identity, consistent with the normative structure and value pattern of each religious group. This factor keeps the Mauritians away from the civil solidarity.

To sum up, on the external axis, the Indo-Mauritians present a case of limited 'inclusion' into the economic, social and religious spheres of the civic solidarity of Mauritius. It is only in the political sphere that they have made their mark. This is evident from their role in the struggle for political independence as well as in political domination in the post-independence era. On the internal axis, their race, kinship and religion have prevented them from being included in the civil solidarity of Mauritius. The only factor that has contributed to their 'inclusion' into the civil solidarity is the language, that is, Creole, which is a commonly shared cultural trait of the masses in Mauritius. As such, the Indo-Mauritians present a case of uneven 'inclusion' into the core solidarity and civil social set-up of Mauritius.

References

Alexander, Jeffrey C. 1978. 'Formal and Substantive Voluntarism in the Work of Talcott Parsons: A Theoretical and Ideological Reinterpretation', *American Sociological Review*, 43(April).

Alexander, Jeffrey C. 1980. 'Core Solidarity, Ethnic Out-Group and Social Differentiation: A Multi-Dimensional Model of Inclusion in Modern Societies', in J. Dofny and A. Kiwowo (eds.): *National and Ethnic Movements*. London: Sage Publications.

Geertz, Clifford. 1973. *The Interpretation of Cultures*. New York: Basic Books.

Goode, William J. 1963. *World Revolution and Family Patterns*. New York: Free Press.

Lipset, S. M. and Reinhard Bendix. 1960. *Social Mobility in Industrial Society*. Berkeley: University of California.

Mauritius. 1976. *Mauritius Economic Review*. Port Louis: Ministry of Economic Planning and Development, Government of Mauritius.

Mehta, S. R. 1981. *Social Development in Mauritius: A Study on Rural Modernisation in an Island Community*. New Delhi: Wiley Eastern.

Parsons, Talcott. 1967. 'On the Concept of Influence', in T. Parsons (ed.): *Sociological Theory and Modern Society*. New York: Free Press.

———. 1971. *The System of Modern Society*. New York: Free Press.

Schemerhorn, R. A. 1970. *Comparative Ethnic Relations*. New York: Random House.

Shils, Edward A. 1975. *Centre and Periphery: Essays in Macro-Sociology*. Chicago: University of Chicago Press.

Shils, Edward A. and Michael Young. 1975. 'The Meaning of the Coronation', in Edward A. Shils (ed.): *Centre and Periphery: Essays in Macro-Sociology*. Chicago: University of Chicago Press.

Varma, Mohinder Nath. 1973. *Indian Immigrants and their Descendants in Mauritius*. Vacoas: Published by Author.

———. 1975. *The Struggle of Dr Ramgoolam*. Quatre Bornos: Published by Author.

Weber, Eugen. 1977. *Peasants into Frenchmen: The Modernisation of Rural France, 1870–1914*. Stanford: Stanford University Press.

10

Outsiders as Insiders: The Phenomenon of Sandwich Culture—Prefatorial to a Possible Theory*

Yogesh Atal

The two most populous societies of the world—China and India—have contributed both men and elements of their civilisation to almost all the cultures in Asia and beyond. Wherever one goes—the Pacific islands, Australia and New Zealand, Western and Eastern Europe, the Americas, and Africa—representatives of these two Asian cultures come to one's notice almost immediately. Their demographic and civilisational spread is so conspicuous that they have attracted attention of the scholars from a wide range of fields, and mostly from nationalities other than the Chinese and the Indian.

In earlier accounts of non-Indian or non-Chinese societies, the migrant Indian or Chinese remained neglected. Anthropological research, for example, focussed on the 'primitive' and was carried out in isolated tribal pockets. Even in India, anthropologists regarded the 200 and odd tribal groups as their intellectual domain.

*Originally published as 'Outsiders as Insiders: The Phenomenon of Sandwich Culture', *Sociological Bulletin*, Vol. 38, No. 1, March 1989, pp. 23–42.

Writing about *Pacific Indians*, Crocombe (1981: 7)—the editor of the book with the same name—informs that 'Indians sailed far and wide across the Pacific last century. They do not receive much mention in history books, partly because most worked in the less prestigious roles as cooks or seamen and partly because most of the histories have been written by and predominantly for Europeans'. This book, *Pacific Indians*, provides profiles of Indians living in the 20 countries of Melanesia, Polynesia, Micronesia and the countries of the Pacific rim (including Australia, New Zealand, Canada, Japan, Hong Kong, Thailand, Singapore, Malaysia, the Philippines and Indonesia). The presence of Indians in many small Pacific Island states is not known even to the Indians living in large congregations in some other Pacific countries. No Pacific Island nation contains as many members of a single language and cultural community (Crocombe 1981: 9). Field studies among Indians have also 'been carried out in varying degrees of completeness in such geographically diverse areas as Mauritius, Guyana, Fiji, Trinidad, Surinam, Guadeloupe, Martinique, Uganda, Kenya, Tanganyika, Natal, British Columbia, Jamaica, the Unites States...' (Schwartz 1967: xv).

The ubiquitous Indian has, of late, become the subject matter of intensive study and research. However, with only a few notable exceptions, such efforts are examples of 'outsiders being studied by outsiders'—of different types. Indians settled abroad are identified as a distinct group of outsiders by the receiving country; and these have been mostly studied by people not belonging to their group—the expatriate researchers from Europe or North America, some Indians from India, and some scholars of the host-country who are 'insiders' as native inhabitants but outsiders for the in-group of Indian settlers. It is only recently that Indian sociologists and anthropologists have begun showing interest in studying 'other' societies, including the Indians abroad. The topics researched so far, to quote Schwartz (ibid.: xv) again, include 'marriage and the family, caste, ethnic interaction, legal systems, social control, magic and religion, social organisation, social and cultural pluralism, population dynamics, differential fertility, migration, indenture systems, economic integration and exploitation, plantation systems, and sociocultural perpetuation and differential adaptation'.

II

Migrations from India have occurred in several waves. For example, 'The first wave of Indians in the Pacific Islands...were sailors' (Crocombe 1981: 8). The second wave consisted of the indentured labourers which began in 1864 with the arrival of Indians from Reunion to New Caledonia, but the massive flow was to Fiji from 1879 to 1916, under the well-known *girmit* system—the *Hindiized* version of the *agreement* that the migrants entered into with the British government to serve as indentured labourers on plantations for a period of five years and a promise of a free passage back home upon the completion of the *girmit* period. Then came the businessmen and traders, missionaries, and preachers and politicians. In most recent years, individual migrations have occurred bringing to the Pacific Islands professionals and technicians on short-term assignments. The colonial era facilitated inter-colony migration. It also encouraged migration to the coloniser countries for education and for employment contributing both to the so-called 'brain drain' and the dislocation of the labour-force. In the post-colonial era that began in the mid-1940s, migration from the countries of the Third World has taken on new forms. Migratory flows are now multidirectional, at times reciprocal, and are caused by a wide variety of factors—both sociocultural and technological. Of late, it is the Middle East that has promoted many Asians—including Indians—to 'jump from bullock carts to jumbo jets' (Atal 1986: 3). Migration to the Middle East (for short, MIME) appears in some ways similar to the *girmit* (indenture) migration of the 19th century. But it is different from the indenture and has added a new dimension to international migration:

> Middle East has amassed enormous money but has limited manpower; its geology is wet with gasoline, but its geography is dry as sand; the restrictions that the religion imposes do not attract fun-loving tourists from affluent societies of the West. It is its geology that has shaped its economy which, in turn, is now prompting the development process. The sudden riches of the region offer attractive pulls to the poor of Asia ... (Atal 1986: 4).

Migration to the Middle East has contributed to the massive exodus of people from India and the migrants have found opportunities to relocate themselves in congregations to develop community life to share their joys and sorrows away from the families left behind. I reproduce below the distinguishing features of MIME:

1. Unlike the migration of labour during the colonial period, this form of migration is neither coercive, nor conscribed, nor indentured. In other words, role of the government of the country of the migrant, in this new context, is indirect and mostly regulatory in character. Government intervention is noticeable in those cases where the government itself enters into a contract and sends its employees to carry out the task with the right to recall.

2. It is not governed by the old colonial ethos. It involves entry into a different administrative set-up.

3. The migration is of a temporary character, creating *dislocation* in the status of the migrant and in the economy of his family. The migrant moves out of his family and the community only temporarily, without severing ties with them and thus becomes dislocated—enjoying the status of an absentee member. Since immigration is granted by the host government for a fixed period of time, the migrant treats the stay abroad as a brief sojourn, an *interlude*, and comes psychologically prepared to 'return' rather than to 'uproot'. The fact that generally the migrant is disallowed to bring his family contributes to this orientation. Demographically, he becomes a non-familial unit; this status influences his time-budgeting and his orientation towards the family left behind.

4. Such an orientation poses special problems for adjustment and promotes distinctive patterns of interaction with people in similar status working on a common site. The 'We-They' distinction gets continually reinforced.

5. The colonial phenomenon of international migration was related largely to the agricultural and mining sectors requiring use of traditional skills. This new form of migration involves work in the modern sector of the economy.

6. The demand for different skills made by the labour-importing countries shows a changing trend. In the initial phase, skills were needed to create infrastructures, involving a great deal of construction activity. Once such facilities are built—hotels, hospitals, airports, school and college buildings, premises for industrial and power generating plants, roads, etc.—the demand for skills required for their construction declines; in its place, the demand for people to man these establishments arises. This accounts for a massive turnover of people—return of immigrants to their origins and arrival of fresh waves of

migrants with different skills. Such relay migration may ultimately change the character of migration; people from urban areas with high literacy and specialised skills may replace the earlier type of migrant who came from the rural areas (Atal 1986: 5).

III

In the literature on migration different typologies of the migrant are proposed based on the method of migration, chronology of migration, source of migration, destination (within country or outside), proportion of migrants to non-migrants, duration, sequence, etc.

In the earlier literature, the theory of migrant behaviour was heavily influenced by Georg Simmel's concept of 'der Fremde' (the stranger). Elaborating the concept, Robert E. Park (1928) coined the term 'marginal man' for the migrant who becomes a 'stranger' to both the worlds—his parent society and the host society. In his introduction to Stonequist's book entitled The Marginal Man (1937), Park further refined his definition thus: 'The marginal man ... is one whom fate has condemned to live in two societies and in two, not merely different but antagonistic, cultures'.

Researching on the Chinese in America, Paul C. P. Siu (1952: 34) introduced yet another term, 'the sojourner', for a special type of migrant which could not be called a 'marginal man':

> The essential characteristic of the sojourner is that he clings to the culture of his own ethnic group as in contrast to the bicultural complex of the marginal man. Psychologically, he is unwilling to organise himself as a permanent resident in the country of his sojourn. When he does, he becomes a marginal man.

Siu finds it convenient to define 'the "sojourner" as a stranger who spends many years of his life time in a foreign country without being assimilated by it. The sojourner is par excellence an ethnocentrist'.

The manner in which Siu has used the word ethnocentrism departs from its original sense in which Sumner first coined the term in 1907. Sumner (1907: 13) regards ethnocentrism as a 'view of things in which one's own group is the centre of everything...each group nourishes its own pride and vanity, boasts itself superior, exalts its own divinities, and looks with contempt on outsiders'. A migrant group, when it moves to a different society for improving its prospects, is more likely to be *xenocentric*, a term proposed by Kent and Burnight in 1951, which refers 'to both basic and favourable orientations to groups other than one's own' (Merton 1972: 17). Since the migrant is an outsider, his orientation to the host group could be either ethnocentric or *xenocentric*—the latter again being divided into 'xenophilia' or 'xenophobia' (ibid.). It is ethnocentrism combined with xenophobia of the receiving society that can explain the phenomenon of host hostility. On the other hand, hospitality implies presence of xenophilia (or, which is the same thing, absence of xenophobia). It may further be noted that xenophobia need not necessarily arise from the feeling of superiority: it may arise because of a certain sense of insecurity, of a fear of being engulfed by the other party.

The concept of the sojourner appears, in my view, to be applicable to cases of individual migration, to transient or passenger migrations. Once a collectivity emerges out of a continued interaction among discrete sojourners originating from the same source, it requires a different nomenclature. Elsewhere, analysing the MIME phenomenon I have employed the term *interlude* (see Atal 1986: 5) for a prolonged period of sojourn by a migrating group that is destined to return to its homeland. Such interludial migration causes a *dislocation*, and not complete severance of ties with the homeland. It also encourages relay migration. 'MIME does not become a factor in uprooting...; his dislocation does not necessarily result in the dislodging of the family from the place of his origin' (Atal 1986: 7).

In a similar fashion, the concept of *marginal man* has been further chiselled by Merton in the context of the reference group theory. Developing the concept of non-members in terms of their attitude towards membership and the eligibility criteria imposed by the group of orientation, Merton provides in the Table 10.1 (1964: 290):

Table 10.1: Group-defined Status of Non-members

Non-members' Attitude toward Membership	Eligible for Membership	Ineligible
Aspire to belong	Candidate for membership	Marginal man
Indifferent to affiliation	Potential member	Detached non-member
Motivated not to belong	Autonomous non-member	Antagonistic non-member (out-group)

The outsiders getting relocated in a receiving country would thus comprise of six possible categories, marginal being just one of them. Merton (1964: 265) posits that in

> a relatively closed social structure [where a person] would not find acceptance by the group to which he aspires and would probably lose acceptance because of his out-group orientation, by the group to which he belongs. This latter type of case will be recognised as that of the marginal man, poised on the edge of several groups but fully accepted by none of them.

Such conceptualisation of marginal man would reject the definition given by Schermerhorn in *A Dictionary of the Social Sciences* (Gould and Kolb 1964: 406) where he says that a marginal man 'may be defined in broadest terms as any individual who is simultaneously a member (by ascription, self-reference, or achievement) of two or more groups whose social definitions and cultural norms are distinct from each other'.

As against the concepts of 'the stranger', 'the sojourner' and 'the marginal man', which mainly focus on the individual migrants, Edna Bonacich (1973) attempted to build 'a theory of middlemen minorities', which was further refined by her in collaboration with Jonathan H. Turner (1980). Granting that most racial and ethnic minorities 'occupy the bottom strata in a society's system of stratification', Turner and Bonacich (1980: 144) proceed to conceptualise and theorise on the phenomenon of minorities that occupy a middle rank. 'Such minorities are "middlemen" in two senses: (1) they are likely to occupy middle rank positions in the stratification system; and (2) they are likely to be economic middlemen, involved in the movement of goods and services in a society'.

These authors do acknowledge the relevance of the concept of 'the sojourner', as developed by Siu and attribute the characteristic of return orientation to 'the middlemen minorities'. They regard 'liquidity' as the essential general occupational characteristic of these groups. Bonacich (1973: 583 and 585) says that such minorities 'began as sojourners in the territories to which they move'. However, sojourning is not regarded as 'a sufficient condition of the middleman...but it is a necessary one...' because it 'leads the individual to select occupations which do not tie him to the territory for long periods'. The authors regard ethnic organisation, host hostility and economic concentration as the key distinguishing features of the middlemen minorities. Around these three pegs, they have woven a set of propositions regarding prerequisites for, and consequences of, becoming a middlemen minority.

An appraisal of all the conceptual frameworks suggests the need to distinguish between individual migrations and the group migrations, and between temporary dislocations (interludes) and migrations for permanent settlement elsewhere. There is, thus, a need for an umbrella concept which can be employed for the migrant communities of different types including the sojourners and the middlemen minorities. For example, how would one describe the Fiji Indians who are not a minority and all of them are not in the middle reaches of the local hierarchy?

The phenomenon of intercultural contact is common to all migrations. The increasing rate of migratory flows has significantly affected not only the demographic profiles of the societies but also changed their cultural contours. In one sense, all the countries of the world have become plural or multicultural societies and their capital cities and other metropolises have assumed a cosmopolitan character. For example, if one were to consult the yellow pages of the telephone directory of any major city in any country of the world one would locate a variegated world of restaurants representing different cultural cuisines. One is equally impressed by the resurgence of a concern for cultural and ethnic identities. In the face of enormous give-and-take, identities have not always blurred. Changes in the material culture occurring as a result of rapid advances in science and technology have created lookalike configurations of material culture and yet there is some thing that distinguishes one metropolis from another. Cultures do receive outside traits and complexes but reinterpret them and endow them with new definitions through the provision of location to external traits in their cultural space.

Movement of people, spread of ideas and diffusion of material culture highlight the phenomenon of co-existence of the processes of continuity and change that characterise all societies. Elements coming from outside—men, materials and messages—are screened by a society's gate keepers, which permit or deny their entry. A society with a powerful *insulatory* mechanism may thwart all entries and maintain its purity; a complete breakdown of the insulators would result in the society's absorption into another bigger powerful social system. This dynamics of interplay of a society's *insulators* and *apertures* determines its degree of integration. Complete insulation depends on the firm closure of all apertures resulting into a fully isolated society and culture—perhaps the ideal type of a primitive society. No real society corresponds to the model of complete insularity, or a total absence of barriers (see Atal 1981 for the explication of the concepts of *insulators* and *apertures*).

The colonisation era broke some such barriers and opened out apertures, thus providing opportunities for exposure to the outside world. This process did not only affect the societies of the Third World which were colonised; it also affected the coloniser cultures. It initiated a process of mass migrations and settlements of people in strange lands—both in coloniser countries and in other colonies of the empires. Despite the onslaught of colonisation, it is striking that the societies and cultures have not lost their identities. The newly independent nations have retained their cultures while pursuing the path of modernisation and development. Theories of social and cultural change, emanating from the West, have failed to adequately capture and explain this phenomenon. Equally, the literature on migration has not adequately dealt with the process through which the migrating groups have been able to demonstrate, to use Simmel's phraseology, 'distance and nearness, indifference and involvement' in the affairs of the host society alongside of retaining their parental identity.

To explain the former phenomenon, Third World scholars have begun using the concept of *resilience*. For the latter phenomenon, that of a stranger community in an alien land, I propose the concept of *sandwich culture*.

Both these concepts—societal resilience and sandwich culture—are in the making and are complementary. They are serious candidates for inclusion in the vocabulary of social sciences and have enormous theoretical potential. Since the two concepts are complementary let me briefly allude to the concept of *resilience* before expanding the concept of *sandwich culture* that I propose to nominate. I first used the concept of sandwich as a metaphor while reviewing Ravindra K. Jain's book entitled *South Indians on the Plantation Frontier in Malaya* (Atal 1973).

The word 'resilience' is being used both as an ideology (advocating the desirability of resilience and suggesting strategies to inject and promote it in relatively rigid social structures) and as an analytical tool. Regarding resilience as an essential component of the 'cultural envelop', the concept has been defined in a variety of ways. In the opinion of some, resilience is the capsule word for the processes that prevent the core of culture from extraneous attack and thus account for the unchangeable; a typical formulation would be something like this: it is the resilience of the society that enabled it to withstand the shock of a culture contact, or of the external forces of change (see e.g., Atal 1979: 231). It is viewed as identical to homeostasis which brings back the system to its normalcy after a pathological aberration or deviance. The forces that do not allow deformation, rupture or fracture of the social and cultural systems are subsumed by some authors in the concept of resilience. Others have used it to envelop the processes of adaptability, plasticity, accommodation and symbiosis. Resilience is likened to a bamboo which bends with the storm but does not break; it reasserts itself when the storm is gone.

Clearly there is a need for proper conceptualisation of the word resilience and formulation of a paradigm to analyse the processes that this concept seeks to encompass. In this exercise it will also be necessary to examine its role in the context of sandwich cultures— a concept that is also in need of elaboration. As the word implies, 'sandwich' refers to the process (as well as the product) of 'laying or placing something between two layers', or 'to fit tight between two others of another kind' (see Chambers 20th century dictionary). Interestingly enough, the Dictionary also defines a 'sandwich man' as one 'who perambulates the streets carrying two advertising boards hung over his shoulders so that one is in front, the other behind'. An immigrant in a society who has a longer period of stay fits the description of a sandwich man, carrying the two tags, one representing the country of his origin and the other, the country of his migration. A Fiji Indian, for example, is a Fiji citizen (I am deliberately not using the Fijian, as it is used for the indigenous population) and he is distinguished as a migrant Indian from the indigenous Fijians. But a Fiji Indian is not the same as the India-Indian (an awkward way of putting it but perhaps it makes the point).

When visiting different countries, one is impressed by the fact that though derived from the same cultural stock, Indians in different lands share not only the 'Indianness' in common but also have peculiar features of their own, which distinguish them from Indian settlers in other countries because of different 'mixes' of host and parent cultures in their ways of life. Skinner (1958) has referred to this phenomenon as an assimilation trap while analysing the situation of 'viable and visible' Chinese communities in the Southeast Asian region. It emerges that the migrating communities make efforts to adopt the practices of the host country with a view to assimilation. In this, they succeed only in degrees. To illustrate the point, let me quote instances of Chinese communities in Indonesia, Thailand and Malaysia which are, incidentally, also the countries with substantial Indian population.

Exhibit-A: In Indonesia, the Chinese are divided into two categories: *Totoks* and *Peranakans*. China-born Chinese are called *Totoks* and local born Chinese are referred as *Peranakans*. In that country,

> there has been considerable amount of intermarriage between Chinese and the indigenous people, and the adoption of Indonesian language and Indonesian names by the Chinese is not uncommon. But Chinese—both *Totoks* and *Peranakans*—remain Chinese, almost 100 per cent identifiable though they may have lost much of the Chinese culture (Ting Chew Peh 1976: 27).

But they 'were stuck halfway in the assimilation'.

Exhibit-B: In Thailand there is no doubt a greater degree of assimilation of the Chinese into Thai society as compared to the Indians. But Coughlin (1955: 312) has this to say about them:

> Judged by any material standard, the Chinese have made an unusually successful economic adjustment.... Yet the Chinese in Bangkok have not been assimilated. The Chinese population remains by and large distinct from the Thai people in occupations, in the formation of voluntary associations, in the use of educational facilities, and in political interests and activities.

At another place, Coughlin (1960: 11) further remarks, 'Culturally and socially, this minority in Thailand has learned to accept Thai ways without, however, losing its attachment to things Chinese'.

Exhibit-C: In Malaysia, the Chinese 'still remain Chinese to all intents and purposes, and live quite apart from the Malays both emotionally and socially' (Ting Chew Peh 1976: 29). Even the Straits Chinese, called *Babas*, who are regarded as 'Malayised', with a 'Sinified' Malay dialect and 'their culture a mixture of both Chinese and Malay cultures' are viewed as having 'remained Chinese despite the fact that they know not a scrap of the high Chinese culture'.

Though all the three exhibits of Chinese communities in three different countries refer to the problem of assimilation, they also exemplify the phenomenon of what Coughlin (1960) has called *double identity.* Pressed between the twin forces of the parent and the host cultures, these communities have assumed double identities through shedding off of some elements of their parent culture and adoption of the host cultural elements with a view to assimilation. This dual process of pulls from two opposite directions—of orientations toward two cultures—leads to accretions and attrition and develops a new pattern of interrelationship between different elements. Such an intercalation gives rise to sandwich cultures.

Without employing the word sandwich culture, what several authors have said about overseas Indians also provides elements for a definition of this concept. Let me cite a few:

1. 'The essential character of an institution lies in the manner in which its component parts are combined to form a distinctive pattern. The pattern gets mangled in the process of emigration and resettlement...what persists is a thing of shreds and patches and the seamless web (that existed) in the ancestral society' (Jayawardena 1971: 114–15).

2. 'Villagers look to India for cultural models and often draw upon Indian books, films and popular music in trying to construct a sense of what it means to be "Indian". Despite this borrowing, the social context of life in Fiji has been radically altered, and Indian themes, values and motifs take on new definitions in Fiji' (Brenneis 1981: 224).

3. 'Fiji Indians, whether in their successes or failures, in their triumphs and tribulations, cannot be treated on their own divorced from their multi-cultural environment...Fiji's development is a consequence of the interplay of Fijian land, European capital and Indian labour' (Ali 1981: 31).

4. Writing about East Indians in Trinidad, Nevadomsky (1980: 44) observes, 'The several well-kept temples and *jandi* prayer flags, and the fields of rice, sugar cane and vegetable crops, convey the impression of a community that has successfully survived that trauma of emigration and the winds of change. Indian food, Bombay music and the seemingly endless round of traditional wedding celebrations also suggest this. But this impression is misleading. Behind the remaining traditional ceremonial and cultural features of rural life, one sees the effects of a modernising economy and the heavy influence of western norms...on local social life'.

5. Philip Singer has this to say of the situation in Guyana, 'The melting pot or creolisation approach to Guyana would like to establish a dialectic between Indian and African social structure with a synthesis into a third or Guyanese culture. It seems to me that the Indian in Guyana is presently engaged in his own identity dialectic in the interplay between the Little (Guyanese) Tradition and the Great Tradition of Hinduism' (Singer 1967: 113–14).

6. For Guyana again, Smith and Jayawardena (1967: 43–44) have this to say, 'More than half the population of Guyana is descended from immigrants from India....The East Indians...recognise themselves, and are recognised, as a differentiated group within the society of Guyana. They retain a considerable amount of Indian culture, including religious belief and practice, but absorption into a new social system marked by sharp ethnic differentiation has profoundly changed the meaning and content of "Indian culture" in the new setting'.

Similar statements about other societies can be culled out, but it will suffice our purpose to indicate that while scholars differ in their assessment of the degree and extent to which institutions transplanted from India have retained their originality, they all seem to hint at the continued presence of 'Indian-ness' that seems to provide these migrant communities an identity distinct from other groups in the plural societies of their relocation. They have carried the 'notions' and reactivated several structural and cultural features of their parent culture alongside of making adjustments and adoption of local customs, thus striking a new equation—a consequence of sandwiching. The different equations provide different profiles and distinguish them not only from the non-Indians of the host society but also from other overseas Indians and the Indians in India.

Here, it must also be said that India itself is a plural society with a multitude of cultures, religions, languages and differing levels of socioeconomic development. No single group migration thus reflects a representative sample of the complex Indian society and civilisation. It is also hazardous to equate Indian with Hindu; and even the word 'Hindu' admits of a large variety of subgroupings. It is, for example, important to note that in Malaysia and in Singapore the Indians use Tamil as their *lingua franca*, which is used by people who came not only from Tamil Nadu (Madras) but from Andhra, Kerala and Sri Lanka. In contrast to this, the Fiji Indians have evolved their own Hindi, which has its own grammar (now systematised and available in a book form) and is spoken not only by those who came from northern India but also by Tamils and Gujaratis; even the native Fijians have picked up the words from the language of this numerically preponderant group. Moreover, all Indian immigrants in a given host culture do not constitute a single grouping. For the outsiders, they may all be clubbed together, but distinctions within remain; these derive from religious, provincial and time-of-arrival differences. Thus, in Fiji, the descendants of Indian indentured labour are different from the latecomer groups, such as the Punjabis and the Gujaratis. If caste had diluted for the indentured people in the 19th century, it has surfaced again in terms of endogamy practised at the level of these different categories of migrants to Fiji. Thailand also offers a similar case. Among the settled Indians (with or without Thai nationality) there are two distinct groups—those who came from Uttar Pradesh and Orissa, and those who came from Punjab (the Sikhs and the non-Sikhs). No doubt, for certain purposes, the inner distinctions melt away, such as celebration of Indian independence day, or visit to Indian restaurants; but for other purposes, these remain different groups with different lifestyles and different patterns of interaction with the members of the host community.

It appears that the concept of sandwich culture is applicable at several levels:

1. *At the country level*: The culture of the entire country may be a result of the process of sandwiching between the powerful pressures from two or more civilisations. Thailand offers a good example of this type, which has emerged as a result of sandwiching between Indian (mainly Buddhist) and Chinese civilisations. The language (vocabulary and the script) and the religion (including the institution of monarchy) represent the influence of Indian civilisation (see Desai 1980). Its food habits, some patterns of dress, and tonality in language as well as business ethic are derived from the Chinese.

2. *Within the country level*:

    (i) Immigrant communities: the instances of Indians and of the Chinese in other countries.

(ii)   Autochthonous communities: those overwhelmed by the invading immigrants also develop sandwich cultures as a result of the breakdown of their isolation. The modern Maori in New Zealand, the aboriginals in Australia and the several tribal communities in India exemplify this type.

(iii) Sandwich cultures created as a result of relay migration: for example, student groups from a foreign country and migrant workers in the Middle East from a foreign country. In such situations the actual demographic composition changes through gradual replacement but the new arrivals enter into an already created sandwich culture. The old inhabitants 'socialise' and 'enculturate' the newcomers and thus make their adjustment in a strange environment relatively smooth. These groups define their own areas of interaction, create aperture points for an interface with the host culture and set-up their membership boundaries.

(iv)   Frontier groups: communities located on the frontiers of a given political system receive influences from the neighbouring country whose frontier is common. For example, the residents of southern Thailand exhibit a mix of Thai and Malay cultures.

(v)   Refugee communities: these constitute another type with a potential for a sandwich culture.

Sandwich cultures that are of our immediate interest are the subcultures of the outside groups in an alien land; their analytical protocol will certainly be different from the one meant for a culture as a whole of a country resulting out of a process of sandwiching, such as that of Thailand. A sandwich culture, in the restricted sense, is thus a subculture of the outside group settled in a different country/ setting and thus contributing to its heterogeneity. By definition, it cannot be completely insulated; of necessity, it has at least double apertures—one linking it to the parent culture and the other to the host culture. Through these apertures, among others, it receives the influences and responds to them. Closing of its apertures to the parent culture leads to its alienation; if it is associated with wide opening of the apertures towards the host society then it accelerates the process of absorption and assimilation with the total loss of independent identity. However, if the host society does not allow its aperture to open and tries to insulate it, the group may remain marginal and face hostility; its response to such a situation will be different: it may either attempt to convert the attitude of the host society or retaliate against it, or may even be ejected out (as happened in the case of Uganda Indians and as the situation seems to be developing in Fiji recently).

It seems that in the cases of conservative migration, where the migrants aim to preserve their way of life, the chances of creating a sandwich culture are greater, as against the cases of what is called 'innovating' migration illustrative of renegade behaviour. Migrants who come with a view to settling down would show a more accommodative attitude towards the host culture (of course, this excludes the 'invaders', or the *en bloc* refugee resettlers). Such migrants would create a sandwich culture—and this will also be true of 'invading' conquerors; and the refugees who are not kept fully insulated by the receiving society. Those who come as sojourners, temporary settlers with a view to returning to their parent societies, also create (perhaps unconsciously) a web of patterns to guide their behaviour during the sojourn and develop a distinctive sandwich culture, which is passed on from the returnee migrants to the new arrivals in instances of chain or relay migration. Upon their return, in their parent society, such groups may succeed in carving out a different way of life that distinguishes them from their original group.

It is necessary to outline the process of the formation of a sandwich culture. Perhaps the beginning is made as a response to 'perceived' or 'real' host 'hostility' or 'hospitality' by the migrants. This leads, on the one hand, to find 'semblances' and 'functional equivalents' in each other's cultures, and on the other to shed off some inconvenient practices (e.g., vegetarians becoming non-vegetarians).

Pending research in this perspective, let me list the two sets of factors which operate to facilitate or hinder the process of formation of sandwich cultures:

1. *Aperture Opening*: Efforts made by the outsiders to become insiders so as to merge/blur their identity and gain certain degree of acceptance by the host society. Some of the possible apertures are: (a) intermarriage (or the breakdown of endogamy); (b) adoption of names of the host society; (c) adoption (or use) of language of the host culture; (d) religious conversion and (e) adoption of food habits and developing taste for host cuisine.

2. *Insulatory Mechanisms*: Efforts made by the incoming group to conserve its identity and maintain some distance from the host culture. The possible insulatory mechanisms are: (a) retention of mother tongue and use of the native script (the oft-quoted case of the Chinese Press in Malaysia is a good example of this); (b) concentration of living quarters to promote greater interaction with the members of the in-group; (c) provision of separate educational facilities for the children, either by opening schools in the host country or sending children to the parent country for schooling; (d) practice of endogamy; (e) concentration in certain occupations; (f) formation of voluntary organisations; (g) pursuit of parental religion; (h) continuation of food habits and taboos associated with eating; (i) retention of cultural diacriticals particularly in the manner of dressing. This is more common with the womenfolk (such as wearing of *sari* and application of *bindi* on the forehead); but in men also this can be conspicuous such as among the Sikhs (who could be easily identified by their turban and the beard). The original UP migrants to Thailand still continue to wear *dhoti* and *kurta* in Bangkok; (j) racial features; (k) keeping apertures open to the parent culture, for example: (a) frequent visits; (b) schooling of children, either in parent society or using the textbooks and reading material in separate schools; (c) affinal relations; (d) exposure to media: books, music, films, videos and (e) postal- and tele-communication.

It is thus obvious that using the concept of sandwich cultures, one will have to respond to different sets of questions rather than merely to address oneself to the query of 'how much of parent culture is found in a migrant group'. The focus is on double orientation, dual apertures, linkages and interactions that a group sandwiched between two cultures encounters. There is a need to develop the empirical profiles of these sandwich cultures with a view to (a) evolving a suitable typology, (b) identifying the process of the creation and maintenance of these subcultures and (c) the role they play in the dynamics of nation building and in the promotion of intercultural understanding.

This chapter is only a prelude to such an exercise. It offers a framework, rather a scaffolding, to initiate work in this challenging and potentially fruitful area of research.

References

Abella, M. and Yogesh Atal (ed.). 1986. *Middle East Interlude: Asian Workers Abroad*. Bangkok: UNESCO.

Ali, Ahmed. 1977. 'The Emergence of Muslim Separatism in Fiji', *Plural Societies*, 8: 57–69.

———. 1981. 'Fiji: The Fiji Indian Achievement', in Ron Crocombe (ed.): *Pacific Indians: Profiles from 20 Countries*. Suva: Institute of Pacific Studies, University of South Pacific.

Atal, Yogesh. 1973. Review of R. K. Jain: *South Indians on the Plantation Frontier in Malaya, The Eastern Anthropologist*, 26: 109–11.

———. 1979. *Changing Frontiers of Caste*. Delhi: National Publishing House (second edition).

———. 1981. *Building a Nation: Essays on India*. New Delhi: Abhinav Publications.

———. (ed.). 1984. *Dynamics of Nation Building*. Bangkok: UNESCO.

———. 1985. *Dynamics of Nation Building*. Bangkok: UNESCO.

———. 1986. 'Asians in the Middle East: A New Dimension to International Migration', in M. Abella and Yogesh Atal (ed.): *Middle East Interlude: Asian Workers Abroad*. Bangkok: UNESCO.

Atal, Yogesh and Luca Dall'Oglio (ed.). 1987. *Migration of Talent: Causes and Consequences of Brain Drain*. Bangkok: UNESCO.

Bharati, Agehanand. 1967. 'Ideology and Content of Caste among the Indians in East Africa', in Barton M. Schwartz (ed.): *Caste in Overseas Indian Communities*. San Francisco: Chandler Publishing Co., pp. 283–320.

Bonacich, Edna. 1973. 'A Theory of Middleman Minorities', *American Sociological Review*, 38(5): 583–94.

Brenneis, Donald. 1981. 'A Comparative View of Overseas Indians', in Ron Crocombe (ed.): *Pacific Indians: Profiles from 20 Countries*. Suva: Institute of Pacific Studies, University of South Pacific.

Coughlin, R. J. 1955. 'The Chinese in Bangkok', *American Sociological Review*, 20(3).

———. 1960. *Double Identity: The Chinese in Modern Thailand*. Hong Kong: Hong Kong University Press.

Crocombe, Ron (ed.). 1981. *Pacific Indians: Profiles from 20 Countries*. Suva: Institute of Pacific Studies. University of South Pacific.

Dahlan, H. M. (ed.). *The Nascent Malaysian Society: Developments, Trends, and Problems*. Kuala Lumpur: University Kebangsaan Malaysia.

Desai, Santosh N. 1980. *Hinduism in Thai Life*. Bombay: Popular Prakashan.

Gould, Julius and William L. Kolb (ed.). 1964. *A Dictionary of the Social Sciences*. London: Tavistock Publications.

Hiatt, L. R. and Chandra Jayawardena. 1971. *Anthropology Oceania*. Sydney: Angus and Robertson, pp. 89–119.

Hossain, Zakir. 1982. *The Silent Minority: Indians in Thailand*. Bangkok: Chulalongkorn University Social Research Institute.

Jayawardena, Chandra. 1971. 'The Disintegration of Caste in Fiji Indian Rural Society', in L. R. Hiatt and Chandra Jayawardena (ed.): *Anthropology Oceania*. Angus and Robertson.

Kent, Donald P. and Robert G. Burnight. 1951. 'Group Centrism in Complex Societies', American Journal of Sociology, 57(3): 256–59.

Kurian, George. 1987. 'Sociocultural Adaptation of South Asian Immigrants: The Canadian Experience', The Journal of Sociological Studies, 6(1): 47–62.

Malik, Yogendra. 1972. East Indians in Trinidad. Oxford: Oxford University Press.

Mayer, Adrian C. 1967. 'Introduction', in Barton M. Schwartz (ed.): Caste in Overseas Indian Communities. San Francisco: Chandler Publishing Co., pp. 1–19.

Merton, Robert K. 1964. Social Theory and Social Structure. Glencoe: The Free Press of Glencoe.

———. 1972. 'Insiders and Outsiders: A Chapter in the Sociology of Knowledge', American Journal of Sociology, 78(1): 9–47.

Nevadomsky, Joseph. 1980. 'Changes in Hindu Institutions in an Alien Environment', The Eastern Anthropologist, 33(1): 839–53.

Niehoff, Arthur. 1958. 'The Survival of Hindu Institution in an Alien Environment', The Eastern Anthropologist, 12(3): 171–87.

Park, Robert E. 1928. 'Human Migration and the Marginal Man', American Journal of Sociology, 33(6): 881–93.

Peterson, W. 1958. 'A General Typology of Migration', American Sociological Review, 23(2): 255–66.

Schermerhorn, R. A. 1964. 'Marginal Man', in Julius Gould and William L. Kolb (eds.): A Dictionary of Social Sciences. London: Tavistock Publications, pp. 406–7.

Schwartz, Barton M. (ed.). 1967. Caste in Overseas Indian Communities. San Francisco: Chandler Publishing Co.

Siddique, Sharon and Nirmala Purushottam. 1982. Singapore's Little India: Past, Present, and Future. Singapore: Institute of South East Asian Studies.

Singer, Philip. 1967. 'Caste and Identity in Guyana', in Barton M. Schwartz (ed.): Caste in Overseas Indian Communities. San Francisco: Chandler Publishing Co., pp. 93–116.

Siu, Paul C. P. 1952. 'The Sojourner', The American Journal of Sociology, 58(1): 34–44.

Skinner, G. W. 1957. Chinese Society in Thailand, Ithaca: Cornell University Press.

———. 1958. 'The Chinese in Java', in M. H. Fried (ed.): Colloquium on Overseas Chinese. New York: Institute of Pacific Affairs.

Smith, Raymond T. and Chandra Jayawardena. 1967. 'Caste and Social Status Among the Indians of Guyana', in Barton M. Schwartz (ed.): Caste in Overseas Indian Communities. San Francisco: Chandler Publishing Co., pp. 43–92.

Stonequist, Everett V. 1935. 'The Problem of the Marginal Man', American Journal of Sociology, 41(1): 1–12.

———. 1937. The Marginal Man. New York: Charles Scribener's Sons.

Sumner, William Graham. 1907. Folkways. Boston: Ginn.

Tingh, Chew Peh. 1976. 'Some Problems of Chinese Assimilation in Peninsular Malaysia', in H. M. Dahlan (ed.): The Nascent Malaysian Society: Developments, Trends, and Problems. Kuala Lumpur: University Kebangsaan Malaysia.

Turner, Jonathan H. and Edna Bonacich. 1980. 'Toward a Composite Theory of Middleman Minorities', Ethnicity, 7(2): 144–58.

Select Bibliography on *The Indian Diaspora*

I

Articles Appearing in the *Sociological Bulletin* (* Included in this Volume)

Atal, Yogesh. 1989. 'Outsiders as Insiders: The Phenomenon of Sandwich Culture', 38(1): 23–41.*

Aurora, G. S. 1965. 'Process of Social Adjustment of Indian Immigrants in Britain', 14(2): 39–49.*

Brown, Carolyn Henning. 1989. 'The Social Background of Fiji's 1987 Coup', 38(1): 95–117.

Buchignani, Norman. 1989. 'Contemporary Research on People of Indian Origin in Canada', 38(1): 71–93.*

Chauhan, I. S. 1965. 'Fiji Today: Political Process and Race Relations in a Plural Society', 14(2): 70–85.

Jain, Prakash C. 1989. 'Emigration and Settlement of Indians Abroad', 38(1): 155–68.

Jain, Ravindra K. 1989. 'Race Relations, Ethnicity, Class and Culture: A Comparison of Indians in Trinidad and Malaysia', 38(1): 57–69.*

———. 1998. 'Reality and Representation: Aspects of the Electronic Media in Contemporary Indian Society and Diaspora', 47(2): 167–84.

Jayaram, N. 2000. 'The Dynamics of Language in Indian Diaspora: The Case of Bhojpuri/Hindi in Trinidad', 49(1): 41–62.*

Malik, Yogendra K. 1969. 'Agencies of Political Socialisation and East Indian Ethnic Identification in Trinidad', 28(1): 101–21.

Mehta, S. R. 1989. 'The Uneven "Inclusion" of Indian Immigrants in Mauritius', 38(1): 141–53.*

Mustapha, Nasser. 1997. 'The Influence of Indian Islam on Fundamentalist Trends in Trinidad and Tobago', 46(2): 245–69.*

Oommen, T. K. 1982. 'Foreigners, Refugees and Outsiders in the Indian Context', 31(1): 41–64.

Sharma, K. N. 1989. 'The "Indian Question" in the Caribbean Sociology', 38(1): 43–56.

Sharma, S. L. 1989. 'Perspectives on Indians Abroad', 38(1): 1–21.*

Siddique, Chaudry M. 1977. 'On Migrating to Canada: The First Generation Indian and Pakistani Families in the Process of Change', 26(2): 203–26.*

Sivakumar, Chitra. 1989. 'Social Origins of the Sri Lankan Tamils' Militant Movement', 38(1): 119–39.

II

Select Bibliography

Abella, M. and Yogesh Atal (eds.). 1986. *Middle East Interlude: Asian Workers Abroad*. Bangkok: UNESCO.

Adamson, Alan H. 1972. *Sugar without Slaves: The Political Economy of British Guiana, 1838–1904*. New Haven: Yale University Press.

Adhopia, Ajit. 1993. *The Hindus in Canada: A Perspective on Hindu-Canadians' Cultural Heritage*. Mississauga: Inderlekh Publications.

Aldrich, H.; John Cater, Trevor Jones and D. Mcevoy. 1981. 'Business Development and Self-Segregation: Asian Enterprise in Three British Cities', in C. Peach, V. Robinson and S. Smith (eds.): *Ethnic Segregation in Cities*. London: Croom Helm.

———. 1983. 'From Periphery to Peripheral: The South Asian Petite Bourgeoisie in England', in I. H. Simpson and R. L. Simpson (eds.): *Research in the Sociology of Work* (Vol. II–Peripheral Workers). Greenwich, Conn.: JAI Press.

Ali, Ahmed. 1977. 'The Emergence of Muslim Separatism in Fiji', *Plural Societies*, 8: 57–69.

Allen, Calvin H. Jr. 1991. 'The Indian Merchant Community of Muscat', *Bulletin of the School of Oriental and African Studies*, 44(1): 39–53.

Amjad, Rashid. 1989. *To the Gulf and Back: Studies on the Economic Impact of Asian Labour Migration*. Geneva: United Nations Development Programme.

Ampalavanar, Rajaswary. 1981. *The Indian Minority and Potential Change in Malaya, 1945–1957*. London: Oxford University Press.

Anderson, Benedict. 1983. *Imagined Communities: Reflections on the Origin and Spread of Nationalism*. London: Verso.

Andrews, E. J. L. 1933. *Indian Labour in Rangoon*. Calcutta: Oxford University Press.

Angelo, Michael. 1997. *Sikh Diaspora: Tradition and Change in an Immigrant Community*. New York: Garland Publishing Inc.

Angrosino, Michael V. 1976. 'Sexual Politics in the East Indian Family in Trinidad', *Caribbean Studies*, 16(1): 44–66.

Appadurai, Arjun. 1997. *Modernity at Large: Cultural Dimensions of Globalisation*. New Delhi: Oxford University Press.

Arasaratnam, Sinnappah. 1970. *Indians in Malaysia and Singapore*. London: Oxford University Press.

Arkin, A. J.; K. P. Magyar and G. J. Pillay (eds.). 1989. *The Indian South Africans*. Pinetown: Owen Burgess.

Arnold, Fred and Nasra M. Shah (eds.). 1986. *Asian Labour Migration: Pipeline to the Middle East*. Boulder and London: Westview Press.

Aurora, Gurdip Singh. 1976. *The New Frontiersmen: Indians in Great Britain*. Bombay: Popular Prakashan.

Bacon, Jean. 1996. *Life Lines: Community, Family, and Assimilation among Asian Indian Immigrants*. New York/Oxford: Oxford University Press.

Bahadoorsingh, Krishna. 1968. *Trinidad Electoral Politics: The Persistence of the Race Factor*. London: Institute of Race Relations.

Bahri, D. and M. Vasudeva (eds.). 1996. *Between the Lines: South Asians and Postcoloniality*. Philadelphia: Temple University Press.

Bains, T. S. and H. Johnston. 1995. *The Four Quarters of the Night: The Life Journey of an Emigrant Sikh*. Montreal: Mcgill-Queen's University Press.

Baksh, Ishmael J. 1979. 'Stereotypes of Negroes and East Indians in Trinidad: A Re-Examination', *Caribbean Quarterly*, 25(1–2): 52–71.

Ballard, R. 1973. 'Family Organization among the Sikhs in Britain', *New Community*, 2(1): 12–24.

Ballard, R. and C. Ballard. 1977. 'The Sikhs: The Development of South Asian Settlements in Britain', in J. L. Watson (ed.): *Between Two Cultures: Migrants and Minorities in Britain*. Oxford: Basil Blackwell.

————. 1994. *Desh Pardesh: The South Asian Presence in Britain*. London: C. Hurst.

Ba'Nikongo, Nikongo. 1994. 'Of Afro-Trinidadians, Indo-Trinidadians and "Apartheid" in a Pseudo-Emancipatory, Accidental Bi-Racial State', *The Eastern Anthropologist*, 47(3): 207–28

Barrier, N. Gerald and Verne A. Dusenbery (eds.). 1989. *The Sikh Diaspora: Migration and the Experience Beyond Punjab*. Delhi: Chanakya Publications.

Barton, S. 1986. *The Bengali Muslims of Bradford: A Study of their Observance of Islam with Special Reference to the Function of the Mosque and the Work of the Imam* (Community Religions Project Monograph). Leeds: University of Leeds.

Basdeo, Sahadeo. 1986. 'Indian Participation in Labour Politics in Trinidad, 1919–1939', *Caribbean Quarterly*, 32(3&4): 50–65.

Baumann, Martin. 2000. 'Diaspora: Genealogies of Semantics and Transcultural Comparison', *Numen* (International Review for the History of Religions), 47(3): 313–37.

————. 2001. *Migration, Religion, Integration: Buddhistische, Vietnamesen Und Hinduistische Tamilen in Deutschland* (in German). Marburg, Germany: Diagonal–Verlag Marburg.

Bell, Robert R. 1970. 'Marriage and Family Differences among Lower Class Negro and East Indian Women in Trinidad', *Race*, 12(1): 59–73.

Benedict, Burton. 1961. *Indians in a Plural Society: A Report on Mauritius*. London: H. M. Stationery Office.

Benedict, Burton. 1964. 'Capital, Saving and Credit among Mauritian Indians', in Raymond Firth and B. S. Yamey (eds.): *Capital, Saving and Credit in Peasant Societies*. London: George Allen and Unwin, pp. 330–46.

———. 1965. *Mauritius: Problems of a Plural Society*. London: Pall Mall.

Bernard, Godfrey St. 1994. 'Ethnicity and Attitudes towards Inter-Racial Marriages in Trinidad and Tobago: An Exploration of Preliminary Findings', *Caribbean Quarterly*, 40(3&4): 109–24.

Bhachu, Parminder. 1984. 'East African Sikhs in Britain: Experienced Settlers with Traditionalistic Values', *Immigrants and Minorities*, 3(3): 276–95.

———. 1985. *Twice Migrants: East African Sikh Settlers in Britain*. London: Tavistock Publications.

———. 1986. 'Work, Dowry and Marriage among East African Sikh Women in the United Kingdom', in C. B. Brettell and R. Simon (eds.): *International Immigrants: The Female Experience*. Totowa, NJ: Rowman and Allenhead.

Bharati, Agehananda. 1964. 'The Indians in East Africa: A Survey of Problems of Transition and Adaptation', *Sociologus*, 14(1): 168–77.

———. 1972. *The Asians of East Africa: Jay Hind and Uhuru*. Chicago: Nelson Hall.

Bhat, Chandrashekhar. 1993. 'Indian Ethnic Associations in London: Search for Unity in Diversity', in Chandrashekhar Bhat, Laxmi Narayan Kadekar, and K. Ranga Rao (eds.): *Sociology of Development and Change*. Delhi: Orient Longman, pp. 210–28.

Bhatia, Prem. 1973. *Indians' Ordeal in Africa*. Delhi: Vikas Publishing House.

Bilimoria, P. 1996. *The Hindus and Sikhs in Australia*. Canberra: Australian Government Publishing Service.

Birbalsingh, Frank. 1986. 'Indians in the Novels of Edgar Mittelholzer', *Caribbean Quarterly*, 32(1–2): 16–24.

———. (ed.). 1989. *Indenture and Exile: The Indo-Caribbean Experience*. Toronto: TSAR in Association with the Ontario Association for Studies in Indo-Caribbean Culture.

———. (ed.). 1993. *Indo-Caribbean Resistance*. Toronto: TSAR in Association with the Ontario Association for Studies in Indo-Caribbean Culture.

———. 1997. *From Pillar to Post: The Indo-Caribbean Diaspora*. Toronto: Tsar Publications.

Bisnauth, Dale Arlington. 1989. 'Hinduism and Islam in the Caribbean', in Dale Arlington Bisnauth: *A History of Religions in the Caribbean*. Kingston, Jamaica: Kingston Publishers Ltd., pp. 140–64.

Bissoondoyal, B. 1968. *The Truth about Mauritius*. Bombay: Bharatiya Vidya Bhavan.

Bolan, Indira. 1994. 'Building Cross Cultural Bridges in Multi-Ethnic Societies: The Role of the Pundit', *Caribbean Quarterly*, 40(3&4): 54–60.

Boodhoo, Ken. 1974. 'The Case of the Missing Majority', *Caribbean Review*, 6(2): 3–7.

———. 1981. 'East Indian Labourers', in Roberta M. Delson (ed.): *Readings in Caribbean History and Economics: An Introduction to the Region*. New York: Gordon and Breach Science Publishers, pp. 143–54.

Bowen, D. 1987. *The Sathya Sai Baba Community in Bradford: Its Origin and Development, Religious Beliefs and Practices* (Community Religions Project Monograph). Leeds: University of Leeds.

Brah, Avtar. 1996. *Cartographies of Diaspora: Contesting Identities*. London: Routledge.

Breman, Jan. 1995. *Taming the Coolie Beast: Plantation Society and the Colonial Order in South East Asia*. New Delhi: Oxford University Press.

Brenneis, Donald. 1991. 'Aesthetics, Performance, and the Enactment of Tradition in a Fiji Indian Community', in A. Appadurai, F. Korom and M. Mills (eds.): *Gender, Genre, and Power in South Asian Expressive Traditions*. Philadelphia: University of Pennsylvania Press, pp. 362–78.

Brereton, Bridget. 1974. 'The Foundations of Prejudice: Indians and Africans in Nineteenth Century Trinidad', *Caribbean Issues*, 1(1): 15–28.

———. 1979. *Race Relations in Colonial Trinidad, 1870–1900*. Cambridge: Cambridge University Press.

———. 1981. *A History of Modern Trinidad, 1783–1962*. Kingston, Port of Spain, London: Heinemann Educational Books.

Brown, Carolyn Henning. 1977. 'Ethnic Politics in Fiji: Fijian Indian Relations', *Journal of Ethnic Studies*, 5(4): 1–17.

———. 1981. 'Demographic Constraints on Caste: A Fiji Indian Example', *American Ethnologist*, 8(2): 314–28.

Buchignani, Norman. 1980a. 'South Asians and the Ethnic Mosaic: An Overview', *Canadian Ethnic Studies*, 11(1): 48–68.

———. 1980b. 'The Social and Self Identities of Fijian Indians in Vancouver', *Urban Anthropology*, 9(1): 75–97.

———. 1987. *Fijian Indians in Vancouver: The Structural Determinants of a New Community*. New York: Ams Press.

Buchignani, Norman and Doreen Marie Indra. 1981a. 'The Political Organization of South Asians in Canada', in J. Dahlie and T. Fernando (eds.): *Ethnicity, Power and Politics in Canada*. Toronto: Methuen, pp. 202–32.

———. 1981b. 'Inter-Group Conflict and Community Solidarity: Sikhs and South Asian Fijians in Vancouver', *Canadian Journal of Anthropology*, 1(2): 149–57.

Burghart, Richard (ed.). 1987. *Hinduism in Great Britain*. London: Tavistock.

Camejo, Acton. 1971. 'Racial Discrimination in Employment in the Private Sector in Trinidad and Tobago: A Study of the Business Elite and the Social Structure', *Social and Economic Studies*, 20(3): 294–318.

Caribbean Quarterly. 1986. Special Issue on 'East Indians in West Indian Literature', 32(1–2).

———. 1994. Special Issue on 'The Indian Presence: Arrival and After', 41(1).

Castles, Stephen and Alastair Davidson. 2000. *Globalization and the Politics of Belonging*. Basingstoke, Hampshire: Palgrave Publishers Ltd.

Castles, Stephen and J. Miller. 1998. *International Population Movements in the Modern World*. London: Macmillan, 1998 (2nd Edition).

Centre for Ethnic Studies, The. 1994a. *Ethnicity and Employment Practices in Trinidad and Tobago*. St. Augustine, Trinidad: The University of the West Indies.

———. 1994b. *A Study of the Secondary School Population in Trinidad and Tobago: Placement and Patterns and Practices* (A Research Report). St. Augustine, Trinidad: The University of the West Indies.

Chadney, James G. 1977. 'Demography, Ethnic Identity, and Decision-Making: The Case of the Vancouver Sikhs', *Urban Anthropology*, 6(3): 187–204.

Chadney, James G. 1984. *The Sikhs of Vancouver.* New York: Ams Press.

Chako, B. J. 1994–95. *NRI: Guide on Taxation, Investment and Incentives.* Agra: Wadhwa and Company Law Publishers.

Chakravarti, N. R. 1971. *The Indian Minority in Burma: The Rise and Decline of an Immigrant Community.* London: Oxford University Press.

Chaliand, Gerard and Jean-Pierre Rageau. 1995. *The Penguin Atlas of Diasporas* (Maps by Catherine Petit and Td. from the French by A. M. Berrett). New York: Penguin Books/Viking.

Chandan, Amarjit. 1986. *Indians in Britian.* New Delhi: Sterling Publishers.

Chandrasekhar, S. (ed.). 1983. *From India to America: A Brief History of Immigration; Problems of Discrimination; Admission and Assimilation.* La Jolla: A Population Review Book.

Chattopadhaya, Haraprasad. 1970. *Indians in Africa: A Socio-Economic Study.* Calcutta: Booklands.

———. 1979. *Indians in Sri Lanka: A Historical Study.* Calcutta: OPS Publishers.

Chauhan, I. S. 1988. *Leadership and Social Cleavages: Political Processes among the Indians in Fiji.* Jaipur: Rawat Publications.

Clarke, Colin G. (ed.) 1978. *Caribbean Social Relations.* London: Centre for Latin American Studies, University of Liverpool.

———. 1986. *East Indians in a West Indian Town: San Fernando, Trinidad, 1930–70.* London: George Allen and Unwin.

Clarke, Colin; David Ley and Ceri Peach (eds.). 1984. *Geography and Ethnic Pluralism.* London: George Allen and Unwin.

Clarke, Colin; Ceri Peach and Steven Vertovec (eds.). 1990. *South Asians Overseas: Migration and Ethnicity.* Cambridge: Cambridge University Press.

Cohen, Robin (ed.). 1995. *The Cambridge Survey of World Migration.* Cambridge: Cambridge University Press.

———. 1997. *Global Diasporas: An Introduction.* Seattle: University of Washington Press.

Collins, Elizabeth Fuller. 1997. *Pierced by Murugan's Lance: Ritual, Power, and Moral Redemption among Malaysian Hindus.* Northern Illinois: University Press.

Coulter, John W. 1942. *Fiji: Little India of the Pacific.* Chicago: University of Chicago Press.

Coward, H.; J. R. Hinnells and R. B. Williams (eds.). 2000. *The South Asian Religious Diaspora in Britain, Canada, and the United States.* Albany: State University of New York Press.

Crocombe, Ron (ed.). 1981. *Pacific Indians: Profiles from 20 Countries.* Suva: Institute of Pacific Studies, University of South Pacific.

Cross, Malcolm. 1972. *The East Indians of Guyana and Trinidad.* London: Minority Rights Group (Report No. 13).

Cumpston, I. M. 1956. 'A Survey of Indian Immigration to British Tropical Colonies till 1910', *Population Studies*, 10(2): 158–65.

———. 1969. *Indians Overseas in British Territories, 1834–54.* London: Dawsons of Pall Mall.

Dabydeen, David and Brinsley Samaroo (eds.). 1987. *India in the Caribbean.* London: Hansib Publishing Limited.

Dabydeen, David and Brinsley Samaroo. (eds.). 1996. *Across the Dark Waters: Ethnicity and Indian Identity in the Caribbean*. London and Basingstoke: Macmillan Education.

Damsteegt, Theo. 1988. 'Sarnami: A Living Language', in R. K. Barz and J. Siegel (eds.) *Language Transplanted: The Development of Overseas Hindi*. Wiesbaden: Harrassowitz.

Das, Chitta Ranjan. 1996. 'Israel's Jews from India', *The Eastern Anthropologist*, 49(3–4): 317–48.

Das, Rajani Kant. 1923. *Hindustani Workers on the Pacific Coast*. Berlin: Walter De Gruyter.

Davids, Leo. 1964. 'The East Indian Family Overseas', *Social and Economic Studies*, 13(3): 383–96.

Debysingh, Molly. 1986. 'Cultural Change and Adaptation as Reflected in the Meat-Eating Habits of the Trinidad Indian Population', *Caribbean Quarterly*, 32(2&4): 66–77.

Deen, Shamsu. 1994. *Solving East Indian Roots in Trinidad*. Trinidad: The Author.

Diesel, Alleyn and Patrick Maxwell. 1993. *Hinduism in Natal: A Brief Guide*. Pietermaritzburg: University of Natal Press.

de Lepervanche, Marie M. 1984. *Indians in a White Australia: An Account of Race, Class and Indian Immigration to Eastern Australia*. Sydney: George Allen and Unwin Australia.

Delf, G. 1963. *Asians in East Africa*. London: Oxford University Press, for the Institute of Race Relations.

Depoo, Tilokie (with Prem Misir and Basdeo Mangru) (eds.). 1993. *The East Indian Diaspora: 150 Years of Survival, Contributions and Achievements*. New York: Asian/American Center, Queens College (Cuny).

Desai, Rashmi. 1964. *Indian Immigrants in Britain*. London: Oxford University Press.

Despres, Leo A. 1967. *Cultural Pluralism and Nationalist Politics in British Guiana*. Chicago: Rand Mc Nally.

Dew, Edward. 1978. *The Difficult Flowering of Surinam: Ethnicity and Politics in a Plural Society*. The Hague: Martinus Nijhoff.

Dey, Mukul K. 1962. 'The Indian Population in Trinidad and Tobago', *International Journal of Comparative Sociology*, 3: 245–53.

Dhruvarajan, Vanaja. 1994. 'Hindu Asian Indian Women, Multiculturalism and Reproductive Technologies', in B. S. Boloria and R. Boloria (eds.): *Racial Minorities, Medicine and Health*. Halifax: Fernwood.

———. 1995. 'Hindu Indo-Canadian Families', M. Lynn (ed.): *Voices: Essays in Canadian Families*. Toronto: Nelson.

Diesel, Alleyn. 1998. 'The Empowering of the Divine Mother: A South African Hindu Woman Worshiping the Goddess', *Journal of Contemporary Religion*, 13(1): 73–90.

Duggal, Ved P. 1970. 'Relations between Indians and Africans in Guyana', *Revista Interamericana*, 3: 55–60.

Durbin, Mridula Adenwala. 1973. 'Formal Changes in Trinidad Hindi as a Result of Language Adaptation', *American Anthropologist*, 75(5): 1290–1304.

Dusenbery, Verne A. 1981. 'Canadian Ideology and Public Policy: The Impact on Vancouver Sikh Ethnic and Religious Adaptation', *Canadian Ethnic Studies*, 8(3): 101–20.

Dusenbery, Verne A. 1987. 'The Sikh Person, The Khalsa Panth and Western Sikh Converts', in J. K. Lele et al. (eds.): *Boeings and Bullock Carts: Rethinking India's Restructuring*. Leiden: E. Brill.

———. 1995. 'A Sikh Diaspora? Contested Identities and Constructed Realities', in Peter van der Veer (ed.): *Nation and Migration: The Politics of Space in the South Asian Diaspora*. Philadelphia: Pennsylvania University Press, pp. 17–42.

East Indians in the Caribbean: Colonialism and the Struggle for Identity (Papers presented to a symposium on East Indians in the Caribbean, The University of the West Indies, June, 1975). 1982. Millwood, New York: Kraus International Publications.

Ehrlich, Allen S. 1971. 'History, Ecology, and Demography in the British Caribbean: An Analysis of East Indian Ethnicity', *Southwestern Journal of Anthropology*, 27(2): 166–80.

———. 1976. 'Race and Ethnic Identity in Rural Jamaica: The East Indian Case', *Caribbean Quarterly*, 22(1): 19–27.

———. 1977. 'East Indian Integration in Rural Jamaica', *Actes Du XLIIe Congress International Des Americanistes*, Paris, 1: 120–36.

Emmer, Peter C. 1984. 'The Importation of British Indians into Surinam (Dutch Guiana), 1873–1906', in S. Marks and P. Richardson (eds.): *International Labour Migration: Historical Perspectives*. London: Temple Simth, pp. 187–207.

———. (ed.). 1986a. *Colonialism and Migration: Indentured Labour Before and After Slavery*. Dordrecht, The Netherlands: Martinus Nijhoff.

———. 1986b. 'The Great Escape: The Migration of Female Indentured Servants from British India to Surinam, 1873–1916', in P. D. Richardson (ed.): *Abolition and its Aftermath*. London: Frank Cass, pp. 245–66.

Erickson, Edgar L. 1934. 'The Introduction of East Indian Coolies into the British West Indies', *The Journal of Modern History*, 6(2): 127–46.

Eriksen, Thomas Hylland. 1992. 'Indians in New Worlds: Mauritius and Trinidad', *Social and Economic Studies*, 41(1): 157–87.

Fenton, J. 1988. *Transplanting Religious Traditions: Asian Indians in America*. New York: Praeger.

Finch, Jacqueline. 1986. 'The East Indian West Indian Male in Naipaul's Early Caribbean Novels', *Caribbean Quarterly*, 32(1–2): 25–37.

Firth, Raymond; David Pocock, H. S. Morris, Adrian C. Mayer and Burton Benedict. 1957. 'Factions in Indian and Overseas Indian Societies', *British Journal of Sociology*, 8(4): 291–342.

Fisher, Maxine P. 1980. *Indians of New York City: A Study of Immigrants from India*. Delhi: Heritage Publishers/South Asia Books.

Fleuret, Anne. 1974. 'Incorporation into Networks among Sikhs in Los Angeles', *Urban Anthropology*, 3(1).

Forbes, Richard H. 1985. *Hindu Organizational Function and Disfunction in an Alien Society*. Trinidad: The Vedanta Society.

Freund, Bl. 1995. *Insiders and Outsiders: The Indian Working Class of Durban*. Pietermaritzburg: University of Natal Press.

Fuglerud, Ivind and Oivind Fuglerud. 1999. *Life on the Outside: The Tamil Diaspora and Long-Distance Nationalism*. London: Pluto Press.

Furtado, Patrick E. 1999. *Impact of Gulf Migration on Family: A Research Study of Catholic Christian Community in Dakshina Kannada.* Honavar (Karnataka): Prathibhodaya, Academy for Art and Literature.

Gabbi, R. S. 1998. *Sikhs in Australia.* Melbourne: Aristoc Press.

Gambhir, Surendra K. 1983. 'Diglossia in Dying Languages: A Case Study of Guyanese Bhojpuri and Standard Hindi', *Anthropological Lingustics*, 25(1): 28–38.

————. 1986. 'Mauritian Bhojpuri: An International Perspective on Historical and Sociolinguistic Processes', in U. Bissoondoyal and S. B. C. Servansing (eds.): *Indian Labour Migration* (Papers presented at the International Conference on Indian Labour Immigration, 23–27 October 1984, held at the Mahatma Gandhi Institute). Moka, Mauritius: Mahatma Gandhi Institute, pp. 189–206.

Gangulee, N. 1947. *Indians in the Empire Overseas.* London: New India Publishing Co.

Ghai, Dharam P. (ed.). 1970. *Portrait of a Minority in East Africa.* Nairobi: Oxford University Press.

Ghosh, Ratna. 1981a. 'Minority Within a Minority: On Being South Asian and Female in Canada', in George Kurian and Ratna Ghosh (eds.): *Women in the Family and the Economy.* Westport, Conn.: Greenwood Press, pp. 413–26.

————. 1981b. 'Social and Economic Integration of South Asian Women in Montreal, Canada', in George Kurian and Ratna Ghosh (eds.): *Women in the Family and the Economy.* Westport, Conn.: Greenwood Press, pp. 59–71.

Gillion, K. L. 1962. *Fiji's Indian Immigrants: A History to the End of Indenture in 1920.* Melbourne: Oxford University Press.

————. 1977. *The Fiji Indians: Challenge to European Dominance, 1920–46.* Canberra: Australian National University Press.

Glasgow, Roy Arthur. 1970. *Guyana: Race and Politics among Africans and East Indians.* The Hague: Martinus Nijhoff.

Gosine, Mahin. 1986. *East Indians and Black Power in the Caribbean: The Case of Trinidad.* New York: Africana Publications.

————. 1990a. *Caribbean East Indians in America: Assimilation, Adaptation and Group Experience.* New York: Windsor Press.

————. (ed.). 1990b. *Dot-Head Americans: The Silent Minority in the United States.* New York: Windsor Press.

————. 1992. *The Coolie Connection: From the Orient to the Occident.* New York: Windsor Press.

————. (ed.). 1994. *The East Indian Odyssey: Dilemmas of a Migrant People.* New York: Windsor Press.

Gosine, Mahin (with Dipak Malik and Kumar Mahabir). 1995. *The Legacy of Indian Indenture: 150 Years of East Indians in Trinidad.* New York: Windsor Press.

Gossai, Hemchand and Nathaniel S. Murrell. 2000. (ed.) *Religion, Culture and Tradition in the Caribbean.* Basingstoke, Hampshire: Palgrave Publishers Ltd.

Gracias, Fatima da Silva. 2000. 'Goans Away from Goa: Migration to the Middle East', *Lusotopie 2000* (Lusophonies Asiatiques, Asiatiques en Lusophonies). Paris: Editions Karthala, pp. 423–32.

Greene, John Edward. 1974. *Race vs. Politics in Guyana: Political Cleavages and Political Mobilization in the 1968 General Election*. Mona, Jamaica: Institute of Social and Economic Research.

Gregory, Robert G. 1971. *India and East Africa: A History of Race Relations within the British Empire, 1890–1939*. Oxford: Clarendon Press.

———. 1993. *Quest for Equality: Asian Politics in East Africa, 1900–1967*. New Delhi: Orient Longman.

Griffith, J. A. G. 1960. *Coloured Immigrants in Britain*. London: Oxford University Press.

Gunatilleke, Godfrey (ed.) 1986. *Migration of Asian Workers to the Arab World*. Tokyo: United Nations University.

Haraksingh, Kusha. 1976. 'Indian Leadership in the Indenture Period', *Caribbean Issues,* 2(3): 17–38.

———. 1988. 'Structure, Process and Indian Culture in Trinidad', *Immigrants and Minorities*, 7(1): 113–22.

Hazareesingh, K. 1966. 'The Religion and Culture of Indian Immigrants in Mauritius, and the Effect of Social Change', *Comparative Studies in Society and History*, 8(2): 241–57.

———. 1975. *History of Indians in Mauritius*. London: Macmillan.

Helweg, Arthur W. 1979. *Sikhs in England: The Development of a Migrant Community*. New Delhi: Oxford University Press.

———. 1983. 'Emigrant Remittances: Their Nature and Impact on a Punjabi Village', *New Community*, 10(3): 435–43.

———. 1985. 'Social Networks among Indian Professionals in Australia', *New Community*, 12(3): 439–49.

———. 1987. 'Why leave India for America? A Case Study Approach to Understanding Migrant Behaviour', *International Migration*, 25: 165–78.

———. 1990. *An Immigrant Success Story*. Philadelphia: University of Pennsylvania Press and London: C. Hurst.

Helweg, Arthur and Usha Helweg. 1982. 'Indians in America: Doing Well', *Span*, 23: 14–19.

Hollingworth, Lawrence W. 1966. *The Asians of East Africa*. London: Macmillan.

Hollup, Oddvar. 1994. *Bonded Labour: Caste and Cultural Identity among Tamil Plantation Workers in Sri Lanka*. New Delhi: Sterling Publishers.

Horowitz, Michael M. 1963. 'The Worship of South Indian Deities in Martinique', *Ethnology*, 2(3): 339–46.

Horowitz, Michael M. and Morton Klass. 1961. 'The Martiniquan East Indian Cult of Maldevidan', *Social and Economic Studies*, 10(1): 93–100.

Hossain, Zakir. 1982. *The Silent Minority: Indians in Thailand*. Bangkok: Chulalongkorn University Social Research Institute.

Hoyt, Edwin P. 1974. *Asians in the West*. Nashville, Tennessee: Thomas Nelson.

Innes, Frank. 1995. 'Indo Caribbean Diaspora in Context: A Prospectus for Comparative Studies in Involuntary Migrations', *Indo-Caribbean Review*, 2(2): 159–63.

Israel, Benjamin J. 1984. *The Bene Israel of India: Some Studies*. Bombay: Orient Longman.

Israel, M. (ed.). 1987. *The South Asian Diaspora in Canada*. Toronto: Multicultural History Society of Ontario.

Israel, Milton and N. K. Wagle (eds.). 1993. *Ethnicity, Identity, Migration: The South Asian Context.* Toronto: Centre for South Asian Studies, University of Toronto.

Jackson, R. 1985. 'Hinduism in Britain: Religious Nurture and Religious Education', *British Journal of Religious Education,* 7(2): 68–75.

Jagpal, S. S. 1994. *Becoming Canadians: Pioneer Sikhs in their Own Words.* Madeira Park: Harbour Publishing.

Jain, Prakash C. 1982. 'Indians Abroad: A Current Population Estimate', *Economic and Political Weekly,* 17(8): 299–304.

———. 1989. *Racial Discrimination Against Overseas Indians.* New Delhi: Concept Publishing Company.

———. 1999. *Indians in South Africa: Political Economy of Race Relations.* New Delhi: Kalinga.

Jain, Ravindra K. 1970. *South Indians on the Plantation Frontier in Malaya.* New Haven: Yale University Press.

———. 1986. 'The East Indian Culture in a Caribbean Context: Crisis and Creativity', *India International Centre Quarterly,* 13(2): 153–64.

———. 1988. 'Overseas Indians in Malaysia and the Caribbean: Comparative Notes', *Immigrants and Minorities,* 7(1): 123–43.

———. 1993. *Indian Communities Abroad: Themes and Literature.* New Delhi: Manohar.

———. 1998. 'Indian Diaspora, Globalisation and Multi-Culturalism: A Cultural Analysis', *Contributions to Indian Sociology,* 32(2): 337–60.

James, A. 1974. *Sikh Children in Britain.* London: Oxford University Press.

James, Clifford. 1994. 'Diasporas', *Cultural Anthropology,* 9(3): 302–38.

James, C. L. R. 1965. *West Indians of East Indian Descent.* Trinidad: Ibis Publications.

Jayaram, N. 1998a. 'Social Construction of the *Other* Indian: Encounters between Indian Nationals and Diasporic Indians', *Journal of Social and Economic Development,* 1(1): 46–63.

———. 1998b. 'The Study of Indian Diaspora: A Multidisciplinary Agenda' (Occasional Paper No. 1). Hyderabad: Centre for the Study of Indian Diaspora, University of Hyderabad.

———. 2003. 'The Politics of "Cultural Renaissance" Among Indo-Trinidadians', in Bhikhu Parekh, Gurharpal Singh and Steven Vertovec (eds.): *Culture and Economy in the Indian Diaspora.* London: Routledge, pp. 123–41.

Jayaraman, R. 1975. *Caste Continuities in Ceylon: A Study of the Social Structure of Three Tea Plantations.* Bombay: Popular Prakashan.

Jayawardena, Chandra. 1960. 'Marital Stability in Two Guianese Sugar Estate Communities', *Social and Economic Studies,* 9(1): 76–100.

———. 1963. *Conflict and Solidarity in a Guianese Plantation.* London: Athlone Press. (London School of Economics Monographs in Social Anthropology No. 25)

———. 1966. 'Religious Belief and Social Change: Aspects of the Development of Hinduism in British Guiana', *Comparative Studies in Society and History,* 8(2): 211–40.

———. 1968. 'Migration and Social Change: A Survey of Indian Communities Overseas', *Geographical Review,* 58(3): 426–49.

Jayawardena, Chandra. 1971. 'The Disintegration of Caste in Fiji Indian Rural Society', in L. R. Hiatt and C. Jayawardena (eds.): *Anthropology Oceania*. Sydney: Angus and Robertson.

———. 1980. 'Culture and Ethnicity in Guyana and Fiji', *Man* (NS), 15(3): 430–50.

Jensen, Joan M. 1988. *Passage from India: Asian Indian Immigrants in North America*. New Haven: Yale University Press.

Jha, Jagdish Chandra. 1972. 'The Indian Mutiny-cum-Revolt of 1857 and Trinidad (West Indies)', *Indian Studies: Past and Present*, 13(4): 419–30.

———. 1976a. 'The Hindu Festival of Divali in The Caribbean', *Caribbean Quarterly*, 22(1): 53–61.

———. 1976b. 'The Hindu Sacraments (*Rites de Passage*) in Trinidad and Tobago', *Caribbean Quarterly*, 22(1): 40–52.

John, De Witt. 1969. *Indian Workers' Associations in Great Britain*. London: Oxford University Press, for The Institute of Race Relations.

Johnston, Hugh. 1979. *The Voyage of the Komagata Maru: The Sikh Challenge to Canada's Colour Bar*. Delhi: Oxford University Press.

———. 1984. *The East Indians in Canada*. Ottawa: Canadian Historical Association.

Joshi, P. S. 1942. *The Tyranny of Colour: A Study of Indian Problem in South Africa*. Durban, South Africa: E. P. and Commercial Printing Co.

Joy, Annamma. 1984. 'Work and Ethnicity: The Case of the Sikhs in the Okanagan Valley of British Columbia', in Rabindra Kanungo (ed.): *South Asians in the Canadian Mosaic*. Montreal: Kala Bharati.

Judge, Paramjit S. 1993. *Punjabis in Canada: A Study of Formation of an Ethnic Community*. Delhi: Chanakya Publications.

———. 2003. 'Social Construction of Identity in a Multicultural State: Sikhs in Canada', *Economic and Political Weekly*, 38(17): 1725–31.

Kalla, Abdool Cader. 1986. 'The Language Issue: A Perennial Issue in Mauritian Education', in U. Bissoondoyal and S. B. C. Servansing (eds.): *Indian Labour Migration* (Papers presented at The International Conference on Indian Labour Immigration, 23–27 October 1984, held at The Mahatma Gandhi Institute). Moka, Mauritius: Mahatma Gandhi Institute, pp. 165–78.

Kanungo, Rabindra (ed.). 1984. *South Asians in the Canadian Mosaic*. Montreal: Kala Bharati.

Kapur, Devesh. 2003. 'Indian Diaspora as a Strategic Asset', *Economic and Political Weekly*, 38(5): 445–48.

Kelly, John. 1991. *A Politics of Virtue: Hinduism, Sexuality, and Counter-Colonial Discourse in Fiji*. Chicago: University of Chicago Press.

Khan, Aisha. 1994. '*Juthaa* in Trinidad: Food, Pollution, and Hierarchy in a Caribbean Diaspora Community', *American Ethnologist*, 21(2): 245–69.

Kirpalani, Murli J.; Mitra G. Sinanan, S. M. Rameshwar and L. F. Seukeran (eds.). 1945. *Indian Centenary Review: One Hundred Years of Progress, 1845–1945, Trinidad, B.W.I.* Trinidad: Indian Centenary Review Committee.

Klass, Morton. 1961. *East Indians in Trinidad: A Study of Cultural Persistence*. Prospect Heights, Illinois: Waveland Press.

———. 1991. *Singing with Sai Baba: The Politics of Revitalization in Trinidad*. Boulder, Colorado: Westview Press.

Kondapi, C. 1951. *Indians Overseas, 1838–1949*. New Delhi: Indian Council for World Affairs. (Bombay: Oxford University Press).

Kuepper, W. G.; G. L. Lackey and E. N. Sinerton. 1975. *Ugandan Asians in Great Britain*. London: Croom Helm.

Kumar, Amitava (ed.). 2003. *Away: The Indian Writer as An Expatriate*. New Delhi: Penguin Books.

Kuper, Hilda. 1960. *Indian People in Natal*. Pietermaritzburg: University of Natal Press. (Republished in 1974 by Westport, Con.: Greenwood Press.)

Kuper, Jessica. 1975. 'The Goan Community in Kampala', in Michael Twaddle (ed.): *Expulsion of a Minority: Essays on Uganda Asians*. London: The Athlone Press, pp. 53–69.

Kuppusami, C. 1983. *Religions, Practices, and Customs of South African Indians*. Durban: Sunray Publishers.

Kurian, George. 1987. 'Socio-Cultural Adaptation of South Asian Immigrants: The Canadian Experience', *The Journal of Sociological Studies*, 6(1): 47–62.

Kurian, George and Ram P. Srivastava (eds.). 1983. *Overseas Indians: A Study in Adaptation*. New Delhi: Vikas Publishing House.

Kurian, Raja. 1979. 'Patterns of Emigration from Kerala', *Social Scientist*, 7(6): 32–53.

La Brack, Bruce. 1988. *The Sikhs of Northern California, 1904–1975*. New York: Ams Press.

La Guerre, John Gaffar. 1976. 'Afro-Indian Relations in Trinidad and Tobago: An Assessment', *Social and Economic Studies*, 25(3): 291–306.

———. (ed.). 1985. *Calcutta to Caroni*. St. Augustine, Trinidad: Extra Mural Studies Unit, The University of the West Indies (2nd Revised Edition).

La Guerre, John Gaffar; Brinsley Samaroo and George Sammy. 1973. *East Indians and the Present Crisis*. Aranguez, Trinidad: Print-Rite.

Lal, Brij V. 1983. *Girmitiyas: The Origins of the Fiji Indians*. Canberra: Journal of Pacific History.

Lal, Vinay. 1999. 'The Politics of History on the Internet: Cyber-Diasporic Hinduism and the North American Hindu Diaspora', *Diaspora*, 8(2): 137–72.

Lall, Marie-Carine 2001. *India's Missed Opportunity: India's Relationship with the Non Resident Indians*. Aldershot (Hampshire): Ashgate Publishing Limited.

Lambert, S. M. 1938. *East Indians and Fijians in Fiji: Their Changing Numerical Relations*. Honolulu, Hawaii: Published by the Museum.

Landis, Joseph Boyd. 1973. 'Racial Attitudes of Africans and Indians in Guyana', *Social and Economic Studies*, 22(4): 427–39.

Laurence, K. O. 1971. *Immigration into the West Indies in the 19th Century* (Chapters in Caribbean History 3). Aylesbury, Bucks, U.K.: Ginn and Co.

———. 1994. *A Question of Labour: Indentured Immigration into Trinidad and British Guiana, 1875–1917*. Kingston, Jamaica: Ian Randle Publishers.

Lemon, Anthony. 1980a. 'Asian Overseas Settlement in the Nineteenth and Twentieth Centuries', in Anthony Lemon and Norman Pollock (eds.): *Studies in Overseas Settlement and Population*. London/New York: Longman, pp. 103–25.

Lemon, Anthony. 1980b. 'The Indian Communities of East Africa and the Caribbean', in Anthony Lemon and Norman Pollock (eds.): *Studies in Overseas Settlement and Population*. London/New York: Longman, pp. 225–41.

Leonard, Karen. 1997. *The South Asian Americans*. Westport, Conn.: Greenwood Press.

Lessinger, J. 1995. *From the Ganges to the Hudson: Indian Immigrants in New York City*. Needham Heights, Mass.: Allyn Bacon.

Logan, P. 1988. 'Practising Religion: British Hindu Children and the Navaratri Festival', *British Journal of Religious Education*, 10: 160–69.

Look Lai, Walton. 1993. *Indentured Labor, Caribbean Sugar: Chinese and Indian Migrants to The British West Indies, 1838–1918*. Baltimore and London: The Johns Hopkins University Press.

Mahajani, Usha. 1960. *The Role of Indian Minorities in Burma and Malaya*. New York: Institute of Pacific Relations. (Bombay: Vora and Co.)

Maharaj, Ashram B. 1991. *The Pandits in Trinidad: A Study of a Hindu Institution*. Couva, Trinidad: Indian Review Press.

Malik, Yogendra K. 1971. *East Indians in Trinidad: A Study in Minority Politics*. London: Oxford University Press, for Institute of Race Relations, London.

Mangat, J. S. 1969. *A History of the Asians in East Africa, 1886–1945*. Oxford: Clarendon Press.

Mangru, Basdeo. 1983 'Disparity in Bengal and Madras Emigration to British Guiana in the Nineteenth Century', *Revista Interamericana*, 13: 99–107.

———. 1986a. 'Abolishing the Return Passage Entitlement under Indenture: Guianese Planter Pressure and Indian Government Response, 1838–1917', *Caribbean Quarterly*, 32(3&4): 1–13.

———. 1986b. 'Aftermath of Indenture: The British Guiana Colonization Scheme, 1915–1927', *Journal of Caribbean Studies*, 5(3): 181–98.

———. 1987. *Benevolent Neutrality: Indian Government Policy and Labour Migration to British Guiana*. London: Hansib.

———. 1993. *Indenture and Abolition: Sacrifice and Survival on the Guyanese Sugar Plantations*. Toronto: TSAR.

Mansingh, Ajai and Laxmi Mansingh. 1995. 'Hosay and its Creolization', *Caribbean Quarterly*, 41(1): 25–39.

Mascarenhas-Keyes, Stella. 1979. *Goans in London: Portrait of a Catholic Asian Community*. London: Goan Association (UK).

———. 1993. 'International and Internal Migration: The Changing Identity of Catholic and Hindu Women in Goa', in Gina Buijs (ed.): *Migrant Women: Crossing Boundaries and Changing Identities*. Providence/Oxford: Berg Publishers, pp. 119–43.

Mayer, Adrian C. 1957. 'Factions in Fiji Indian Rural Settlements', *British Journal of Sociology*, 8(4): 317–27.

———. 1958. 'Association in Fiji Indian Rural Society', *American Anthropologist*, 14(1): 97–108.

———. 1961. *Peasants in the Pacific: A Study of Fiji Indian Rural Society*. Berkeley, LA: University of California Press.

———. 1963. *Indians in Fiji*. London: Oxford University Press.

Mcleod, W. H. 1986. *Punjabis in New Zealand*. Amritsar: Guru Nanak Dev University.

Mearns, David James. 1987. 'Caste Overseas: Does it Matter? Urban Indians in Malaysia', *Contributions to Indian Sociology*, 21(2): 285–306.

———. 1995. *Shiva's Other Children: Religion and Social Identity Amongst Overseas Indians.* New Delhi: Sage Publications.

Meer, F. 1969. *Portrait of South African Indians.* Durban: Avon House.

Metcalf, Thomas R. 1986. 'Indian Migration to South Africa', in M. S. A. Rao (ed.): *Studies in Migration: Internal and International Migration in India.* Delhi: Manohar Publications, pp. 345–62.

Min, Pyong Gap (ed.). 1995. *Asian Americans: Contemporary Trends and Issues.* Beverley Hills: Sage Publications.

Mishra, Vijay (ed.). 1979. *Rama's Banishment: A Centenary Tribute to the Fiji Indians, 1879–1979.* Auckland, Heinemann Educational Books (NZ).

Mohammed, Patricia. 1994. 'Gender as a Primary Signifier in the Construction of Community and State among Indians in Trinidad', *Caribbean Quarterly*, 40(3&4): 32–43.

Mohan, Peggy and Paul Zador. 1986. 'Discontinuity in a Life Cycle: The Death of Trinidad Bhojpuri', *Language*, 62: 291–319.

Mohapatra, Prabhu P. 1995. '"Restoring the Family" Wife Murders and the Making of a Sexual Contract for Indian Immigrant Labour in the British Caribbean Colonies, 1860–1920', *Studies in History*, 11(2): 227–60.

Moodley, K. A. 1975. 'South African Indians: The Wavering Minority', in L. Thompson and J. Butler (eds.): *Change in Contemporary South Africa.* Berkeley: University of California Press, pp. 250–79.

Moore, Brian L. 1977. 'The Retention of Caste Notions among the Indian Immigrants in British Guiana during the Nineteenth Century', *Comparative Studies in Society and History*, 19(1): 96–107.

———. 1987. *Race, Power and Social Segmentation in Colonial Society: Guyana after Slavery, 1838–1891.* New York: Gordon and Breach Science Publishers.

———. 1995. *Cultural Power, Resistance and Pluralism: Colonial Guyana, 1838–1900.* Jamaica: The Press University of the West Indies, and Montreal: Mcgill Queen's University Press.

Moore, Dennison. 1995. *Origins and Development of Racial Ideology in Trinidad: The Black View of the East Indian.* Tunapuna, Trinidad: Chakra Publishing House.

Morris, H. S. 1968. *The Indians in Uganda.* London: Weidenfeld and Nicolson.

Motwani, Jagat K. and Jyoti Barot-Motwani (eds.). 1993. *Global Migration of Indians: Saga of Adventure, Enterprise, Identity and Integration.* New York: Global Organization of People of Indian Origin.

Motwani, Jagat K.; Mahin Gosine and Jyoti Barot-Motwani (eds.). 1993. *Global Indian Diaspora: Yesterday, Today and Tomorrow.* New York: Global Organization of People of Indian Origin.

Muthanna, I. M. 1975. *People of India in North America.* Bangalore: Lotus Printers.

Naidoo, Josephine C. 1985. 'Contemporary South Asian Women in the Canadian Mosaic', *International Journal of Women's Studies*, 8(4): 338–50.

———. 1986. 'Value Conflicts for South Asian Women in Multicultural Canada', in Lars H. Ekstrand (ed.): *Minorities and Immigrants in a Cross-Cultural Perspective.* Berwyn: Swets North America, pp. 132–46.

Naidoo, M. B. 1960. 'The East Indian in Trinidad: A Study of an Immigrant Community', *Journal of Geography*, 59(4): 175–81.

Nair, P. R. Gopinathan. 1989. 'Incidence, Impact and Implications of Migration to the Middle East from Kerala (India)', in Rasid Amjad (ed.): *To the Gulf and Back: Studies on the Economic Impact of Asian Labour Migration*. New Delhi: Ilo-Artep, pp. 343–64.

————. 1994. 'Migration of Keralites to the Arab World', in B. A. Prakash (ed.): *Kerala's Economy: Performance, Problems, Prospects*. New Delhi: Sage Publications.

Nath, Dwarka. 1970. *A History of Indians in Guyana*. London: Butler and Tanner (2nd Revised Edition).

Nayagam, Xavier S. Thani. 1969. 'Tamil Emigration to the Martinique', *Journal of Tamil Studies*, 1(2): 75–123.

Nayyar, Deepak. 1994. *Migration, Remittances and Capital Flows: The Indian Experience*. Delhi: Oxford University Press.

Nevadomsky, Joseph J. 1980a. 'Changes in Hindu Institutions in an Alien Environment', *The Eastern Anthropologist*, 33(1): 39–53.

————. 1980b. 'Abandoning the Retentionist Model: Family and Marriage Change among the East Indians in Rural Trinidad', *International Journal of Sociology of the Family*, 10(2): 181–98.

————. 1981a. 'Cultural and Structural Dimensions of Occupational Prestige in an East Indian Community in Trinidad', *Journal of Anthropological Research*, 37: 343–59.

————. 1981b. 'Wedding Rituals and Changing Women's Rights among the East Indians in Rural Trinidad', *International Journal of Women's Studies*, 4(5): 484–96.

————. 1982a. 'Changing Conceptions of Family Regulation among the Hindu East Indians in Rural Trinidad', *Anthropological Quarterly*, 55(4): 189–98.

————. 1982b. 'Social Change and the East Indians in Rural Trinidad: A Critique of Methodologies', *Social and Economic Studies*, 31(1): 90–126.

————. 1983a. 'Changing Patterns of Marriage, Family and Kinship among the East Indians in Rural Trinidad', *Anthropos*, 78: 107–48.

————. 1983b. 'Economic Organization, Social Mobility and Changing Social Status among East Indians in Rural Trinidad', *Ethnology*, 22(1): 63–79.

————. 1984. 'Marital Discord and Dissolution among the Hindu East Indians in Rural Trinidad', *Anthropos*, 79: 113–28.

————. 1985a. 'Developmental Sequences of Domestic Groups in an East Indian Community in Rural Trinidad', *Ethnology*, 24(1): 1–11.

————. 1985b. 'Domestic Cycles in an East Indian Community in Rural Trinidad', *The Eastern Anthropologist*, 38(2): 99–116.

Nicholls, David G. 1971. 'East Indians and Black Power in Trinidad', *Race*, 12(4): 443–59.

Niehoff, Arthur. 1959. 'The Survival of Hindu Institutions in an Alien Environment', *The Eastern Anthropologist*, 12(3): 171–87.

Niehoff, Arthur and Juanita Niehoff. 1960. *East Indians in The West Indies* (Milwaukee Public Museum Publications in Anthropology No. 6). Milwaukee, Wisconsin: Milwaukee Public Museum.

Norton, Robert. 1977. *Race and Politics in Fiji*. New York: St. Martin's Press.

Norton, Robert. 1986. 'Colonial Fiji: Ethnic Divisions and Elite Conciliation', in Brij V. Lal (ed.): *Politics in Fiji: Studies in Contemporary History.* Sydney: Allen and Unwin Australia, pp. 52–73.

Oberai, A. S. and H. K. Manmohan Singh. 1980. 'Migration Remittances and Rural Development: Findings of a Case Study in the Indian Punjab', *International Labour Review*, CIX (2): 229–41.

Palmer, M. 1957. *The History of the Indians in Natal* (Natal Regional Survey Vol. 10). Cape Town: Oxford University Press.

Pant, Girijesh. 1987. 'South Asian Migration to the Gulf: Problems and Prospects', in Bhabani Sen Gupta (ed.): *The Persian Gulf and South Asia.* New Delhi: South Asia Publishers.

Paranjape, Makarand (ed.). 2001. *In-Diaspora: Theories, Histories, Texts.* New Delhi: Indialog.

Parekh, Bhikhu; Gurharpal Singh and Steven Vertovec (eds.). 2003. *Culture and Economy in the Indian Diaspora.* London: Routledge.

Parmasad, Ken. 1994. 'Searching for Continuity: The Ancestral Impulse and Community Identity Formation in Trinidad', *Caribbean Quarterly*, 40(3–4): 22–29.

Pearn, B. R. 1946. *The Indians in Burma.* Ledbury: U.M. Lee Play House Press.

Persaud, Kamal. 1988. *Racism Against the Indians in the Eastern Caribbean.* Trinidad and Tobago: Battlefront Pointers.

———. 1996. *The Indian Spectre or Crisis in the Media.* Couva, Trinidad: The Indian Review Committee.

Petievich, Carla (ed.). 1999. *The Expanding Landscape: South Asians and the Diasporas.* New Delhi: Manohar.

Pfaffenberger, Bryan. 1982. *Caste in Tamil Culture: The Religious Foundations of Sudra Domination in Tamil Sri Lanka.* Syracuse, New York: Foreign and Comparative Studies.

Prasad, Shiu. 1971. *Indian Indentured Workers in Fiji.* Suva: Mayfair Printers for South Pacific Social Sciences Association.

Prashad, V. 2000. *The Karma of Brown Folk.* Minneapolis: University of Minnesota Press.

Premdas, Ralph R. 1986. 'Ethnic Conflict Management: A Government of National Unity and Some Alternative Proposals', in Brij V. Lal (ed.): *Politics in Fiji: Studies in Contemporary History.* Sydney: Allen and Unwin Australia, pp. 107–38.

———. 1995a. *Ethnic Conflict and Development: The Case of Fiji.* Aldershot, Hants, England: Avebury/Ashgate Publishing Ltd.

———. 1995b. *Ethnic Conflict and Development: The Case of Guyana.* Aldershot, Hants, England: Avebury/Ashgate Publishing Ltd.

———. 1996a. 'Ethnicity and Elections in the Caribbean: A Radical Realignment of Power in Trinidad and the Threat of Communal Strife' (Working Paper 224). The Helen Kellogg Institute for International Studies, University of Notre Dame.

———. 1996b. 'Ethnic Identity in the Caribbean: Decentering a Myth' (Monograph Series No. 1). New Haven, Connecticut: Center for Latin American and Caribbean Studies, Yale University.

Premdas, Ralph R. 1996c. 'Ethnic Conflict and Religion: The Christian Challenge of Reconciliation' (Occasional Paper Series, 10: OP: 5). The Joan B. Krock Institute for International Peace Studies, University of Notre Dame.

Prorok, Carolyn V. 1986. 'The Canadian Presbyterian Mission in Trinidad: John Morton's Work among East Indians', *National Geographical Journal of India*, 33(3): 253–62.

Radhakrishnan, R. 1996. *Diasporic Mediations: Between Home and Location.* Minneapolis: University of Minnesota Press.

Rahman, A. 2001. *Indian Labour Migration to the Gulf.* New Delhi: Rajat.

Rajkumar, N. V. 1951. *Indians Outside India: A General Survey.* Madras: Commercial Printing and Publishing House.

Ralston, Helen. 1988. 'Ethnicity, Class and Gender among South Asian Women in Metro Halifax: An Exploratory Study', *Canadian Ethnic Studies*, 20(3): 63–83.

Ramchandani, R. R. 1976. *Uganda Asians: The End of an Enterprise.* Bombay: United Asia Publications.

Ramdin, Ron. 1994. *The Other Middle Passage: Journal of a Voyage from Calcutta to Trinidad, 1858.* London: Hansib.

Ramesar, Marianne D. Soares. 1976a. 'Patterns of Regional Settlement and Economic Activity by Immigrant Groups in Trinidad, 1851–1900', *Social and Economic Studies*, 25(3): 187–215.

————. 1976b. 'The Impact of the Indian Immigrants on Colonial Trinidad Society', *Caribbean Quarterly*, 22(1): 5–18.

————. 1976c. 'The Integration of Indian Settlers in Trinidad after Indenture', *Caribbean Issues*, 11(3): 52–69.

————. 1994. *Survivors of Another Crossing: A History of East Indians in Trinidad, 1880–1946.* St. Augustine, Trinidad and Tobago: School of Continuing Studies, The University of the West Indies.

Rao, M. S. A. (ed.). 1986. *Studies in Migration: Internal and International Migration in India.* Delhi: Manohar Publications.

Rauf, N. 1974. *Indian Village in Guyana: A Study of Cultural Change and Ethnic Identity.* Leiden, The Netherlands: E.J. Brill.

Rayaprol, Aparna. 1997. *Negotiating Identities: Women in the Indian Diaspora.* New Delhi: Oxford University Press.

————. 2001. '"Can You Talk Indian?": Shifting Notions of Community and Identity in the Indian Diaspora', in Surinder S. Jodhka (ed.): *Community and Identities: Contemporary Discourses on Culture and Politics in India.* New Delhi: Sage Publications, pp. 163–90.

Reddock, Rhoda. 1986. 'Indian Women and Indentureship in Trinidad and Tobago, 1845–1917: Freedom Denied', *Caribbean Quarterly*, 32(3–4): 27–49.

————. 1994. 'Douglarisation and the Politics of Gender Relations in Contemporary Trinidad and Tobago: A Preliminary Exploration', in Ramesh Deosaran, Rhoda Reddock and Nasser Mustapha (eds.): *Contemporary Issues in Social Science: A Caribbean Perspective.* St. Augustine, Trinidad: The ANSA McAL Psychological Research Centre, UWI, pp. 98–127.

————. 1995. 'Contestations Over National Culture in Trinidad and Tobago: Considerations of Ethnicity, Class and Gender', in Ramesh Deosaran and Nasser Mustapha (eds.): *Contemporary Issues in Social Science: A Caribbean*

Perspective (Vol. 2). St. Augustine, Trinidad: The ANSA MCAL Psychological Research Centre, Uwi, pp. 106–45.

Rex, John and Sally Tomlinson. 1979. *Colonial Migrants in a British City: A Class Analysis*. London: Routledge and Kegan Paul.

Rhoodie, Nic (ed.). 1978. *Intergroup Accommodation in Plural Societies* (A Selection of Conference Papers with Special Reference to The Republic of South Africa). London: Macmillan.

Robinson, Vaughan. 1981. 'The Development of South Asian Settlements in Britain and The Myth of Return', in C. Peach, V. Robinson and S. Smith (eds.): *Ethnic Segregation in Cities*. London: Croom Helm.

———. 1982. 'The Assimilation of South and East African Asian Immigrants in Britain', in D. A. Coleman (ed.): *Demography of Immigrants and Minorities in the United Kingdom*. London: Academic Press.

———. 1984. 'Asians in Britain: A Study in Encapsulation and Marginality', in Colin Clarke, David Ley and Ceri Peach (eds.): *Geography and Ethnic Pluralism*. London: George Allen and Unwin, pp. 231–57.

———. 1986. *Transients, Settlers, and Refugees: Asians in Britain*. Oxford: Oxford University Press.

Roopchand, T. 1976. 'The Hindu Temple Service: A Functionalist Approach', *Guyana Journal of Sociology*, 1: 93–122.

Rubin, Vera. 1962. 'Culture, Politics and Race Relations', *Social and Economic Studies*, 11(4): 433–55.

Ruhomon, Peter. 1947. *Centenary History of the East Indians in British Guiana, 1838–1938*. George Town: *The Daily Chronicle*.

Ryan, Selwyn. 1972. *Race and Nationalism in Trinidad and Tobago: A Study of Decolonization in a Multiracial Society*. St. Augustine, Trinidad: Institute of Social and Economic Research, The University of the West Indies.

———. (ed.). 1988. *Trinidad and Tobago: The Independence Experience, 1962–1987*. St. Augustine, Trinidad: Institute for Social and Economic Research, The University of the West Indies.

———. (ed.). 1991. *Social and Occupational Stratification in Contemporary Trinidad and Tobago*. St. Augustine, Trinidad: Institute of Social and Economic Research, The University of the West Indies.

———. 1996. *Pathways to Power: Indians and the Politics of National Unity in Trinidad and Tobago*. St. Augustine, Trinidad: Institute of Social and Economic Research, The University of the West Indies.

Safran, William. 1991. 'Diasporas in Modern Societies: Myths of Homeland and Return', *Diaspora*, 1(1): 83–99.

Saha, Panchanan. 1970. *Emigration of Indian Labour, 1834–1900*. New Delhi: People's Publishing House.

Sahadevan, P. 1995. *India and Overseas Indians: The Case of Sri Lanka*. Delhi: Kalinga Publications.

Saintsbury, G. 1972. *East Indian Slavery*. Dublin: Irish University Press.

Salick, Roydon. 1986. 'The East Indian Female in Three West Indian Novels of Adolescence', *Caribbean Quarterly*, 32(1–2): 38–46.

Samaroo, Brinsley. 1975. 'The Presbyterian Canadian Mission as an Agent of Integration in Trinidad during the Nineteenth and early Twentieth Centuries', *Caribbean Studies*, 14(4): 41–55.

Samaroo, Brinsley et al. (eds.) 1995. *In Celebration of 150 Years of the Indian Contribution to Trinidad and Tobago*. Arima, Trinidad: D. Quentrall-Thomas.

Sandhu, Karnial Singh. 1969. *Indians in Malaysia: Some Aspects of their Immigration and Settlement, 1786–1957*. London: Cambridge University Press.

Sandhu, Karnail Singh and A. Mani (eds.). 1993. *Indian Communities in Southeast Asia*. Singapore: Times Academic Press.

Santhiram, R. 1999. *Education of Minorities: The Case of Indians in Malaysia*. Selangor, Malaysia: Child Information, Learning and Development Centre.

Saran, Parmatma. 1985. *The Asian Indian Experience in the United States*. Cambridge, Mass.: Schenkman Publishing Company/New Delhi: Vikas Publishing House.

Saunders, Kay (ed.). 1984. *Indentured Labour in the British Empire, 1834–1920*. London: Croom Helm.

Sax, William S. (ed.). 1995. *The Gods at Play: Lila in South Asia*. New York/Oxford: Oxford University Press.

Schwartz, Barton Morley. 1964a. 'Ritual Aspects of Caste in Trinidad', *Anthropological Quarterly*, 37(1): 1–15.

———. 1964b. 'Caste and Endogamy in Trinidad', *Southwestern Journal of Anthropology*, 20(1): 58–66.

———. 1965a. 'Extra-Legal Activities of the Village Pandit in Trinidad', *Anthropological Quarterly*, 38(2): 62–71.

———. 1965b. 'Patterns of East Indian Family Organization in Trinidad', *Caribbean Studies*, 5(1): 23–36.

———. (ed.). 1967a. *Caste in Overseas Indian Communities*. San Francisco, California: Chandler Publishing Co.

———. 1967b. 'Differential Social and Religious Adaptation', *Social and Economic Studies*, 16(3): 237–48.

Seecharan, C. 1993. *India and the Shaping of the Indo-Guyanese Imagination, 1890s–1920s*. Leeds and Coventry: Peepal Tree Press/University of Warwick.

Sekhar, T. V. 1993. 'Migration Selectivity from Rural Areas: Evidences from Kerala', *Demography India*, 22(2): 191–202.

———. 1996. 'Male Emigration and Changes in the Family: Impact on Female Sex Roles', *The Indian Journal of Social Work*, 57(2): 277–94.

Seshadri, V. 1990. *Hindus Abroad: The Dilemma—Dollar or Dharma?* Delhi: Suruchi Prakashan.

Shankar; L. Dhingra and R. Srikanth (eds.). 1998. *A Part, Yet Apart: South Asians in Asian America*. Philadelphia: Temple University Press.

Sharma, Kailash Nath. 1986. 'Changing Forms of East Indian Marriage and Family in the Caribbeans', *The Journal of Sociological Studies*, 5: 20–58.

Shepherd, Verene A. 1986. 'The Dynamics of Afro Jamaican–East Indian Relations in Jamaica, 1845–1945: A Preliminary Analysis', *Caribbean Quarterly*, 32(3&4): 14–26.

———. 1986a. 'From Rural Plantations to Urban Slums: The Economic Status and Problems of East Indians in Kingston, Jamaica', *Immigrants and Minorities*, 5(2).

———. 1988. 'Indians and Blacks in Jamaica in the Nineteenth and Early Twentieth Centuries: A Micro Study of the Foundations of Race Antagonisms', *Immigrants and Minorities*, 7(1): 95–112.

Shepherd, Verene A. 1993. *Transients to Settlers: The Experience of Indians in Jamaica, 1845–1950*. Leeds, England: Centre for Research in Asian Migration, The University of Warwick and Peepal Tree Books.

Sheth, Pravin. 2001. *Indians in America: One Stream, Two Waves, Three Generations*. Jaipur: Rawat Publications.

Siddique, Sharon and Nirmala Purushottam. 1982. *Singapore's Little India: Past, Present, and Future*. Singapore: Institute of South East Asian Studies.

Siegel, Jeffrey. 1975. 'Fiji Hindustani', *Working Papers in Linguistics*, University of Hawaii, Honolulu, 7(3): 127–44.

Silverman, M. 1980. *Rich People and Rice: Factional Politics in Rural Guyana*. Leiden, The Netherlands: E.J. Brill.

Singaravelou. 1976. 'Indian Religion in Guadeloupe, French West Indies', *Caribbean Issues*, 2(3): 39–51.

———. 1987. *Les Indiens de la Caraibe* (3 Vols.). Paris: Editions L'Harmattan.

Singer, Philip and Enrique Araneta. 1967. 'Hinduization and Creolization in Guyana: The Plural Society and Basic Personality', *Social and Economic Studies*, 16(3): 221–36.

Singh, Gurharpal. 1999. 'A Victim Diaspora? The Case of The Sikhs' (Review article on Tatla 1999), *Diaspora*, 8(3): 293–307.

Singh, I. J. Bahadur (ed.). 1979. *The Other India: The Overseas Indians and Their Relationship with India (Proceedings of a Seminar)*. New Delhi: Arnold-Heinemann.

———. (ed.) 1982. *Indians in South-East Asia*. New Delhi: Sterling Publishers.

———. (ed.) 1984. *Indians in South Asia*. New Delhi: Sterling Publishers.

———. (ed.) 1987. *Indians in the Caribbean*. New Delhi: Sterling Publishers.

Singh, Kelvin. 1988. *Bloodstained Tombs: The Muharram Massacre, 1884*. London: Macmillan.

———. 1994. *Race and Class Struggles in a Colonial State: Trinidad, 1917–1945*. Kingston, Jamaica: The University of the West Indies.

Singh, Karnial. 1969. *Indians in Malaya*. Cambridge: Cambridge University Press.

Singh, Kunwar Maharaj. 1925. *Indian Immigration to British Guiana*. Calcutta: Government of India.

Singh, Shubha. 2001. *Fiji: A Precarious Coalition*. New Delhi: Har-Anand Publications.

Sinha-Kerkhoff, Kathinka and Ellen Bal. 2003. 'Eternal Call of the Ganga: Reconnecting with People of Indian Origin in Surinam', *Economic and Political Weekly*, 38(38): 4008–21.

Smillie, E. E. 1923. 'A Historical Survey of Indian Migration within the Empire', *The Canadian Historical Review*, 4: 217–57.

Smith, M. G. 1965. *The Plural Society in the British West Indies*. Berkeley, California: University of California Press.

Smith, Raymond T. 1957. 'Economic Aspects of Rice Production in an East Indian Community in British Guiana', *Social and Economic Studies*, 6(4): 502–22.

———. 1959. 'Some Social Characteristics of Indian Immigrants to British Guiana', *Population Studies*, 13(1): 34–39.

Smith, Raymond T. 1964. 'Ethnic Difference and Peasant Economy in British Guiana', in Raymond Firth and B. S. Yamey (eds.): *Capital, Saving and Credit in Peasant Societies*. London: George Allen and Unwin, pp. 305–29.

———. 1971. 'Race and Political Conflict in Guyana', *Race*, 12(4): 415–27.

———. 1996. *The Matrifocal Family: Power, Pluralism, and Politics*. New York/London: Routledge.

Smith, Raymond T. and Chandra Jayawardena. 1958. 'Hindu Marriage Customs in British Guiana', *Social and Economic Studies*, 7(2): 178–94.

———. 1959. 'Marriage and the Family amongst East Indians in British Guiana', *Social and Economic Studies*, 8(4): 321–76.

Speckmann, Johan Dirk. 1963. 'The Indian Group in the Segmented Society of Surinam', *Caribbean Studies*, 3(1): 3–17. .

———. 1965. *Marriage and Kinship among the Indians in Surinam*. Assen, The Netherlands: Royal Van Gorcum and Co.

———. 1975. 'Ethnicity and Ethnic Group Relations in Surinam', *Caribbean Studies*, 15(3): 5–15.

Srivastava, Ram P. 1975. 'Family Organization and Change among the Overseas Indians with Special Reference to Indian Immigrant Families of British Columbia, Canada', in George Kurian (ed.): *Family in India: A Regional View*. The Hague: Mouton.

St. Bernard, Godfrey. 1994. 'Ethnicity and Attitudes towards Inter-Racial Marriages in Trinidad and Tobago: An Exploration of Preliminary Findings', *Caribbean Quarterly*, 40(3–4): 109–25.

Steele, Beverley A. 'East Indian Indenture and the Work of the Presbyterian Church among the Indians in Grenada', *Caribbean Quarterly*, 22(1): 28–39.

Subramani (ed.). 1979. *The Indo-Fijian Experience*. St. Lucia, Queensland: University of Queensland Press.

Sudama, Trevor. 1983. 'Class, Race, and the State in Trinidad and Tobago', *Latin American Perspectives*, 10(4): 75–96.

———. 1993. *The Political Uses of Myth* or *Discrimination Rationalized: A Collection of Articles*. Trinidad: The Author.

Takaki, Ronald. 1989. *Strangers from a Different Shore: A History of Asian Americans*. New York: Penguin.

Tambs-Lyche, H. 1980. *London Patidars: A Case in Urban Ethnicity*. London: Routledge and Kegan Paul.

Tandon, Y. and A. Raphael. 1973. *East Africa's Asians*. London: Minority Rights Group.

Tatla, Darshan Singh. 1999. *The Sikh Diaspora: The Search for Statehood*. Seattle: University of Washington Press.

Thakur, Andra P. 1995. 'The Impact of Emigration and Remittances on an Indo-Guyanese Village Economy in Guyana', *Indo Caribbean Review*, 2(2): 105–25.

Thomaz, Luis Filipe. 1985. 'The Indian Merchant Communities in Malacca under the Portuguese Rule', in Teotonio R. de Souza (ed.): *Indo-Portuguese History: Old Issues, New Questions*. New Delhi: Concept Publishing Co., pp. 56–72.

Tikasingh, Gerad. 1980. 'Social Change in the Emerging East Indian Community in Late 19th Century Trinidad', *Journal of Caribbean Studies*, 1(2–3): 120–39.

Tinker, Hugh. 1974. *A New System of Slavery: The Export of Indian Labour Overseas, 1830–1920.* London: Oxford University Press (2nd Edition Published in 1993 by Hansib Publishing Limited, London).
———. 1976. *Separate and Unequal: India and The Indians in The British Commonwealth, 1920–1950.* Vancouver: University of British Columbia Press.
———. 1977. *The Banyan Tree: Overseas Emigrants from India, Pakistan and Bangladesh.* Oxford: Oxford University Press.
Van den Berghe, P. 1962. 'Indians in Natal and Fiji: A "Controlled Experiment" in Culture Contact', *Civilizations*, 12: 75–87.
Van der Burg, Corstian and Peter van der Veer. 1986. 'Pundits, Power and Profit: Religious Organization and the Construction of Identity among the Surinamese Hindus', *Ethnic and Racial Studies*, 9(4): 514–29.
Van der Veer, Peter (ed.). 1995. *Nation and Migration: The Politics of Space in the South Asian Diaspora.* Philadelphia: University of Pennsylvania Press.
Van der Veer, Peter and Steven Vertovec. 1991. 'Brahmanism Abroad: On Caribbean Hinduism as an Ethnic Religion', *Ethnology*, 30(1): 149–66.
Varma, Mohinder Nath. 1973. *Indian Immigrants and Their Descendants in Mauritius.* Vacoas, Mauritius: The Author.
Varma, Sushma J. and Radhika Seshan (eds.). 2003. *Fractured Identity: The Indian Diaspora in Canada.* Jaipur and New Delhi: Rawat Publications.
Vasil, Raj K. 1984. *Politics in Bi-Racial Societies: The Third World Experience.* New Delhi: Vikas Publishing House.
Vatuk, Ved Prakash. 1964. 'Protest Songs of East Indians in British Guiana', *Journal of American Folklore*, 77: 220–35.
Vedalankar, Pandit Nardev and Manohar Somera. 1975. *Arya Samaj and Indians Abroad.* New Delhi: Sarvadeshik Arya Pratinidhi Sabha.
Verma, Archana B. 2002. *The Making of Little Punjab in Canada: Patterns of Immigration.* New Delhi: Sage Publications.
Vertovec, Steven. 1984. 'Oil Boom and Recession in Trinidad Indian Villages', in Colin Clarke, David Ley and Ceri Peach (eds.): *Geography and Ethnic Pluralism.* London: George Allen and Unwin, pp. 89–111.
———. 1989. 'Hinduism in Diaspora: The Transformation of Tradition in Trinidad', in Günther D. Sontheimer and Hermann Kulke (eds.): *Hinduism Reconsidered* (South Asian Studies No. 24). New Delhi: Manohar Publications, pp. 157–86.
———. 1990. 'Religion and Ethnic Ideology: The Hindu Youth Movement in Trinidad', *Ethnic and Racial Studies*, 13(2): 225–49.
———. (ed.). 1991. *Aspects of the South Asian Diaspora* (Oxford University Papers on India, Vol. 2, Part 2). New Delhi: Oxford University Press.
———. 1991a. 'East Indians and Anthropologists: A Critical Review', *Social and Economic Studies*, 40(1): 133–69.
———. 1991b. 'Inventing Relgious Tradition: *Yagnas* and Hindu Renewal in Trinidad', in Armin Geertz and Jeppe Sindung Jensen (eds.): *Religion, Tradition and Renewal.* Aarthus: Universitetsforlag, pp. 77–95.
———. 1992a. *Hindu Trinidad: Religion, Ethnicity and Socio-Economic Change.* London: Macmillan.
———. 1992b. 'Community and Congregation in London Hindu Temples: Divergent Trends', *New Community*, 18: 251–64.

Vertovec, Steven. 1994. '"Official" and "Popular" Hinduism in Diaspora: Historical and Contemporary Trends in Surinam, Trinidad and Guyana', *Contributions to Indian Sociology*, 28(1): 123–47. [Also in Dabydeen and Samaroo
1996: 108–30]

————. 1997. 'Three Meanings of "Diaspora", Exemplified among South Asian
Religions', *Diaspora*, 6(3): 277–99.

————. 2000. *The Hindu Diaspora: Comparative Patterns*. London: Routledge.

Vertovec, Steven and Robin Cohen (eds.). 1999. *Migration, Diasporas and
Transnationalism*. Cheltenham, UK: Edward Elgar Publishing Ltd.

Visram, R. 1986. *Ayahs, Lascars and Princes: Indians in Britain, 1700–1947*.
London: Pluto.

Waghorne, Joanne Punzo. 1999. 'The Diaspora of the Gods: Hindu Temples in
the New World System, 1640–1800', *The Journal of Asian Studies*, 58(3):
648–86.

Waiz, S. A. (ed.). 1927. *Indian Abroad*. Bombay: Imperial Indian Citizenship
Association.

Warner, Stephen R. and Judith G. Wittner (eds.). 1998. *Gatherings in Diaspora:
Religious Communities and the New Immigration*. Philadelphia: Temple
University Press.

Weil, Shalva. 1996. 'Religious Leadership vs. Secular Authority: The Case of the
Bene Israel', *The Eastern Anthropologist*, 49(3–4): 301–16.

Weiner, Myron. 1982. 'International Migration and Development: Indians in the
Persian Gulf', *Population and Development Review*, 8(10): 1–36.

————. (ed.). 1993. *International Migration and Security*. Boulder, Westview
Press.

Weller, Judith Ann. 1968. *The East Indian Indenture in Trinidad* (Caribbean
Monograph Series 4). Rio Piedras: Institute of Caribbean Studies, University
of Puerto Rico.

Williams, Brackette F. 1991. *Stains on My Name, War in My Veins: Guyana and
the Politics of Cultural Struggle*. Durham, N.C.: Duke University Press.

Williams, Raymond B. 1988. *Religions of Immigrants from India and Pakistan*.
Cambridge: Cambridge University Press.

Wood, Donald. 1968. *Trinidad in Transition: The Years After Slavery*. Oxford:
Oxford University Press.

Wood, John R. 1981. 'A Visible Minority Votes: East Indian Electoral Behaviour
in the Vancouver South Provincial and Federal Elections of 1979', in J. Dahlie
and T. Fernando (eds.): *Ethnicity, Power and Politics in Canada*. Toronto:
Methuen, pp. 177–201.

Yelvington, Kevin A. 1990. 'Ethnicity "Not Out": The Indian Cricket Tour of the
West Indies and the 1976 Elections in Trinidad and Tobago', *Arena Review*,
14(1): 1–12.

————. (ed.). 1993. *Trinidad Ethnicity*. Knoxville: The University of Tennessee
Press.

Zaidman, Nurit. 1996. 'The American Iskon Temple as a Global Site: The Forms
of Interaction of Western Converts with Indian Immigrants', *The Eastern
Anthropologist*, 49(3–4): 373–96.

Compiled by N. Jayaram

About the Editor

N. Jayaram is Professor of Research Methodology at the Tata Institute of Social Sciences, Mumbai. He has previously taught Sociology at Bangalore University (1972–99) and Goa University (1999–2003). His areas of interest include the sociology of education, political sociology and the sociology of diaspora. He has visited and lectured at various universities and institutions outside India including as Visiting Professor of Indian Studies at The University of the West Indies (St. Augustine), Trinidad and Tobago (1994–96). His previous books are: *Higher Education and Status Retention*; *Housing in India* (co-edited); *Introductory Sociology*; *Sociology: Methods and Theories*; *Sociology of Education in India*; and *Social Conflict* (co-edited).

About the Contributors

Yogesh Atal was formerly UNESCO's Regional Adviser for Social and Human Sciences in Asia and the Pacific, Bangkok, and its Principal Director in charge of co-ordination work related to the World Summit for Social Development held in Copenhagen (1995). He now lives in Gurgaon, Haryana.

G. S. Aurora was formerly Professor of Sociology at the University of Hyderabad. He is currently a freelance consultant sociologist based in Bangalore.

Norman Buchignani is Professor of Anthropology at the University of Lethbridge, Atlanta, Canada.

Ravindra K. Jain was formerly Professor of Sociology at Centre for the Study of Social Systems, Jawaharlal Nehru University, New Delhi.

S. R. Mehta was formerly Professor of Sociology at Punjab University, Chandigarh. He now lives in Panchkula, Haryana.

Nasser Mustapha is on the faculty of the Department of Behavioural Sciences at The University of the West Indies (St. Augustine, Trinidad and Tobago).

S. L. Sharma was formerly Professor of Sociology at Punjab University, Chandigarh. He now lives in Panchkula, Haryana.

Chaudry M. Siddique was on the faculty of the Department of Sociology at the University of Toronto, Canada.

Index

D-k/ 33663
19/10/04